Gender and Migration in Southern Europe

Mediterranea Series

GENERAL EDITOR: Jackie Waldren, *Lecturer at Oxford Brookes University; Research Associate CCCRW, Queen Elizabeth House, Oxford; and Field Co-ordinator, Deya Archaeological Museum and Research Centre, Spain.*

This series features ethnographic monographs and collected works on theoretical approaches to aspects of life and culture in the areas bordering the Mediterranean. Rather than presenting a unified concept of 'the Mediterranean', the aim of the series is to reveal the background and differences in the cultural constructions of social space and its part in patterning social relations among the peoples of this fascinating geographical area.

ISSN: 1354-358X

Other titles in the series:

Marjo Buitelaar
Fasting and Feasting in Morocco: Women's Participation in Ramadan

William Kavanagh
Villagers of the Sierra de Gredos: Transhumant Cattle-raisers in Central Spain

Aref Abu-Rabia
The Negev Bedouin and Livestock Rearing: Social, Economic and Political Aspects

V. A. Goddard
Gender, Family and Work in Naples

Sarah Pink
Women and Bullfighting: Gender, Sex and the Consumption of Tradition

David E. Sutton
Memories Cast in Stone: The Relevance of the Past in Everyday Life

Paloma Gay y Blasco
Gypsies in Madrid: Sex, Gender and the Performance of Identity

Gender and Migration in Southern Europe

Women on the Move

Edited by

FLOYA ANTHIAS AND
GABRIELLA LAZARIDIS

Oxford • New York

First published in 2000 by
Berg
Editorial offices:
150 Cowley Road, Oxford OX4 1JJ, UK
70 Washington Square South, New York NY 10012, USA

© Floya Anthias and Gabriella Lazaridis 2000

Berg is the imprint of Oxford International Publishers Ltd.

Library of Congress Cataloging-in-Publication Data

A catalogue record for this book is available from the Library of
Congress.

British Library Cataloguing-in-Publication Data

A catalogue record for this book is available from the British Library.

ISBN   1 85973 231 3 (Cloth)
       1 85973 236 4 (Paper)

Typeset by JS Typesetting, Wellingborough, Northants.
Printed by WBC Book Manufacturers Limited, Bridgend

Contents

Acknowledgements

This volume is the first to be entirely devoted to the analysis of gender and migration in southern Europe and therefore fills an important gap in the available literature. The initial impetus for this book arose from a conference we organized at the University of Greenwich in December 1995 with the support of the Department of Political Science and Social Policy at the University of Dundee and the School of Social Sciences at the University of Greenwich. An edited volume has already been prepared from this conference on migration and exclusion in southern Europe, published by Ashgate, 1999.

We would like to thank all the participants in that conference who contributed to discussing some of the issues raised in the present book. We would also like to thank Lynne Beeson from the School of Social Sciences of the University of Greenwich and Maria Koumandraki from the Department of Political Science and Social Policy of the University of Dundee for helping us with the preparation of the final manuscript.

Contributors

Jacqueline Andall is lecturer in Italian studies in the Department of European Studies and Modern Languages at the University of Bath, UK.

Floya Anthias is Professor of Sociology at the University of Greenwich, London, UK.

Victoria Chell completed her doctoral research at Queen Mary Westfield College, University of London and now lives in the US researching South West and Californian immigration policies.

Angeles Escrivá has a PhD in sociology from the Universitat Autonoma de Barcelona, Spain.

Francesca Gattullo is a researcher at the University La Sapienza in Rome, Italy.

Gabriella Lazaridis is Lecturer in European and Gender studies at the Department of Political Science and Social Policy, University of Dundee, UK.

Karen O'Reilly is Lecturer in the Department of Sociology, at the University of Aberdeen, UK.

Marina Orsini-Jones is subject leader for Italian and teaches on contemporary Italy at Coventry University, UK.

Iordannis Psimmenos teaches sociology at the Panteion University, Athens and at the American College Deere, Athens, Greece.

Natalia Ribas-Mateos is a researcher at the Department of Sociology at the Universitat Autonoma de Barcelona, Spain.

Introduction: Women on the Move in Southern Europe

FLOYA ANTHIAS AND
GABRIELLA LAZARIDIS

Both within Europe and beyond, millions are on the move, 'their journeys reshaping the human mosaic' (King and Oberg 1993: 1).

> Albanian boat people on the Adriatic, Pakistanis occupying a disused spaghetti factory in Rome, Filipinas fleeing an erupting volcano, migrants from the East gathering in the grim splendour of Budapest's railway station – these are just some of the images recalled from the past couple of years (King and Oberg 1993: 1).

Women have been particularly affected by transnational global processes (see Anthias, this volume) and are an increasingly important component of the new migrations to southern Europe. This book aims to explore the gendering of migration. Whilst gender cannot be reduced to looking at women, as Floya Anthias argues in the first chapter, which provides an overall conceptual basis for this book, the specific situation of women needs to be examined, particularly given the extent to which women still remain largely invisible in the migration literature (for exceptions see amongst others, Buijs 1993, Lutz, Pheonix and Yuval-Davis 1995, Indra 1999). The papers in this book explore the processes that produce and reproduce multiple forms of marginalization and exclusion of female migrants in southern Europe.

Despite the fact that some have cast doubt on the extent of feminization, on the basis of official figures (Zlotnik 1995), others argue that there are large numbers of undocumented women who are testimonies to an increasingly feminized migrant workforce. Many of these women

1

are migrating to southern Europe. Although over the past few years there has emerged a plethora of academic and other literature on migration in the European context (Koser and Lutz 1993: 1), the literature on migration in the southern European context is far less impressive and the writing on the feminization of migration in the southern European context is scant. A theme that unites much of the writing in southern Europe is the recent change of character from emigration to immigration and the generic term "new migration". The latter, according to Koser and Lutz (1993: 4–5), seems plausible only at an empirical level; as they write, 'at a more conceptual level historical analysis shows us that the application of the term "new" to a social phenomenon is arbitrary and therefore debatable – tensions are permeable and boundaries can be blurred. It is a concept which is poorly understood ' (Koser and Lutz 1993: 4–5).

Certainly, it is possible to argue that migration to southern Europe challenges traditional migration theory on a number of counts as Floya Anthias argues in the opening chapter of this book. The prototype migrant actor within these is seen to be a male who is economically motivated, either choosing to migrate, or being subject to the vicissitudes of capitalist production. Moreover, such migration is seen as one way, involving either a journey *from* or a *return to* a particular locale. Little attempt has been made to link these locales in terms of what now has become known as transnationalism (for example see Faist 1998, Cohen 1997).

Although traditionally an area that exports migrants, in recent years southern Europe has witnessed a major reversal of historical patterns, which gathered momentum in the early 1990s. Italy, Spain, Greece, Portugal and Cyprus became receivers of relatively large numbers of migrants (both poverty migrants and of highly qualified experts) and of refugees, from non-European countries (see King and Black 1997; Anthias and Lazaridis 1999). Italy has around one million migrants from diverse origins, including the Mahreb, Dominican Republic and the Philippines. In Spain there are over 850,000 foreigners, half from the EU and half from the Third World. Greece has an estimated half million migrants, half from Albania and the rest a mix from eastern Europe and Third World countries, about 70,000 of whom are legal. The estimate is that there are around 30,000 legal migrants in Cyprus with another 10,000 who have entered illegally. These are estimates only because of the vast amount of undocumented migrants who are not included in the official statistics (for more details see King and Black 1997; Anthias and Lazaridis 1999). Despite attempts by Spain and Italy to regularize the state of foreign workers, it is argued that these have been largely unsuccessful due to a continual demand for unregularized labour. In Greece, the first and so far only attempt made towards regularization was in 1998. It is too early however to make a valuable generalization about its success.

This migration to southern Europe has been explained in terms of a combination of factors; geographical location (long coast lines, numerous islands and mountainous borders), the residual effects of African colonial influences, the inadequacies of methods of surveillance and control used in southern Europe (see Fielding 1993: 50) and the economic and social transformation of the region to post-Fordist structures (tertiarization, flexibility, informality). An important aspect here is southern Europe's labour-market segmentation.

Within Europe, the single market has given a boost to mobility through the lifting of restrictions on movement between the member states of the Union. In addition, substantial transfers of population are taking place from less-developed countries outside Europe, to Europe. There are people on the move from a range of countries: southeast Asia, Eritrea, Somalia, Sri Lanka and Latin America; countries like Algeria, Morocco, Tunisia, which are situated just across the Mediterranean; and, particularly since the late 1980s, there are large scale migration flows from eastern and central Europe.

Ethnic tensions, low living standards, poverty and unemployment, economic restructuring, political repression and ecological problems are some of the factors impelling people to leave. The dismantling of the Iron Curtain and the geopolitical and economic changes that followed opened new possibilities for migration between East and West; around four million people have migrated from East to West (Fassman and Munz 1994). At the same time, ethnic cleansing has triggered the flight of around five million refugees from former Yugoslavia, plus others from the former Soviet Union. These phenomena, together with increasing mobility within the EU, and the emergence of new types of migration such as transit migration (Wallace, Choumliar and Sidorenko 1996), migration of students and of highly skilled workers, trafficking of women and children and so on has resulted in 'the distinction between countries of origin and countries of destination within Europe [becoming] increasingly blurred, as traditional countries of emigration have become countries of immigration at the same time' (Koser and Lutz 1993: 2). These tendencies have taken place in the context of the restructuring of the international labour market and the national labour markets implicated. Contemporary migration in southern Europe needs to be seen within quite particular historical contexts.

Borders with southern Europe allow entry by specific groups of migrants fleeing from their countries on the one hand (such as Kurds and Albanians in Greece) and Third World migrants on the other, many of whom enter illegally and are therefore undocumented. Others enter on short-term work contracts. These forms exist side by side with extensive return migration and family reunification processes. Much migration is illegal and therefore undocumented, hence it is difficult to estimate, with many states periodically regularizing particular groups (see various chapters in this volume as well as Anthias and Lazaridis 1999). Many of these migrants are women, coming in as domestic maids or as 'cabaret' artists and to take part in the flourishing sex industry. The migratory flows into southern Europe comprise mostly undocumented migrants whose only possibility for work is in the informal economy. The migrant population is heterogeneous, characterized by ethnic and gender specialization in different sectors. Women usually are found in the lowest levels of the employment hierarchy in the service industry (maids, nurses, entertainers in the sex industry, and cleaners in the tourist industry).

The migratory phenomenon in southern Europe must be understood in the context of a large informal economy where irregular employment is very common and which absorbs the great majority of migrants. As Iosefides (1997: 62) points out, the informal sector, which constitutes activities outside the legally registered formal production methods and money flows, can take many forms; one form is unpaid labour within the family; it can also take the form of hidden or underground activities and is greatly facilitated by clientelism, a feature which all southern European states share in abundance. It is estimated that the informal sector accounts for over 35 per cent of the gross domestic product (GDP) in Greece and about 25 per cent in Italy (Iosefides 1997: 82). This process manifests itself through the creation of a primary and secondary labour market, the secondary offering unstable, undesirable jobs with no security and with uncertain prospects. Such jobs play a major role in helping small family businesses achieve flexibility and survive pressures towards cost cutting in order to remain competitive. This need has led to the rise in demand for a labour force that is available when needed, cheap, flexible, non-demanding; in other words, a labour force that is squeezable. Flexible forms of production have increased labour market segmentation along age, gender and ethnic lines and have created niches for which inexpensive forms of labour are ideally suited. Such niches can be found in traditional activities organized along lines recognized as 'informal' (agricultural activities, petty trade), including informal activities that will never be formalized because of their clandestine nature (street-vending, sex industry).

These changes have been accompanied by an increase in female employment amongst local women since the early 1980s and a concomitant increase in demand for traditional female jobs particularly in domestic and sex-related services. In particular, women on the move come primarily from two sources: the Third World, in a search for economic roles and economic improvement, or fleeing their countries because of war (as in the case of Somalia): much of this is solo migration but it includes women entering as part of the family reunification process. As Ribas Mateos shows in this volume, socio-economic changes in the country of origin have contributed to pushing women towards migration, and as other papers in this volume show, such changes in the host countries have made women an attractive source of labour. The second category consists of women from eastern Europe, escaping the difficulties and problems faced by these. Indeed, migrant women who come to work in southern Europe are from a wide variety of countries and origins, including Morocco, Eritrea and Ethiopia and the Philippines in Italy, from the Dominican Republic, Morocco and Peru in Spain, from Poland, Albania, Bulgaria, Ukraine, Ethiopia, Somalia and the Philippines in Greece and from the Philippines, Sri Lanka, Bulgaria and Russia in Cyprus. Although the majority of these women can be found in the large urban centres, like Athens, Rome, Barcelona, Lisbon, Thessaloniki, Madrid and Nicosia, they can also be found in less-developed coastal regions like Sicily, as well as in agricultural areas like Crete, Valencia, Catalonia, Emilia-Romana and in areas where tourism flourishes, like Corfu, and Santorini. It can be seen, therefore, that migration and settlement have involved different groups from different parts of the world, although most have some dependency relation to the country of migration. These do not only constitute different identities but have distinct cultural practices, language needs, different religious behaviour and values and different gender relations, work traditions and attitudes.

Wages and work conditions depend, of course, on the legal status of these women, on whether or not they have work permits and on the forms of exclusion and racialization linked to women's ethnic, legal and class positions. Some migrate alone for work purposes (for example, Filipinas), whereas others accompany their men (for example,

Moroccans, Tunisians). Both find themselves in a strongly gendered labour market, where they take up precarious, insecure jobs in areas where illegal economic activities flourish, jobs rejected by southern Europeans themselves, like domestic work, sex and 'entertainment' industries. Many of these women are on short-term contracts or are undocumented, subjected to the vagaries of their employers.

The unique contribution of this book lies in the wealth of concepts and qualitative material relating to an under explored area, gender and migration in southern Europe. There is no doubt that not all the important issues have been covered, and not all countries in southern Europe have been included for a variety of reasons; chapters cover Italy, Greece, Spain and Cyprus. Nonetheless, we hope that this book is able to provide an impetus for strengthening the whole area of gender and migration studies. A number of foci are found in this book: the experiences of women as domestic workers (Chell, Lazaridis, Escrivá), the importance of family and household strategies in explaining female migration (Chell, Lazaridis, Ribas Mateos, Escriva), the use of women in the trafficking of prostitution (Psimmenos in particular), the diverse experiences of different groups and men and women within them (Chell, Lazaridis, Orsini Jones and Gattullo, Ribas Mateos, Escrivá), the disadvantages relating to illegality, the issue of divisions between different groups of women in the context of the domestic work sector (Andall, Lazaridis) and so on.

In the next chapter, Floya Anthias stresses the importance of locating migration within transnational processes in terms of global economies and the formation of transnational migratory groups. In addition, she argues that migration should be seen in relation to three locales: the homeland, the country of destination and the local and transnational migrant group. Moreover, although the role of women for transnational, national and ethnic groups is important, the position of women should also be located in terms of ethnic and national boundaries (Anthias and Yuval Davis 1989), and in terms of the intersection of gender, race and class (Anthias and Yuval Davis 1992, Anthias 1998).

Some attempts to gender migration have tended to overemphasize the role of structures and constraints and at times have produced an impression that women are victims of circumstances. Introducing agency into migration theory, whilst also recognizing that such agency is conducted in given structural and institutional contexts, enables a more multifaceted approach that can pay attention to the lived experiences of migrant women. As some of the authors in this volume point out, the narratives of women migrants, whilst referring to the enforced response to economic hardship, also talk about migration as an escape route from patriarchal structures as well as being motivated by the search for economic improvement for their families. This involves a multi-layered approach (also found in the chapters by Lazaridis, Andall, and Escriva) which is able to attend to the intersections of gender, ethnicity and class. The majority of the chapters in this volume critique economistic accounts of migration, inserting the importance of gendered households and social networks that support migration.

The role of migrant women as domestic workers constitutes one of the main forms and characteristics of the feminization of migration flows to southern Europe. A number of papers in this volume in fact address migrant women's experiences as domestic workers. The maid industry in southern Europe has expanded enormously in recent years, filling the gaps created by the increasing numbers of local women in paid employment and the lack of state provision for the very young and the very old. Many of these women, as well as suffering poor conditions of work and super-exploitation and abuse (see Anderson and Phizacklea 1997), suffer from social isolation (see Chell and Escrivá's contributions), although friendship groups and other informal networks serve to provide important social and other support. Similar arguments are put forward by Lazaridis in relation to the growing demand for cheap flexible domestic workers in Greece. Given the significance of domestic work for women migrants to southern Europe, Andall looks at the organization of the sector by observing the changing ideology and strategy of a national domestic workers' association in Italy; her chapter highlights how class and ethnicity affect women's experience of domestic work, whether as employees or employers.

The multiple forms of oppression that migrant women face have often been noted (Phizacklea 1983, Anthias 1993). Lazaridis, writing on Greece on the experience of Filipina and Albanian women, shows how racism interacts with sexist relations within Greek society and how the interplay between them produces different outcomes, however subtle these may be. This is also found in a particularly extreme way in Psimmenos's chapter on young Albanian women in the sex industry of Athens. An important feature of female migration to southern Europe is the degree to which many of the women are recruited into the sex industry. Psimmenos, examining female migrant prostitution in Greece, argues that this is linked to new global economic formations and the resulting structuration of a new type of labouring force. Most of these prostitutes are Albanian minors who suffer both physical and psychological abuse. Using the notion of 'periphractic' space (from the Greek 'fencing in'), to denote the spatial dimensions of marginalization and social exclusion, Psimmenos posits the production of a slave labour force, existing on the margins and 'fenced in' by society. This treats the city-place as the command point between the global and the local. Within this intersection, migrant women are particularly marginalized and this is expressed in their self-presentations and the narratives they use. The extent to which this constitutes forced migration becomes apparent in the context of the trafficking to which they are subjected.

Issues of 'difference' and diversity are now central dimensions for all feminist research as well as research on ethnicity and racism. Gender and ethnic groups are not homogeneous and it is important to pay attention to the rich complexity of experiences and positions. Chell, Lazaridis and Escriva all examine gender and ethnic segregation in the migrant labour force. For example, in Italy, Moroccans, who are mainly men, are concentrated in construction and agriculture whereas women are predominantly in service work. At the heart of Victoria Chell's chapter on migrant women in Italy is the issue of ethnic diversity. She highlights the difficulty of making generalizations about the impact of migration, but stresses, like Lazaridis and others in this book, the active and independent roles of women and that they need to be considered as social and economic actors in their own right. Chell looks at Filipina and Somalian domestic workers in Rome and at the role of networks in the migration flow and in assisting their subsequent integration in the host country's informal economy. She is able to show the differences between Filipina women who are predominantly Catholic, and Somalian women who are Muslims, and how this acts as one factor in explaining their reception in Italian society. Whilst the former have a higher income than the latter (a finding also in Lazaridis's paper on Greece), they are additionally regarded as more desirable domestic workers (see also Anderson and Phizacklea 1997). Other differences relate to the fact that the motivation to migrate for Filipina women was primarily economic, whereas Somalian women were forced to flee from their country because of civil war. This is a clear case of 'forced migration' (Indra 1999). The role of intermediaries, like the Catholic Church, is important and the personal networks, which particularly exist for Filipina women, go some way in explaining their different forms of adaptation, a point also found in other chapters in this book (for example, Lazaridis). However, despite the differences between these groups of women, they both shared the experience of deskilling, although Filipina women who migrated earlier were moving to the top of domestic work beginning to act in a nursing capacity. Both groups also suffered by being divided from their families and being compelled to live in an isolated nuclear family unit imposed by Western norms. Both groups moreover had prime responsibility for supporting their families back home, a common feature of the burden placed on migrant women.

There is no doubt that national and local contexts provide particular conditions for the enablement of migrant women's agency. The national and local states within each country will determine their ability to find a fertile environment for the pursuit of their aspirations in the new migration setting. Given the economic and other disadvantages faced by migrant women, and poor service and other provision, social mobilization to pursue their interests vis-à-vis the state is vital. Marina Orsini Jones and Francesca Gattulo compare the experiences of migrant women in Bologna with those in Florence. A large number of women come in as domestic maids, particularly from the Philippines and Eritrea, with the next largest category being women who come for family reunification purposes who are mainly from Morocco and Pakistan. Prostitution is also an important category and involves mainly Nigerian, East European and Albanian women. Bologna and Florence provide different contexts that shape women's migration project. Whilst Bologna has a strong tradition of migrant women's associationism and feminism, in Florence there are fewer such structures and a greater degree of racism and disadvantage is experienced by migrant women. This resembles the situation of migrant women in Bologna at an earlier period, at the beginning of the 1990s. On the front of equal opportunities, the chapter highlights the potential of inter-ethnic communication, in the context of enabling local structures. Jacqui Andall's chapter focuses also on how migrant domestic workers organize in Italy and the important role that the national and local context plays. She raises the important issue of the potential for coalition between migrant women and Italian women. In the 1970s the organization that she focuses on had a clear class perspective, but in the 1980s more attention was given to the problems relating to migration and ethnicity. Moreover, increasingly there is a recognition within the organization of the intrinsic value of the female relationship between employer and employee. The interrelationship between gender, class and ethnicity is being recognized to a greater extent over time.

Conditions in the country of origin as well as a long history of colonial dependency have often been pointed to as factors that 'push' people to migrate. Natalia Ribas Mateos focuses on just this issue. Migration to Spain from the Philippines, Gambia and Morocco is looked at in the context of the factors in the country of origin that have contributed to migratory exodus. Whilst recognizing the gendered demand in the Spanish labour market and the role of the state, particularly through the quota system covering domestic service, she argues that in order to understand the 'hows' and 'whys' of migration it is important to have a dual perspective: country of origin as well as country of destination. The three groups she has researched differ in terms of the degree of female participation in migration: the Filipina group is predominantly female, the Moroccan is mainly male but moving towards feminization, and the Gambian group is predominantly male. Like other contributors to this book, she shows the importance of transnational connections for all these groups and that household strategies are as important as economic factors in explaining why particular people, male or female, migrate. For example in the Gambia, there is a male cyclical migration pattern, shared by men within the family, depending on the needs of the compound and the extended family. In all cases, migratory networks, a common theme in this book, are important. With regard to countries of origin, Ribas Mateos argues that labour market disintegration produces female proletarianization, which then leads to migration. Like Orsini Jones and Gattullo, amongst other, she stresses the diversity of outcomes resulting from different local markets and immigration policies.

One of the central issues raised by the migration of women is the degree to which they experience a decline or an improvement in their social position through migration. The chapters in this book show the multifaceted and complex nature of women's position and that it is not possible to see migration in simple terms as either leading always to a loss or always to a gain in social status. Angeles Escrivá shows how the migration experience has impacted differently on different groups of migrant women, in terms of the role of state and labour market practices and the way women have responded to the challenges they face. Women, given the regularization of the domestic sector in Spain, achieve a higher legal status than men, but they none the less face more constraints than men in their everyday life. However, migration may give women more autonomy and control over economic resources than in their country of origin. Because of the role of the ethnic group in controlling women, many women avoid contact with the male members of their migrant group. However, domestic work, while offering some security, also means stigmatization and low social status as well as social isolation. Escrivá reinforces the observation made by others in this volume that many domestic maids have experienced downward social mobility with migration, as many are highly educated and have university diplomas. Despite this, most of the women she researched saw the migration experience as positive because of improved welfare provision and educational opportunities for themselves and their children.

Most migration theorists have concentrated on migrants from less-developed regions to more developed regions, searching for an improvement in their social and economic position. However, there is a long history of reverse movements where residents of the wealthier nations in the West seek to migrate, particularly at retirement, to sunnier and more welcoming climes and environments. Karen O'Reilly analyses the experiences of British women on the Costa Del Sol (Fuengirola). Life in Spain is often associated with freedom from social and physical restrictions, a slower pace, and therefore a better quality of life. Some women, however, experience feelings of isolation and marginalization. This is due to their inability to speak Spanish, 'never being quite part of things' in Spain, the confusing way in which the local bureaucratic mechanisms work and the absence of political representation. This illustrates the diversity of experience of different groups of women 'on the move'.

As we argued earlier, the unique contribution of this book lies in the wealth of concepts and qualitative material relating to an under explored area, gender and migration in southern Europe. We can summarize the common themes found in the various contributions to this book in the following way:

- there is a particular concentration of women in the service sector and a growing concentration in domestic service, particularly as live in domestic maids;
- there are large numbers of undocumented workers; for example, few domestic workers have legal status as individuals and their legality is dependent on the permits held by employers;
- the demand for maids is linked to the increasing full-time employment of local women and to poor welfare provisions and state facilities for child care;
- women migrants are more often than not a main source of family support and see their role in terms of a family strategy;
- migrant women provide sexual services as cabaret dancers cum prostitutes, recruited through trafficking, and in these roles they are in an extremely dangerous and vulnerable position;
- it is important to recognize diversity and look at the crosscuttings of gender, ethnicity and class, as sexism intersects with different forms of 'othering' and racialization;

- women must be seen as active agents rather than passive victims;
- there are divisions between different groups of women, particularly local women and migrant women, given that the demand for migrant women is linked to the increasing full-time employment of local women and to poor welfare provisions and state facilities for child care;
- the importance of transnational connections requires us to look beyond the interaction between countries of origin and destination towards wider migratory networks;
- the importance of different conditions in the countries of origin and the various countries of destination requires a contextual and situational analysis;
- there are particular ways in which women are affected by migratory experiences in terms of losses and gains, without this being a homogenous process.

In this way, although there may be some common themes, it is difficult to argue that one can produce a general theory about the role of gender in the migration process. However, what is clear is that it is always important, in developing an understanding of migration, to make sure that we look at the processes through gender- and 'race'-sensitive concepts as well as paying attention to forms of economic and social inequality in general. The agenda for the future of research on migration must include concerns with the ways in which, increasingly, transnational processes are gendered, as well as new citizenship issues prompted by these processes.

References

Anderson, B. and Phizacklea, A. (1997), *Migrant Domestic Workers: a European Perspective*, Unpublished report, Dept of Sociology, University of Leicester.

Anthias, F. (1993), 'Gender, Ethnicity and Racialisation in the British Labour Market' in H. Rudolph and M. Morokvasic (eds), *Bridging States and Markets*, Berlin: Sigma.

Anthias, F. (1998), 'Evaluating Diaspora: Beyond Ethnicity?' in *Sociology*, Vol. 32, No 3, August, pp. 557–580

Anthias, F. and Yuval Davis, N. (1989): Introduction in Yuval Davis and Anthias (eds) *Woman, Nation, State*, Basingstoke: Macmillan.

Anthias, F. and Yuval Davis, N. (1992), *Racialised Boundaries: Race, Nation, Gender, Colour and Class and the Anti-racist Struggle*, London: Routledge.

Anthias, F. and Lazaridis, G. (eds) (1999), *Into the Margins: Migration and Exclusion in Southern Europe*. Aldershot: Ashgate.

Buijs, G (ed.) (1993), *Migrant Women: Crossing Boundaries and Identities*, Oxford: Berg.

Cohen, R. (1997), *Global Diasporas: an Introduction*, London: UCL Press.

Faist, T. (1998), 'Transnational Social Spaces Out of International Migration: Evolution, Significance and Future Prospects', *European Journal of Sociology*, Vol. 39, No. 2, pp. 213–47.

Fassman, H. and Munz, R. (1994), *European Migration in the Late Twentieth Century*, Aldershot: Edward Elgar.

Ferrera, M. (1996), The Southern Model of Welfare in Social Europe, in *Journal of European Social Policy*, Vol. 6, No.1, pp.17–37.

Fielding, A. (1993), Mass Migration and Economic Restructuring, in R. King (ed.) *Mass Migration in Europe*. London: Belhaven.

Indra, D. (ed.) (1999), *Engendering Forced Migration*, Oxford: Berghahn.

Iosefides, T. (1997), *Recent Immigration and the Labour Market in Athens*. PhD thesis, University of Sussex, UK.

Iosefides, T. and King, R. (1996), Recent Immigration to Southern Europe: The Socio-economic and Labour Market Contexts, in G. Lazaridis (ed.), *Southern Europe in Transition*, special issue of the Journal of Area Studies, Vol. 9, pp. 70–94.

King, R. and Oberg, S. (1993), Introduction: Europe and the Future of Mass Migration, in R. King (ed.) *Mass Migration in Europe*. London: Belhaven Press.

King, R. and Black, R. (eds) (1997), *Southern Europe and New Immigrations*, Brighton: Sussex Academic Press.

Koser, K. and Lutz, H. (1998), The New Migration in Europe: Contexts, Constructions and Realities, in H. Koser and H. Lutz (eds), *The New Migration in Europe*, Basingstoke: Macmillan.

Lutz, H., Phoenix, A. and Yuval Davis, N. (eds) (1995), *Crossfires*, London: Pluto.

Phizacklea, A. (1983), *One Way Ticket*, London: Routledge.

Wallace, C., Chmouliar, O. and Sidorenko, E. (1996) The Eastern Frontier of Western Europe: Mobility in the Buffer Zone, in *New Community*, Vol. 22, No. 2, pp. 259–86.

Zlotnick, H. (1995), 'The South-to North Migration of Women', *International Migration Review*, Vol. 29, No. 1, pp. 229–254.

Metaphors of Home: Gendering New Migrations to Southern Europe

FLOYA ANTHIAS

Introduction

The title of this chapter refers to how the migration of women involves 'metaphors of home', that is movement of homes in terms of a movement physically in space, the movements and inter-relationships between these spaces and the impacts that the related symbolic and identity shifts have on women's lives in different ways. Migration, if nothing else, is both an escape (forced or otherwise) from the original homeland and a search for a better life and some kind of new home if not a new homeland. In one sense it is not difficult to gender new transnational migrations to southern Europe because, unlike earlier migrations which were, paradigmatically, predominantly male (although women have always also migrated on their own), much migration today is female, particularly migration from the Philippines, Sri Lanka and Latin America.

Gender is a relational concept as well as a central organizing principle of social relations (Anthias 1998a, Indra 1999). Within most approaches to women in migration, there has been a tendency to treat gender as additive and to reduce it to looking at women migrants. However, gendering migration is not just a question of recognizing the proportions of women *migrants* or their economic and social roles. It is also important to consider the role of *gender* processes and discourses, as well as identities, in the migration and settlement process. This requires looking at the new processes that have given rise to the feminization of migration as well as the particular forms of insertion and mobilization that this involves. The extent to which this feminization may be

15

part of the transformation of gender relations more broadly also needs addressing. The family is a unit of reproduction and cultural transmission and women within the family play a central role in this. This involves what Walby (1997) amongst others now calls 'gender regimes' (as a substitute for the much-criticized notion of patriarchy), meaning broader sets of social relationships whose object of reference is the construction and reproduction of gendered social practices. I prefer using the term gendered social relations, treating gender as an ingredient that enters into different societal mechanisms rather than being constituted as a discrete system (see also Anthias 1998a).

Moreover, as I have argued before, there are two sets of gender relations to consider with ethnic and migrant women: those within their own society/group and those within the dominant group in the state (see Anthias 1992, 1994, 1998a and 1998b). The focus on feminization not only needs to be done within this context (which includes the differential positioning of men), but must also pay attention to 'difference' of social positioning in terms of migration, racialization and class subordination. In other words, the use of the gender category must avoid homogenizing women's experiences and practices and must be undertaken in relation to how gender intersects with other social divisions, such as ethnicity, 'race' and class (Anthias and Yuval Davis 1983, 1992). Indeed, many of the chapters in this book point to the diversity of experiences and positionings of men and women in the migration process. However, the discourse and practice of 'otherness', on the basis of racism and ethnicity, defines the otherness of migrant women, where the European woman serves as the ideal woman. Although some migrant women are pathologized as victims (for example domestic maids from Sri Lanka), others are desired for their supposed submissive nurturing natures (for example mail order brides from the Philippines) and others for their exotic beauty and as fitting better into Western lifestyles (for example Russian women). According to Helma Lutz (1997), Muslim women, on the other hand, are regarded as the 'other other', thus representing a dichotomy with the western European model of womanhood.

Although discussion of gender issues certainly cannot be reduced to looking at the role of women, the latter has not been addressed adequately by most migration approaches, as we noted in the introduction to this book. As Buijs (1993: 1) states: 'Women were invisible in studies on migration and when they did emerge tended to do so within the category of dependants on men.'

This is echoed in the European Forum of Left Feminists statement

(1993: 3), that 'black and migrant women's concerns are largely ignored in policy, in campaigns and in research'. So although it is important not to reduce gender to 'women', given the relative lack of focus on women, it is imperative to make them visible, paying attention to difference. There are at least 6.4 million women in Europe who are not full citizens of the countries where they live. It is estimated that there are more than one million domestic workers who are dependent on the good will of their employers (Lutz 1997). Indeed, more than 14 million non-nationals constitute second class citizens in 'Fortress Europe' (Lutz *et al.* 1995).

In this chapter, I will attempt to provide a conceptual framework for gendering the migration process. I will draw on the case of Cyprus (the Greek-Cypriot sector in the south, as the north of the island is under the military control of Turkey) to explore more substantively some of the issues relating to the feminization of migration within new migration processes, particularly as they relate to southern Europe.

Theories of Migration: Gender-blind?

Ethnic pluralism exists in all societies to a greater or lesser extent, but the phenomena of migration, as well as diasporization (see Cohen 1997), produce ethnic diversity in new ways. Nation state formation usually involves the domination by one group, usually the larger or the most powerful economically, over other groups and the hegemony of its 'world view' and its conception of boundaries of belonging. Migration can be seen as important in terms of testing the boundaries of 'who belongs to the community' or the nation. Moreover, migration from outside Europe tests the boundaries of inclusion and exclusion within Europe itself.

Although migration is a world phenomenon, it is also a diverse one (Moch 1992; Cohen 1995; Castles and Miller 1993). There have been and still are different stages and forms of migration although they are not necessarily either analytically or substantively distinct: the terms *gastarbeiter*, settler, refugee, exile, sojourner, denizen all denote partic- ular forms, as well as ways, in which the phenomena of migration have been distinguished. Much migration stems from economic imperatives linked to rural or urban poverty and tends to be from societies with a link to colonial powers, or involves people fleeing or forcibly expelled from political regimes (Castles and Miller 1993). This has certainly been the case with regard to European migration in the post-war period.

For a long time, the push–pull model, dependent on neo-liberal economic theory, was used as the classic explanation for migration to Europe, starting from the observation that individuals migrated primarily for economic reasons and to better themselves and their families. Although at the descriptive level this approach seemed to capture the dual imperatives involved, it made a number of assumptions that are pertinent to issues of gender. In other words, gender was not absent in this approach, but deeply embedded in it. Firstly, men were the prototype migrant, being regarded as the decision makers and bread winners. Women entered, therefore, as dependants. Secondly, migration was seen as a rational choice (cf. Indra's 1999 use of 'forced migration'). Whilst giving a central role to human agency, that agency was treated in the light of the ideal typical rational economic action. Not only did this ignore the role of constraints around choice (for example why did some individuals migrate when others did not in similar circumstances) but it also ignored wider structural constraints imposed by a long history of colonialist or imperialist forms of domination. Moreover, it underplayed the role of the *mythology of the West* (not even adequately captured by the idea of adventure migration found in the work of writers like Dench 1975) and the continuing interaction between migrants and homelands (captured better by the notion of diaspora (for example see Cohen 1997; Clifford 1994; Anthias 1998b). There is a case for looking at migration in terms of a threefold positioning of social actors: within the relations of the homeland, within the relations of the country of migration and within their own ethnic communities and networks.

As an alternative, some of the important work by Marxists sought to emphasize the role of the mode of production – the macro or system level – as opposed to focusing on individual choices. The seminal text that gave an impetus in this direction was that of Castles and Kosack (1973). In this the focus was on migrants, not as discrete individuals who made choices but as particular categories of labour power, linked to the internationalization of the labour market. Broadly speaking, Marxist political economy, particularly through the work of Castles and Kosack (1973) and Castells (1975) focused on migrants as a sub-proletariat forged out of the uneven development of capitalism. Such work has treated migrants as a reserve army of labour subjected to the power of capital, or as in Phizacklea and Miles's (1980) work, as a class fraction of the working class. The use of Marxist economic categories (like that of the reserve army of labour) for particular population categories, (like women or ethnic minorities) is itself problematic (Anthias 1980). This analysis was not only economistic but gender blind.[1]

Moreover, although mainstream approaches to migration saw the actor as exercising free choice, the Marxist approaches erred in the opposite direction and deprived actors of any agency, thereby reducing the migrant to a category of labour power in the global labour market. Neither of these approaches consider how decision making takes place within family and broader social networks, both within the sending and receiving countries, nor the ways in which knowledge and communication channels and opportunities for work are mediated by social actors in specific social locations. The longing for return may also fundamentally influence settlement (Dahya 1974). Class outcomes are also related to the ways in which migrants may be oriented in complex ways to a number of geographical locales including the homeland (Anthias 1982, 1992). Similarly imaginaries of the *boundaries of the nation* have been as important if often contradictory to class or economic relations in understanding migration and its reception. For example the imaginary of the colonial power as a potential home from home is found in much colonial migration. Most important, the ways in which migrants have been received by the countries of destination (involving, for example, practices of discrimination and racism) cannot be explained fully by economistic explanations, whether neo-liberal or Marxist (Solomos 1986; Anthias 1990).

The bulk of the literature produced in Europe has been on post-war migration to western Europe. More recently, the focus has shifted to refugees and undocumented migrants (for example see Koser 1997). The most important tendency, however, is the shift away from a migration problematic altogether with the permanent settlements of population that western Europe has experienced. This tendency is characterized by a focus on incorporation and exclusion in the receiving countries and has tended to take a problem-oriented approach. In Britain in particular, the 'race relations' and ethnic studies problematic have dominated the field (see Anthias 1982, 1992; Miles 1989). Even more recently, a concern with identity, with new ethnicities, with difference and diversity has characterized debates in the area (see Anthias and Yuval Davis 1992). Theories of diasporization and of new diaspora social forms, including consciousness, have emerged (Cohen 1997; Anthias 1998b). The issue of gender has become an increasingly relevant issue (for example Phizacklea 1983; Anderson and Phizacklea 1997; Anthias 1983, 1992; Brah 1996) as is the role that women play in the reproduction of the ethnic boundary (Anthias and Yuval Davis 1989; Wilford and Miller 1998; Charles and Hintjens 1998).

New Migrations

New migration to Europe and particularly southern Europe in the 1990s has turned the attention of scholars once again to migration processes (see King 1997; Koser and Lutz 1997, for example). The paradigms used to explain earlier forms of migration, with their focus on economic migrants from poorer sectors of their communities, primarily men or families led by men, can no longer yield a fruitful conceptual basis for understanding migration today. Such migration is more *diverse* and includes large numbers of educated people from the old Eastern bloc (Rudolph and Hillman 1997). Some of these may experience downward economic mobility on migration (see Ribas Mateos, this volume) rather than an improvement. It is diverse also because large numbers of the older type economic migrants have to come in as undocumented, as modern economies do not formally want them within their territories, despite needing them; this is particularly the case in Greece, for example, with its large informal and unregulated sector. In addition a large part of this migration is made up of women who migrate on their own, being involved in what can be termed a solo migration project. *The diversity* of these new forms of migration has therefore gone hand in hand with *feminization*. Migrant women, however, have strong transnational family links and major responsibilities for providing for families left in the homelands. Migration is also diverse in terms of motivation: some migrate for family reunification, some migrate simply for work; others are asylum seekers (Koser 1997) and also what Mirjana Morokvasic (1994) has called commuter and brain drain migrants. The increasing diversity of the people on the move is linked to the disintegration of eastern Europe and crisis in various world economies. This is particularly the case with regard to the more educated and 'brain drain' migrants. Return migration and family reunification processes have also been important in southern Europe, as in Europe as a whole, being one of the few ways in which women can migrate legally (Lutz 1997).

As Castles and Miller (1993) argue, in the wake of so many people on the move, the old distinction between refugees, economic migrants and exiles is diminishing. The notion of 'forced migration' has been advanced by others (for example Indra 1999). Such a notion however, does not capture the multilayered processes for individuals and groups in the migration process. Examples from Spain, Italy, Greece and Cyprus (all in this book) show the extent to which movements are multiple and statuses, both legal and other, of individual migrants unstable and precarious. It is this tension between migrants as travellers and migrants as settlers in new territories, that produces the new phenomena of migration.

New approaches to migration, therefore, require us to avoid the binary focus of traditional migration theory with it's emphasis on the process of migration *from* and migration *to* particular nation states. Migration needs to be seen as part of the globalizing tendencies in the modern world and in terms of transnational processes. This involves a set of contradictions between the continuing imperatives of nation-hood, on the one hand, and increasing economic and cultural global-ism on the other. Moreover, all transnational population movements entail contradictory processes relating to particular forms of exclusion and inclusion. These processes involve competing discourses: the idea of human rights and equality of treatment of all persons is accomp-anied by exclusion from full citizenship rights as well as the differential racisms experienced by different categories of migrants. In the case of southern Europe, as in much of the history of migration in the post-war period generally, there are contradictions that lie, on the one hand, in terms of the perceived needs of the economy (or at least action by employers to fill cheaply their needs) and the perceived needs of the 'integrity of the nation' and the borders of 'otherness' or alterity, that will construct migrants as a threat. Different discourses and practices around ethnicity, or around civic rights, may be deployed in excluding and including differentially different groups of migrants in different countries and from different countries (for example see Triantafillidou 1997). This is particularly important where national identity is an important part of the agenda as it is within many societies; this is certainly the case in Cyprus, which will be drawn on substantively in this chapter.

Transnational and global processes provide the context within which new forms of gendered migration to southern Europe need to be located. I will now examine them.

Transnationalism, Globalization and Exclusion

Transnational social spaces mean that the problematic of assimilation and ethnic pluralism may not be adequate. Whilst the assimilation problematic posits the potential disappearance of a migrant popula-tion, the newer ethnic pluralism problematic found in multiculturalist discourse (see Anthias and Yuval Davis 1992) posits the reproduction of ethnic culture. Both of these positions are no longer sustainable, given that transnational processes involve border crossings where migrants have complex relations to different locales and form new and different communities. These include migrant networks involving social, symbolic and material ties between homelands, destinations and relations between destinations. Transnationalism is centred in two or more national spaces; this is found particularly in the case of Filipina maids, for example, discussed in many of the chapters in this volume.

Transnational *population* movements may be seen as part of the globalizing tendencies in the modern world (Walters 1995). Globalization involves a number of related processes: movement of capital in its various forms; the global penetration of new technologies, forms of communication and media; transnational political developments and alliances (such as the European Union (EU), the European Court of Human Rights and the Beijing Conference of Women); and the penetration of ideologies producing a 'world system' (Wallerstein 1990) or Global Village (McLuhan 1964). Appadurai's (1990: 297) conception of the ethnoscape provides one way of understanding the movement of people: 'By ethnoscape, I mean the landscape of persons who constitute the shifting world in which we live; tourists, immigrants, refugees, exiles, guest-workers and other moving groups and persons.'

Globalization challenges social scientific analysis with changing forms of governance and political participation, changing identities, values and, allegiances. These have a profound effect on social life and our understanding of it, with serious implications for the future of democracy, citizenship and nationalism (Eisenstein 1997). Some categories have emerged excluded from society, through new technology and new flexible employment patterns. Many of those most affected by these processes are women. This is partly because the drive to attain greater flexibility in employment practices has encouraged casualized employment practices and especially the feminization of migration.

Although globalized economic structures potentially break national borders, as well as established gender/patriarchal ones, they cannot ensure the equality and growth of status and respect to all groups equally and may reinforce borders in new ways. The state/welfare system has become dominated by increasing *privatization*, dismantling the welfare states of liberal democratic societies and prohibiting the development of welfare regimes in southern Europe. Moreover, privatization and free markets are redefining the relationship between the state and their economies, families and public life and political and cultural life (Eisenstein 1997). This is likely to reinforce divisions between rich and poor nations, on the one hand, and between different categories of people within them on the other.

Moreover, despite globalization, the reconfiguration of ethnic boundaries and exceptions such as the European court of human rights, nation states are still the determinants of juridical, social citizenship and cultural citizenship (Turner 1990) and the ethno-national project remains central. The borders of the nation state are still policed against undesirable others in formal and informal ways through migration controls, racism and the desire for the integration and management of minorities within (in the present phase of multiculturalism) while excluding others on the outside and the inside (such as Gypsies). Many nation states wish to retain the ethnic identity of their diaspora populations and encourage their reproduction as well as their return to the homeland (unrecognizable for those who were born outside it), a home no longer 'a home' or a place where they may feel 'at home'.

It may be the case that globalism as an ideology demands one culture which can be shared (what has been termed a global village), found in a more limited sense within the notion of Europe, but this involves a particular construction of 'Europe' as Christian and White, thus excluding Third World migrants and Muslims. Freedom of movement and trade have made boundaries between one European Union country and another less important, but in practice this is reserved for majority ethnic group members who have full citizenship. For many Third World and other migrants this process means that they need to carry additional identification, with passport controls at airports reinforced to exclude non-Europeans (Anthias and Yuval Davis 1992). Being Black or obviously foreign is therefore an impediment to movement as racialized minorities within Europe may be targeted because of the growing ideology of Europeanism/whiteness (Lutz et al. 1995).

Moreover, there are different layers of citizenship and residence/work permits for different groups and inequality both between the countries of the European Union and between western Europe and southern Europe. Therefore, in practice, privatization and exclusionary nation state citizenships sit alongside differential border controls in the management of movements of population within Appadurai's ethnoscape. Nation states have always had ethnic 'outsiders' or minorities within, who have demanded recognition of their practices. Within eastern Europe, for example in Latvia, Rumanians are excluded from eligibility for citizenship. In ex-Yugoslavia this has been particularly horrendous. 'Ethnic cleansing' may be a relatively new term but it is an old experience. The European framework provides different instances of ethnic and racist practices: racism and hostility in Spain and Greece towards migrants from Tunisia (see Daly and Barot 1999) and Albania (Lazaridis 1999 and Psimmenos this volume); in Germany and the Netherlands the Turks have been targets of racist hostility but more recently Rumanians and Poles in Germany have been the subject of neo-Nazi attacks; in France, target populations are increasingly Muslims and Jews (see Lloyd 1998); in Britain there has been a growth of anti-Muslim racism (see Modood 1996). Such processes are essentially gendered (see Anthias and Yuval Davis 1992, Brah 1996, Lutz *et al.* 1995).

Gendering Migration

The idea of migration as a male phenomenon has been seriously questioned since the mid-1980s by the focus on women migrants making independent choices or taking the initiative for their own families (for example, Phizacklea 1983; Anthias 1992; Buijs 1993; Lutz *et al.* 1995; Indra 1999). The empirical picture of women that has emerged shows the diversity of social positioning entailed. There are class and ethnic differences amongst women migrants and the different countries of origin and destination provide heterogeneous contexts that need to be taken into account, but there are some broad areas that allow us to posit some general features of the new feminization of migration. It is not the case that women migrants migrate primarily as dependants or for family reunification. Instead, women migrants are more often than not a main source of family support and see their role in terms of a family strategy. All the chapters in this volume show instances of this role.

However, as noted previously, gendering migration is not simply attending to women migrants. For gender as a relational social category is implicated in a range of social relations linked to the process of migration. Therefore it is necessary to look beyond merely economic processes for understanding the position of migrant women and to attend to ethnic and national boundaries. Whilst nationalism, as Benedict Anderson (1983) notes, constructs imagined communities with a sense of belonging, it also requires an 'other' from which it can imagine itself as separate. The migrant 'other 'is gendered as well as racialized and classed. Gender is a significant component of ethnic landscapes. Cultural groups, nations and ethnic groups are imagined as woman (see Anthias and Yuval Davis 1989) and women are particular objects of national and ethnic discourses and policies, in terms of the biological reproduction of the group/nation, its social and cultural reproduction and its symbolic figuration. In addition women are active participants in economic processes and are particular political actors, often playing specific roles within the nation. It is necessary to incorporate women as active agents and to focus on the different ways in which they manage the migration process. Women as social actors are located at the intersection of their country of origin and country of destination, as they are economic and ethnic subjects within both locales. A contextual and situational analysis is therefore needed. Moreover, the importance of transnational connections require us to look beyond the interaction between countries of origin and destination towards wider migratory networks.

The role of the state is central in understanding women's position. This entails more than looking at legal rules or social provision, although these are of fundamental importance. The public/private divide, reflected within state practices, with the relegation of women to the private space of the home and the family, has been extensively critiqued by feminists (for example Lister 1997). In the receiving countries, the personal lives and experiences of women are socially constructed as private, so that for example, experiences of women migrants in rape and 'trafficking' (for example see Campani 1997) is treated as private, although the women who are discovered to be illegally working in the sex trade, or who enter illegally as refugees, may be punished if this comes to the attention of the police. Rape and other forms of sexual abuse become explained as products of individual pathology rather than emanating from social processes of gender hierarchy and subordination.

Women Migrants and Gendered Work

There is no doubt that economic incorporation into particular sectors of the economy provides an important context for understanding the position of migrant women, albeit in a heterogeneous manner. Women migrants provide the flexibility that global capital needs. Approximately two-thirds of all part-time and temporary workers are women (Eisenstein 1997). Women fill particular functions in the labour market, being cheap and flexible labour for the service sectors, and in some countries, small/light manufacturing industries. They are located within a secondary, service-oriented or hidden labour market that is divided into male and female sectors and reproduces an ethnically and gendered divided labour market. Moreover, ethnic/migrant groups can use women as an economic resource. For example, family labour was one central pattern for many migrant groups in the post war period in western Europe (Anthias 1983; Ward and Jenkins 1984).

In terms of the economic role of migrant women in southern Europe, there is a diversity in female participation, but there is a concentration in the service sector, particularly domestic service and within the sex or leisure industry. Moreover, many migrant women are either illegal or do not have legal status as individuals, their legality being dependant on the permits held by employers. This places them under the control of their employer and potentially and actually leads to super-exploitation and other forms of abuse (see Anderson and Phizacklea 1997). The undocumented nature of much migration is therefore important in structuring its relation to the market, in terms of the hidden or private economies within the service sector, the household (as in domestic service) and the sex industry. This raises the issue of the ways in which being deprived rights of entry and settlement, as well as broader rights of citizenship, are central reasons for the forms of domination faced by migrant men and women.

Domestic Maids   The use of foreign domestic servants, many of whom live in, constitutes a significant growth industry in southern Europe. Sri Lanka, the Philippines, Albania and Latin America are favoured countries for this form of female labour migration. Southern Europe has increasing numbers of working women, many of whom are mothers. The inadequacy of state provision for the care of the very young and the elderly, or the inability of the state to actually provide those services has resulted in a massively increased demand for domestic workers. Local women with more disposable family incomes turn to poorer women, many of them migrant women, to take on the domestic role and responsibilities traditionally associated with women's role in the private sphere. Few domestic maids have a migration status separate from their work entitlement on entry as domestic workers, and they are therefore vulnerable; if they leave their employer they could be deported. Some women are undocumented, which makes them particularly vulnerable and exploitable. Lack of formal regulation and person rights deprives them of any ways of countering potential forms of abuse and may trap them in unhappy and at times dangerous dependencies on the families that employ them. Often their employers complain loudly of the presence of too many foreigners in their country on the one hand and yet happily employ a foreigner in their own home because they are cheap (Anderson and Phizacklea 1997).

The multiple domestic tasks such maids are given 'as part of the family' means the extension of the subordinate role of women as unpaid family workers to paid family workers. The expectations that families have on the wife and mother now are placed onto the domestic maid but without the potential emotional and other rewards as well as the reciprocities involved in family structures. Women from poorer countries such as Eritrea, Sri Lanka, Albania and the Philippines are subjected to oppression by women from more affluent countries. This problematizes the view that the source of women's oppression is men and shows how power relations not only exist between men and women but also amongst women. This supports the view that many of the gains that indigenous women have made have depended on the exploitation of other women from poorer countries in the international division of labour. It also shows the importance of state processes in the facilitation of subordination within the employer/employee relationship.

This is an important instance of how differential labour market incorporation can be divisive for women. While women of the majority improve their position it is at the expense of migrant women. Moreover, this pattern reproduces traditional family arrangements where women remain responsible for the domestic sphere, even though they work. The employment of maids facilitates changes in the female participation of indigenous women whose reliance on the family (for example their mother and other unpaid female kin) can no longer be guaranteed. Women migrants also often bear the responsibility for supporting their families back home and are an important familial resource. They thus carry the 'burden of reproduction' for their families and for its survival in the homeland or in the society of migration. Changing class relations and the importance of material display also mean maids are part of status symbolism in many societies such as Greece, Italy, Spain and Cyprus.

Sex Related Migration   There has also been a growth of the entertainment industry linked to sexual services such as in cabaret, dancing, and massage parlours etc. The feminization of flows to southern Europe is linked to changes in women's employment, with the restructuring of labour markets towards the service sector (see King 1997), but the sex industry is also linked to continuing traditional maintenance of the family for local women (see Vassiliadou 1999; Campani 1997). Prostitution, in fact, is hidden by some of these activities and has become very lucrative, sometimes for co-ethnic employers or pimps. Traditionally such women tended to come from south-east Asia and Africa, but today it is women from eastern Europe and the former Soviet Union who are increasingly used in this way, being preferred as well as being more available with the collapse of eastern Europe. The traffic in women in the sex industry is largely illegal and undocumented. Where women are not illegal entrants they may be documented as cabaret artistes and musicians as in the case of Cyprus (Anthias forthcoming). Many of these women are promised jobs in clubs and other forms of leisure but find themselves forced into prostitution on arrival (see Psimmenos, this volume). If they are illegal entrants any attempt to avoid prostitution could lead to deportation (see Campani 1997). This shows how the illegality of women and the fact that the abuse they face may be defined as stemming from the private realm of relations with men, means that they cannot be protected by the state.

A related growth industry is that of mail order brides (Anderson and Phizacklea 1997). In the past, women from south-east Asia were favoured for their submissiveness and as good housewives. Eastern European women are increasingly preferred, being promoted on grounds that they will fit in and they are not physically distinguishable. Some of these are educated women who may be escaping from countries that may be in political or economic disarray, searching for a dream in the West. The need to search for new homes involves recognizing individual and subjective components of choices being made by some of these women. If a mail-order bride wishes to leave the relationship that secured her entry to the migration setting, she too will be liable for deportation. Once women are shifted out of the private sphere, it is immigration law that determines their status, not family law or the laws against trafficking.

The Economy and Gendering Migration in Cyprus

We can see some of these processes at work in the small country of Cyprus. It was traditionally a country of migration (see Anthias 1992), but the tables have now turned. In the 1990s Cyprus has become a country that receives migrants from the Third World and from eastern Europe. Like much of southern Europe it has experienced a feminization of migration, with a strong distinction between the calls upon men and women who migrate. More and more Cypriot women have been incorporated into the labour force, along with growing urbanization and the continuation of a gendered division of labour within the Cypriot economy and within the home. Migrant women are therefore important in terms of the changing configuration of gender relations for Cypriot women. Cypriot women are more likely to be in *full time employment*, unlike many married women workers in western Europe (Crompton 1997), whereas care and services for families are not provided through state agencies. This also relates to changing relationships with elderly parents who can no longer be looked after by their married daughters and who need a full time nurse at home. The demand for child care is high given the increase in the proportion of children under 5.5 years who are in child care: 60 per cent in 1996 compared to 27 per cent in 1987 according to published data (Dept of Statistics). The expectations of women in the labour force[2] are for greater parity, but there is continuing relative low pay for women compared with men. There is a shortage of local women going into nursing and care work but there are additional factors relating to the cost of labour (cheapness) and the greater comfort felt by many women in employing foreign maids compared with indigenous ones (also cited in Anderson and Phizacklea 1997). The use of Filipina and Sri Lankan maids and nannies can be understood in this context.

Women became an important source of labour after the 1974 invasion, particularly after 1978. The increasing participation of women in higher education (the latter had to be abroad by necessity, until the recent establishment of the University of Cyprus) provides opportunities for alternative lifestyles and concomitantly the development of less traditional conceptions of gender relations.[3] However, there is a disparity between the attitudes and practices/experiences of women in Cyprus *vis-á-vis* an emancipatory and feminist consciousness (Vassiliadou 1999). Although, as more and more Greek-Cypriot women become active in the labour market (see House, Kyriakidou and Stylianou 1989) some aspects of patriarchal control will be modified, there has not been any great transformation of gender relations to accompany economic participation. This issue has yet to be fully explored through extensive empirical research, but there is a continuation of women's responsibility for household and child care, particularly as the employment of maids has put on the back burner a transformation of social roles within the family.

The latest figures show 27,500 legal migrants and calculate an additional 10,000 illegal migrants resident in Cyprus in 1997 (Ministry of Labour 1997). The employment of artists, maids and foreigners working for offshore companies (calculated at 17,000) is regulated by the Immigration Office, whilst other categories are regulated by the Ministry of Labour. Over one-third of these are maids with about one-eighth as artists and musicians (all likely to be women); that is, women constitute approximately 50 per cent of migrants who come into Cyprus in this way. Major countries of migration to Cyprus are Greece, Bulgaria, The Philippines, Sri Lanka and Syria. Of these the growth over the last few years has been primarily maids from the Philippines and Sri Lanka.[4] There has been an increasing need for foreign workers over the last six years or so and this has extended to a need for domestic workers, governesses, gardeners, barmen and workers in offshore companies, which already employ a significant number of foreign personnel.[5]

Following the pattern found in the rest of southern Europe, women generally come in as maids for middle class professional families, or as artists and musicians, a euphemism for the sex industry, which in Cyprus caters largely for the indigenous population although it is also used by tourists. Sex-related migration has been very profitable and an integral part of tourism in many countries in southern Europe as noted earlier in this chapter. Sex workers come particularly from south-east Asia, Thailand, eastern Europe and Russia. They come in as cabaret dancers but may be recruited as prostitutes. Because their activity is illegal they are heavily dependent on their employers. They are only allowed to come in for six months and then they must be away for six months before they are allowed to return (verbal communication, Ministry of Labour, June 1997). In the case of domestic workers, they come in on short-term contracts. Their employer has to apply for an employer permit for up to three years with the possibility of renewal for another year. At the end of the period, women may send a female relative in their place or change employer. The likelihood is that a large number of women are also operating illegally. The issue of mail-order brides from south-east Asia and eastern Europe has not arisen in Cyprus, although there is some evidence that domestic maids who are brought in by single men may be used as mistresses and there have been some publicized cases of marriages taking place with Filipina women.

There is little regulation of the terms of employment of many of these women. Regarding domestic maids who come largely from the Philippines and Sri Lanka, for example, there is some evidence of super-exploitation (see Anthias, forthcoming). They are also a status symbol: in one middle class neighbourhood I visited in Nicosia out of 26 families living in a new prestigious development, 24 had a foreign maid. This is not only confined to women who work, but women who prefer leisure to doing their own child care and domestic work.

In addition, more and more women are taking maids as part of a materialist status symbol, even within the lower middle classes. Filipinas are regarded as top-class maids for status, being generally seen as cleaner, more deferential and more sensitive to privacy. Many are educated women, some of whom have degrees and were teachers or accountants in their own country. The issue of racialization is relevant here as they are regarded as less of an 'other' than Sri Lankans, largely because they are Christian. Many of these women not only service the family that employs them but that of the employer's elderly parents, so they may be given tasks of cleaning parental homes and looking after sick relatives, as well as looking after the children of brothers and sisters. Bartering in maids is not unknown and a particularly pleasing maid may be passed on to other relatives or friends. The sisters and mothers of maids may also be brought in either concurrently or sequentially and there are cases where a mother may replace her daughter within a particular family. Most maids are not treated as part of the family and eat separately, often sharing a bedroom with the children, and they are not allowed boyfriends. They may be used for the dirtiest work and have little protection.

Like maids, particularly Filipinas, in other countries, remittances home form an important part of the transnational financial aspects of female migration. Women also save to buy consumer goods (particularly good electrical equipment) and fashionable clothes and jewellery to send back home. Networking gives maids strong systems of support (Campani 1997). A usual practice is renting a flat where they meet and eat on their days off and they may be seen in the town squares on Sunday morning congregating and picnicking together.

The different treatment of different groups of women from different origins suggests that economic incorporation cannot fully account for some of the ways in which migrant women have been received by the countries to which they migrate. Issues of nation and ethnicity are also important factors that structure women's lives and I shall now turn to these issues.

Migrant Women and the Ethnic Boundary

There is much evidence that women are central transmitters of ethnic culture: they reproduce the culture and tradition of the group and its religious and familial structures and ideologies. They reproduce the group biologically and are used as symbols of the nation or ethnic group. They are important as 'mothers' of patriots and represent the nation (see Anthias and Yuval Davis 1989 for an analysis). For example in both Bosnia and in Cyprus, the rape of women involved the project of forcing them to bear the children of the enemy and being violated as mothers of the national enemy.

Migration can be seen in the context of the reproduction of national identity and the boundaries of belonging, both for the receiving countries (where it may lead to ethnic exclusion and racism) and the sending countries (where it may lead to a concern with retaining the ethnic bonds of migrants with their countries of origin). These processes are not given or static; they change around specific economic and political conditions. Gender processes may be regarded as important in understanding how nationhood and belongingness are retained and reconstituted, particularly through the role of women as ethnic actors (see Walby 1996; Anthias and Yuval Davis 1989; Yuval Davis 1997). However, it could be argued, that women function as objects of discursive practices and social relations whereas men are its active agents. Wetherall and Potter (1992) argue that men are given the authentic voice to represent their communities (see also Anthias and Yuval Davis 1992).

It is not surprising that women as biological reproducers of the nation play a central role given the importance that ideas of 'blood' and 'common origin' have for constructing ethnic and national collectivities. The importance of this for the formation of nations, however, varies, from societies like Germany, which are based on ideas of essential 'volknation' or true Germanness decided by blood and family, to ideas of common culture (found in France; see Lloyd 1998) and civic virtues that best characterize the Swiss and Belgian context where several ethnic groups constitute a nation, as well as Italy (see Trantafyllidou 1997). Societies like the US, Canada, South Africa and Australia are largely what may be termed White settler societies (see Stasiulis and Yuval-Davis 1995) and contain several ethnicities; nationhood is constructed out of the acceptance of the *political* reality of the nation and identification with its future. This could be seen in terms of the importance of 'collective destiny' rather than origin and common parameters regarding cultural, political and legal rules. But this may exclude those who are regarded as not being able to share in this: Aboriginals in Australia are a case in point.

In all societies, women of different groups are encouraged to reproduce the nation differentially and some are encouraged to 'grow and flourish' whereas others are seen as undesirable. For example, in many Western societies ethnic minority women's fertility may be seen as a threat to the nation, involving demographic and nationalist policing

and ideologies (Anthias and Yuval Davis 1989) and the use of depo-
provera and sterilization techniques against some (Anthias and Yuval
Davis 1992). Indigenous mothers who give birth to many children
(termed polytechna mothers in Cyprus) may be rewarded whereas
migrants and their descendants in this situation may be subjected to
policies and discourses of inferiorization. Although women are members
of collectivities they are subjected to *different* rules and *experience them*
differently.

As well as functioning as biological reproducers, with state policies
being geared to different women in these terms, women also reproduce
the nation culturally. Women may be seen as targets and agents of
national acculturation. The education of women becomes a key dimension in producing loyal citizens and in some cases there have been
highly publicized attempts to assimilate women into the dominant
culture, such as in France through the notorious scarf affair (Silverman
1992). As Anastasia Karakasidou (1996) points out, the education of
women in the Greek language and tradition was central after the
incorporation in 1913 of Thrace into Greece, in order to make women
suitable mothers. She quotes as an example a 1924 report to the
Governor General of Macedonia, the Superintendent of the Florina
Educational district, who maintained that it 'was imperative to educate
women and very young children who spoke no Greek'. He warned
that children would come to harm if they lived in a 'foreign speaking'
home environment (1996: 104). Deniz Kandiyioti (1989), on the other
hand, shows how the modernization project of Turkey, at both political
and cultural levels, used the emancipation of women as a strategic
tool. She also argues that because the domestic sphere represents the
continuation of tradition, it becomes most subject to state discourses
under situations of political change (Kandiyoti 1991).

Women are also symbolic of the nation, but modesty and motherhood are key elements of this as in the French Patria and the symbol
of Cyprus as a martyred mother mourning for her loss (Anthias 1989).
In Nicaragua, the revolution was symbolized by a woman carrying a
baby in one hand and a gun in the other (Charles and Hintjens 1998:
4). Those women who are regarded outside the national collectivity,
unable to reproduce or symbolize it, may face particular forms of
racism and exclusion. Racism against women intersects with sexism
to produce particular forms of exclusion against different ethnic and
class groups. Filipina maids may experience it differently from women
involved in the 'porn' trade and differently from women 'brain drain'
migrants from eastern Europe.

Gender and the Ethnic Boundary in Cyprus

In Cyprus, as in other societies, women may be seen as the direct transmitters of the 'cultural stuff' of ethnicity because of their domi-nant day-to-day role in domestic and familial life and in child rearing. Amongst other cultural values, women transmit the values of 'good' Greek-Cypriots or 'patriots': those of sexuality, the 'work-ethic' and nationalist consciousness.[6] The mother–nation twin is important here as is the notion of 'mother' of 'fighting men' (see Anthias and Yuval Davis 1989).

Women may be seen as definers of the ethnic boundary. This works in terms of the legal definition of citizenship. Only particular women can reproduce citizens within the 'national boundary' (see WING 1985; Anthias and Yuval Davis 1989; Anthias 1989); in Cyprus those who are married to men of Cypriot origin. However another aspect of ethnic boundary definition is entailed in conceptions about desirable sexual or gender behaviour. This works in relation to processes of reproduction of the group. For women, one of the ways of being a good 'ethnic' subject entails behaving in ethnically appropriate ways by conforming to the principle of sexual purity. For men it entails maintaining control over women. In the case of Cypriot migrants in Britain, for example, women have been the bearers, keepers and symbolic signifiers of ethnic identity and constitute one of the most important boundary markers between English and Cypriot ethnicity (Anthias 1992).

In many Western societies, migrants are feared for importing foreign cultural and moral elements, particularly if they are Muslims or Asians. This is the case in Cyprus, with many reports in the press that Cypriot culture is in danger of being undermined by undesirable foreign influences. Maids are employed mainly for their physical work in cook-ing, cleaning and menial child care, but public discourses (Trimikliniotis 1999) show how the fear of importing foreign culture is directed at these women. There are different discourses around this, however, and tourism is also seen as a threat (see Ayres 1999). In Cyprus, eastern European women, on the other hand, are treated as morally loose or likely to be involved in drugs or the porn trade. In addition, when national feeling is strong such as during the recent events in the buffer zone between Greek and Turkish Cyprus, more obvious hostility is shown to foreign workers. The Cypriot press has made reference to foreign workers with terms such as 'we are swamped' (for example *Agon* 18 September 1996 and *Philelleftheros* 1 September 1996) and talking about a 'flood of foreign workers'. The failure of people in

Cyprus to accept the co-existence of foreign workers on equal terms has been noted in a number of public events and has prompted the recent formation of an anti-racist group in Cyprus. The concern with the national heritage found in public discourse is intimately linked to the dominance of the national problem in public life for a large part of the immediate Cyprus past.

Therefore new migration is in tension with the present phase of the national problem with its imperatives with regard to the use of ideas of 'national identity' in pursuing broader human rights with reference to a solution to the Cyprus problem. In other words, economic interests legitimize foreign workers whereas nationalist discourse sees them as undesirable. This also relates to how globalization and Europeanization figure in Cypriot political discourse, with Cypriots increasingly seeing themselves as European with their initiation into the European Union and negotiations about entry. This requires the reformulation of Cyprus as containing multiple ethnicities and new forms of European citizenship (see Kostakopoulou 1999); as such what is posed in Cyprus is the challenge of an increasingly ethnically and culturally diverse society, over and above the ethnic divisions between Turkish Cypriots and Greek Cypriots.

However, to locate women at the intersection between economic and ethnic processes is not enough and it is important to consider them as active agents and in terms of their links to social networks, households and families. In the next part of the chapter, I will look at some of the issues that need to be added to the concerns I have outlined above with regard to economic and ethnic processes, drawing on a range of literature.

Women as Social Agents

Some attempts to gender migration have tended to overemphasize the role of structures and constraints and at times have produced an impression that women are victims of circumstances. Agency is conducted in given structural and institutional contexts, but as Anderson and Phizacklea (1997) point out, the narratives of women migrants, whilst referring to the enforced response to economic hardship, also talk about migration as an escape route from patriarchal structures as well as a motivation towards economic improvement for their families. Therefore, women are not just passive receivers of social processes.

Women's agency can be explored in terms of household strategies and the formation of social networks. Although many women suffer from social isolation (see Chell and Escrivá in this volume), friendship groups and other informal networks serve to provide important social and other support. There is no doubt that national and local contexts provide particular conditions for the enablement of migrant women's agency. The national and local governments within each country will determine their ability to find a fertile environment for the pursuit of their aspirations in the new migration setting, as Orsini Jones and Francesca Gattulo argue in this volume.

Nor are the links between migration and gender relations always negative. Many approaches to women and migration examine the extent to which migration may serve to counter patriarchal forms of social control (see the volume by Buijs 1993). This relates both to women's social power and to the relationships between men and women; what may be regarded as both the public and private social realms. Literature on these issues has not produced simple answers to the effects that transnationalism and migration have on women. Thomas Faist (1998) writing about Turkish migrants in Germany says:

> while communal reciprocity undoubtedly furthered the economic success of Alihan residents, it also cemented gender relations controlled by patriarchs of extended families . . . relatively immobile women, most of whom stayed behind in Turkey, shouldered the transnational life style of Alihan men. [p. 228]

This example is one where men have been the main actors in the transnational sphere. However, with women migrating, there may be changes in the distribution of power in the family: for example, there is some evidence that the new economic and social responsibilities of Filipina women serves to give them a more powerful role in their families (Campani 1997; Escrivá and Ribas in this volume). Bhachu (1985) refers to the transformative powers of migration on Asian women. In the case of Filipina and East European women, migration involves women running away from their allotted place. For example, Escrivá in this volume discusses the avoidance of Somalian women of men from their own group as does Walker (1990) when discussing South African women. Analysis of migration also needs to take into account women's hopes in terms of the concerns quoted in Buijs's (1993) volume: the remaking of homes, the effects of individual circumstances, the growth of independence, the pleasure as well as the pain in the crossing of boundaries. The multi-faceted and complex nature of women's position does not permit us to see migration in simple terms as either leading always to a loss, or always to a gain, in social status. The migration experience impacts differently on different groups of migrant women, in terms of the role of state and labour market practices and the way women have responded to the challenges they face (Escrivá, this volume). Nevertheless, migration may give women more autonomy and control over economic resources than in their country of origin.

Issues of 'difference' and diversity are now central dimensions for all feminist research as well as research on ethnicity and racism. The differences between Filipinas, who are predominantly Catholic, and Somalian, Sri Lankan and Albanian women who are Muslims, shown by various chapters in this volume, indicate the importance of religious identity in relation to processes of 'othering'. The former not only tend to have a higher income than the latter (a finding also reported in Anderson and Phizacklea 1997), but they are regarded as more desirable domestic workers. However, irrespective of differences, most women suffer by being divided from their families and being compelled to live in an isolated nuclear family unit imposed by Western norms. Moreover, they shoulder the responsibility for supporting their families back home, a common feature of the burden placed on migrant women.

Independent wage labour has a strong impact on the opening up of choices for women although in practice socially learnt constraints may limit the exercise of these choices (Anthias 1992). However, even with changes in economic power, there may be pressure on women to maintain customs of the group, for example the pressure or desire to marry husbands or brides from the homeland is quoted as an example of the retention of cultural traditions in Buijs (1993). Some of the forms of agency may therefore be contradictory. Migration sometimes indicates a willingness to cross class boundaries in a downward direction. This is the case for some Russian or Bulgarian women with university degrees working in Greece and Cyprus as cabaret artistes or as domestic cleaners and waitresses (Anthias, forthcoming). Escrivá shows in this volume how many domestic maids have experienced downward social mobility with migration, as many are highly educated and have university diplomas. Despite this, most of the women she researched saw the migration experience as positive because of improved welfare provision and educational opportunities for themselves and their children.

As Atsuko Matsuoka and John Sorenson say, talking about Eritrean women in Canada (1999: 238):

> the redefinition of gender roles among the diaspora population most certainly were shaped by practical constraints that led to the loss of economic control over the household by some men, more financial

independence for some women, legal prohibitions against formerly
accepted practices, the absence of other family members and alternative
media images

It has also been argued that Iranian migrant and refugee women
have greater possibilities to find jobs and this 'provides women with
the feeling of self' (Ahmadi 1997: 3). Hollands, writing about refugees
in the Netherlands (1996: 120), suggests: 'Refugee men tend to refer
to the past in which they were something, whereas women refer to
the present and future where they might become something.'

Moreover, Bhattacharjee (1997) has seen the sites of family, ethnicity
and nation as sites of gendered struggle where women challenge the
status quo. This might imply that such challenges are most effective
in the migration setting when the institutional apparatus for specific
patriarchal controls via these forms is absent. Orsini Jones and Gattullo,
for example, in this book, also highlight the potential of inter-ethnic
communication, in the context of enabling local structures. Indra
(1999) also suggests the potential for feminist transnational alliances.
In other words, there are possibilities for escaping oppressive social
codes and a basis for solidarity with other women. Such processes,
however, can go hand in hand with the persistence, albeit in a transformed way, of gendered social relations that serve to subordinate
women, as well as racialized social relations. Assumptions that the
migration of women leads to more egalitarianism, as a *general* principle,
given the discussion above and the predominance of domestic work
and sex related activities in migrant women's lives, may therefore be
questioned.

Concluding Remarks: Citizenship Issues

Access to citizenship is a crucial issue relating to the experience of
southern European minorities, including women who are excluded
on different terms from full citizenship, and the provision of legal
and social rights could resolve some of the difficulties such women
face. Debates on citizenship in relation to minority or racialized groups
entail looking at civil, political and social rights. Citizenship can be
defined as sets of rights and responsibilities but these must also
be seen in a less narrow way than political rights and include social
rights. The classic work of T.H. Marshall (1950) has been the starting
point of many feminist critiques and developments of the notion of
citizenship (see Lister 1997). It has been argued that Marshall's idea
of citizenship as entailing full membership of the community assumes

a homogeneous community: how is the latter to be defined? Who constitutes the membership and who defines the boundaries? Who are its representatives? Who is able to speak within it (Anthias and Yuval Davis 1992, Anthias 1997, Feminist Review 1997)? Moreover, the notion of citizenship in terms of individual rights (still very far off for migrant groups in southern Europe anyway) raises problems for the attainment of rights for groups who experience ethnic, race or gender discrimination.

Perhaps the most central aspect for migrants in the new migrations (given the large numbers of undocumented) is the right to enter, or, once having entered, the right to stay. The racialized nature of border restrictions is indicated by the differential rules relating to different categories of individuals on the basis of European membership (the freedom of movement within the European Union) and ethnocentric rules found in many countries. Cypriots and Greeks born abroad, for example, are permitted entry to Cyprus as they are treated as potential members of the nation state. Black nationals in Britain are restricted, on the other hand, through changing patriality rules or the informal policing of borders.

The notion of citizenship, recently much debated (Turner 1990; *Feminist Review* 1997, Lister 1997; Roche and van Berkel 1997), therefore needs to pay attention to inclusions and exclusions of entry, as well as settlement. Furthermore, inclusive models of citizenship require a split between notions of nationality (and therefore ethnic and national belonging) and ideas about relations to the state or polity and to the society more generally. Thus issues are raised about civic entitlements, rights and obligations, which may be divorced from nationality and notions of national belongingness and identification. The political dimensions of participation, the social dimensions of social entitlement and the national identities and sentiments attached to these therefore need to be disassociated.

The European project of consolidation is dedicated to containing migrant populations as well as reducing the number of people that might eventually have to be recognized as having legal rights to some form of citizenship. Undocumented workers, however, pose no such problems and can be confined to the least desirable and lowest paid jobs within the large unregulated sector of many southern European countries. Moreover, instead of being encouraged to develop policies of social inclusion for new migrants, southern European countries are being urged to follow the increasingly powerful European Union (EU), which wants them to secure and control the southern frontiers of

Europe. This goes hand in hand with specific forms of ethnocentrism and xenophobia in each country (see Anthias and Lazaridis 1999). Allied to economic interests these produce a situation whereby large numbers of people are subjected to increasingly unacceptable conditions of human existence. The legalization of these workers has begun in some countries but is patchy and uneven, as other chapters in this volume show.

Moreover, the desire on the part of other states to join the EU and the negotiations around entry, for example in the case of Cyprus, is pulling them in two opposite and contradictory directions. On the one hand, there is the impetus toward the recognition of interculturality with the breaking of national borders and the potential impact of this (for Turkish Cypriot and Greek Cypriot rapprochement in Cyprus for example); the development of multiculturalism is one side of this. On the other side, is the need to develop policies in harmony with the powerful countries of the EU that involve the policing of the borders of Europe against undesirable 'others'. Many of those already in these countries are illegal 'undesirables' and yet are needed by the economy. Turning a blind eye to these may no longer be possible and threats of deportation and state violence are issues that may very well come to the fore increasingly. However, even if issues of illegality are resolved, there still remain broader issues of citizenship that will need addressing, issues that still remain unresolved within Europe as a whole.

This chapter has tried to show that migration needs to be located in terms of the globalization of labour, as well as the continuing bonds with ethnic and national territories and identities, on the one hand and gender relations on the other. Any discussion of migration and it's relationship to the economy and to ethnicity requires looking at the issue of gender and ethnic difference; it must also attend to women as active agents within these processes rather than treating them as passive victims. This is quite an agenda to gender!

Notes

1. Although in much Marxist work the family is treated as a precondition or a condition of existence of the capitalist mode of production (see the critique made by Beechey 1979, for example)

2. The Census of Population of 1960 showed that 41 per cent of women aged 15 and over were participating in economic activity, primarily in agriculture. This compares with 29 per cent in 1976, 41 per cent in 1981, 47 per cent in 1987 and 43 per cent in 1992 (compared with around 75 per cent since 1981 for men) (Dept of Statistics and Research). There has been an increase in the proportion of women in the professional, technical and related categories, which are relatively well paid. There has also been an increase in the proportion of women who are working proprietors from 12 per cent in 1976 to 21 per cent in 1995 (Dept of Statistics and Research). The dual labour market is indicated by the fact women constitute 99 per cent of typists and maids and 80 per cent of computer operators, building caretakers, spinners/weavers, tobacco preparers, dressmakers and machinists. Out of 90 groups of two digit ISCO occupational groups (that is excluding agricultural occupations) about 84 per cent of women were concentrated in only 19 such groups (House 1986), which are low paid jobs. The average level for women's wages in 1989 was 54 per cent below that of men compared to 83 per cent in 1975.

3. In 1960 only 1 per cent of women and 2 per cent of men achieved tertiary level education with 11 per cent of women and 21 per cent of men achieving secondary education. In 1987, 12 per cent of women and 16 per cent of men had reached this level and in 1992 the figure was 16 per cent of women and 19 per cent of men (with 34 per cent of women and 42 per cent of men at secondary level) (Dept of Statistics and Research).

4. The information for 1996, issued by the Ministry of Labour, gives the following figures for countries of origin: after Greece with 3,500, are Sri Lanka (3,500), Philippines (3,300), Bulgaria (2,500), Rumania (1,900), Syria (1,800) UK (1,300), Serbia (1,200), Egypt (1,000), Lebanon (900), Georgia (500), India (460) with a category of 1,800 others over and above from the following countries: Ukraine, Germany, Sweden, Jordan Poland, Finland, France, China, Australia, Canada, Holland, Austria, Denmark, Iran, Iraq, Libya and Norway.

The biggest increase between 1993 and 1996 is the number of maids from the Philippines and Sri Lanka.

5. Decision No 33.210 of the 15 March 1990 of the Ministry of Council of Ministers, and the agreement that was made between various social agents of December 1991, stipulates the criteria that have to be met in order that the employer can be granted a licence to employ foreigners (for further details, see Anthias, forthcoming, Trimikliniotis 1999).

6. For an analysis of this issue in detail regarding women and the nation in Cyprus see Anthias 1989.

References

Ahmadi, F. (1997), 'The problem of identity crisis among female Iranian refugees', paper presented to the *3rd European Feminist Research Conference, University of Coimbra*, Portugal 8–12 July.

Anderson, B. (1983), *Imagined Communities*, London: Verso.

Anderson, B. and Phizacklea, A. and (1997), *Migrant Domestic Workers: a European perspective*, Department of Sociology, University of Leicester.

Anthias, F. (1980), Women and the reserve army of labour' in *Capital and Class*, No. 10, pp. 50–63.

Anthias, F. (1982), *Ethnicity and Class among Greek Cypriot migrants – a study in the conceptualisation of ethnicity*. Ph.D. Thesis, University of London.

Anthias, F. (1983), 'Sexual Divisions and Ethnic Adaptation: greek Cypriot women in Britain' in A. Phizacklea (ed.), *One Way Ticket*, London: Routledge.

Anthias, F. (1989), Women and nationalism in Cyprus in N. Yuval Davis and F. Anthias (eds), *Woman, Nation, State*, London: Macmillan.

Anthias, F. (1990), 'Race and Class Revisited-conceptualising Race and Racisms', *Sociological Review*, Feb. 1990, Vol. 38, No. 1, pp. 19–42.

Anthias, F. (1992), *Ethnicity, Class, Gender and Migration-Greek Cypriots in Britain*, Aldershot: Avebury.

Anthias, F. (1993), 'Gender, Ethnicity and Racialisation in the British Labour Market' in H. Rudolph and M. Morokvasic (eds), *Bridging States and Markets*, Berlin: Sigma, pp. 165–91.

Anthias, F. (1997), 'Antiracism, Multiculturalism and Struggles for a Multicultural Democracy' in M. Roche and R. van Berkel, *European Citizenship and Social Exclusion*, Aldershot: Ashgate, pp. 247–61.

Anthias, F. (1998a), 'Rethinking Social Divisions: some notes towards a theoretical framework' in *Sociological Review*, Vol. 46, No. 3, pp. 505–35.

Anthias, F. (1998b), 'Evaluating Diaspora: Beyond Ethnicity?' in *Sociology*, Vol. 32, No. 3, August, pp. 557–80.

Anthias, F. (forthcoming), 'Home and Away: transnational migration to and from Cyprus and the issue of gender,' in T. Stavrou and J. Joseph (eds), *Cyprus: Towards the 21st Century*, Basingstoke: Macmillan.

Anthias, F. and Yuval Davis, N. (1983), 'Contextualising Feminism – ethnic gender and class divisions', in *Feminist Review*, No. 15, pp. 62–75.

Anthias, F. and Yuval Davis, N. (1989), 'Introduction' in N. Yuval Davis and F. Anthias (eds), *Woman, Nation, State*, Basingstoke: Macmillan.

Anthias, F. and Yuval Davis, N. (1992), *Racialised Boundaries: Race, Nation, gender, Colour and Class and the Anti-racist Struggle*, London: Routledge.

Anthias, F. and Lazaridis, G. (eds), (1999), *Into the Margins: Migration and Social Exclusion in Southern Europe*, Aldershot: Ashgate.

Appadurai, A. (1990), 'Disjuncture and Difference in the Global Cultural Economy' in M. Featherstone (ed), *Global Culture*, London: Sage, pp. 295–310.

Ayres, R. (1999), 'Tourism as a passport to development in small states: reflections on Cyprus' in *International Journal of Economics*, forthcoming.

Beechey, V. (1979), 'Women and production: a critical analysia' in A. Kuhn and A.-M. Wolpe (eds), *Feminism and Materialism*, London: Routledge & Kegan Paul.

Bhachu, P. (1985), *Twice Migrants*, London: Tavistock.

Bhattacharjee, A. (1997), 'The public/private mirage: Mapping homes and undomesticating violence work in the South Asian immigrant community' in *Feminist Genealogies, Colonial Legacies, Democratic Futures*, M. Alexander and C. Mohanty (eds), New York: Routledge.

Brah, A. (1996), *Cartographies of the Diaspora*, London: Routledge.

Buijs, G. (ed.) (1993), *Migrant Women: Crossing Boundaries and Identities*, Oxford: Berg.

Campani, G. (1997), 'Immigrant Women in S. Europe, Social Exclusion and Gender' Paper given to conference on *Non-military aspects of security in S. Europe: migration, employment and labour market*, Santorini, 19–21 September.

Castells, M. (1975), 'Immigrant Workers and Class Struggle in Advanced Capitalism', in *Politics and Society*, Vol. 5, No. 1.

Castles S. and Kosack, G. (1973), *Immigrant Workers in the Class Structure in Western Europe*, Oxford: University Press.

Castles, S. and Miller, M.J. (1993), *The Age of Migration*, London: Macmillan.

Champion, A.G. (1994), 'International migration and demographic change in the developed world', *Urban Studies*, Vol. 31, No. 4–5, pp. 653–77.

Charles, N. and Hintjens, H. (1998), *Gender, Ethnicity and Political Ideologies*, London: Routledge.

Clifford, J. (1994), 'Diasporas', *Cultural Anthropology*, Vol. 9, No. 30, pp. 302–38.

Cohen, R. (ed.) (1995), *The Cambridge Survey of World Migration*, Cambridge: Cambridge University Press.

Cohen, R. (1997), *Global Diasporas: an introduction*, London: UCL Press.

Crompton, R. (1997), *Women and Work in Modern Britain*, Oxford: Oxford University Press.

Dahya, B. (1974), 'The nature of Pakistani ethnicity in industrial cities' in A. Cohen, *Urban Ethnicity*, London: Tavistock.

Daly, F. and Bharot, R. (1999), 'Economic Migration and Social Exclusion: The Case of Moroccans in Italy' in F. Anthias and G. Lazaridis (eds), (1999), *Into the Margins: Migration and Social Exclusion in Southern Europe*, Aldershot: Ashgate.

Dench, G. (1975), *The Maltese in London*, London: Routledge & Kegan Paul.

Dept of Statistics, Republic of Cyprus (miscellaneous).

Eisenstein, Z. (1997), 'Women's Publics and the search for new democracies' in *Feminist Review*, special issue on Citizenship: pushing the boundaries, No. 57, pp. 140–67.

European Forum of Left Feminists (1993), 'Confronting the Fortress', report to the eighth conference of the European Forum of Left Feminists, *Nationalism, Racism and Gender in Europe, Amsterdam 19–21 November.*

Faist, T. (1998), 'Transnational social spaces out of international migration: evolution, significance and future prospects', *European Journal of Sociology*, Vol. 39, No. 2, pp. 213–47.

Hollands, M. (1996), 'Of crowbars and other tools to tackle Dutch society' paper presented to Second *International Conference on New Migrations in Europe*, Utrecht, 18–20th April.

House, W.J. (1986), *Labour Market Segmentation and Sex Discrimination in Cyprus*, Statistics and Research Department Ministry of Finance, Nicosia, Cyprus.

House, W.J., Kyriakidou D. and Stylianou, O. (1989), *'The Changing Status of Female Workers in Cyprus'*, Dept of Statistics and Research, Nicosia.

Indra, D. (ed.) (1999), *Engendering Forced Migration*, Oxford: Berghahn.

Kandiyoti, D. (1989), ' Women and the Turkish State: Political Actors or Symbolic Pawns?' in N. Yuval Davis and F. Anthias (eds) *Women, Nation, State*, Basingstoke: Macmillan.

Kandiyoti, D. (ed.) (1991), *Women, Islam and the State*, Basingstoke: Macmillan.

Karakasidou, A. (1996), 'Women of the family, women of the nation', in *Women's Studies International Forum*, Vol. 19, Nos. 1/2, pp. 99–109.

King, R. (1997), 'Southern Europe in the changing Global map and typology of migration', paper given to conference on *Non-Military aspects of security in S. Europe: migration, employment and labour market*, Santorini, 19–21 September.

Koser, K. and Lutz, H. (eds) (1998), *The New Migration in Europe: Social Constructions and Social Realities*, Basingstoke: Macmillan.

Koser, K. (1997), 'Out of the frying pan into the fire: a case study of illegality among asylum seekers' in Koser and Lutz, (eds) (1998), *The New Migration in Europe: Social Constructions and Social Realities*, Basingstoke: Macmillan.

Kostakopoulou, D. (1999), 'European Union Citizenship: exclusion, inclusion and the Social Dimensions' in F. Anthias and G. Lazaridis, (eds), (1999), *Into the Margins: Migration and Social Exclusion in Southern Europe*, Aldershot: Ashgate.

Lazaridis, G. (1999), 'The Helots of the New Millennium: Ethnic-Greek Albanians and 'Other' Albanians in Greece' in F. Anthias and G. Lazaridis (eds), (1999), *Into the Margins: Migration and Social Exclusion in Southern Europe*, Aldershot: Ashgate.

Lister, R. (1997), *Citizenship: A feminist perspective*, London: Macmillan.

Lloyd, C. (1998), *Discourses on Anti-Racism in France*, Aldershot: Ashgate.

Lutz, H., Phoenix, A. and Yuval Davis, N. (eds) (1995), *Crossfires*, London: Pluto.

Lutz, H. (1997), 'The Limits of Europeanness: Immigrant women in Fortress Europe', *Feminist Review*, special issue on 'Citizenship: Pushing the boundaries ', No. 57, pp. 93–112.

McLuhan, M. (1964), *Understanding Media*, London: Routledge.

Marshall, T.H. (1950), *Citizenship and Social Class*, Cambridge: Cambridge University Press.

Matsuoka, A. and Sorenson, J. (1999), 'Eritrean Canadian Refugee Households as Sites of Gender Renegotiation' in D. Indra (ed.), *Engendering Forced Migration*, Oxford: Berghahn.

Miles, R. (1989), *Racism and Migrant Labour*, London: Routledge.

Ministry of Labour (1997), *Statistics on Recent Migrants*, Republic of Cyprus.

Moch, L. 1992, *Moving Europeans*, Bloomington and Indiana: Indiana University Press.

Modood, T. (1996), 'The changing context of 'race' in Britain' in *Patterns of Prejudice*, Vol. 30, No. 1, pp. 3–42.

Morokvasic, M. (1984), 'Birds of Passage are also Women' in *International Labour Review*, Vol. 18, No. 68.

Phizacklea, A. (ed.) (1983), *One Way Ticket*, London: Routledge.

Phizacklea, A. and Miles, R. (1980), *Labour and Racism*, London: Routledge & Kegan Paul.

Roche, M. and van Berkel, R. (eds), *European Citizenship and Social Exclusion*, Aldershot: Ashgate.

Rudolph, H. and Hillman, F. (1997), 'The invisible hands need visible heads: managers, experts and professionals from Western countries in Poland' in Koser and Lutz (eds) (1998), *The New Migration in Europe: Social Constructions and Social Realities*, Basingstoke: Macmillan.

Solomos, J. (1986), 'Varieties of Marxist conceptions of race, class and the state: a critical analysis', J. Rex and D. Mason (eds), *Theories of Race and Ethnic Relations*, Cambridge: Cambridge University Press.

Silverman, M. (1992), *Deconstructing the Nation*, London: Routledge.

Stasiulis, D. and Yuval Davis, N. (eds), *Unsettling Settler Societies*, London: Sage.

Summerfield, H. (1993), 'Patterns of adaptation: Somalian and Bangladeshi women in Britain' in G. Buijs, (ed.), (1993), *Migrant Women: Crossing Boundaries and Identities*, Oxford: Berg.

Stylianou, O. (1989), 'Women in Development Policy in Cyprus', unpublished paper.

Triantafillidou, A. (1997), 'Racists? Us? Are you joking?, the discourse of social exclusion in Greece and Italy', paper to conference on *Non-Military aspects of Security in S. Europe:migration, employment and labour market*, Santorini, 19–21 September.

Trimikliniotis, N. (1999), 'Racism and New Migration to Cyprus: the racialisation of migrant workers', in F. Anthias and G. Lazaridis, G. (eds), (1999), *Into the Margins: Migration and Social Exclusion in Southern Europe*, Aldershot: Ashgate.

Turner, B. (1990), 'The Two Faces of Sociology: Global or National?' In M. Featherstone (ed.), *Global Culture*, London: Sage.

Vassiliadou, M. (1999), *A Struggle for Independence: attitudes and practices of the women of Cyprus*, unpublished Ph.D thesis, the University of Kent.

Walby, S. (1994), 'Is citizenship gendered?', *Sociology*, Vol. 28, No. 2, pp. 379–95.

Walby, S. (1997), *Gender Transformations*, London: Routledge.

Wallerstein, I. (1990),' Culture as the Ideological Battleground of the Modern World-System', in M. Featherstone (ed.), *Global Culture*, London: Sage.

Walker, A. (1990), *Women and Gender in South Africa to 1945*, London: James Currey.

Walters, M. (1995), *Globalization*, London: Routledge.

Ward, R. and Jenkins, R. (eds) (1984), *Ethnic Communities in Business*, London: Cambridge.

Wetherall, M. and Potter, J. (1992), *Mapping the Language of Racism,* Hampstead: Harvester Wheatsheaf.

Wilford, R. and Miller, R. (eds), (1998), *Women, Ethnicity and Nationalism,* London: Routledge.

WING, (1985), *Worlds Apart, Women under Immigration and Nationality Law,* London: Pluto Press.

Yuval-Davis, N. and Anthias, F. (eds), (1989), *Woman, Nation, State,* Basingstoke: MacMillan.

Yuval Davis, N. (1997), *Gender and Nation,* London: Sage.

three

Filipino and Albanian Women Migrant Workers in Greece: Multiple Layers of Oppression

GABRIELLA LAZARIDIS

Introduction

In southern Europe, as already mentioned in the introductory chapter in this book, a major reversal of historical patterns has developed in recent years. Italy, Spain, Portugal and Greece became receivers of migrants (both poverty migrants and highly qualified experts) and of refugees from non-European countries (see King and Black 1997; Anthias and Lazaridis 1999). This phenomenon has been explained in terms of their geographical location, the residual effects of African colonial influences and the inadequacies of methods of surveillance and control of immigration used in southern Europe (see Fielding 1993: 50). Moreover, as Castles and Miller (1993: 267) rightly argue, 'in an increasingly international economy, it is difficult to open borders for movements of information, commodities and capital and yet close them to people'. Women occupy a central position in these migration flows, both as 'dependent' and, more importantly, as 'independent' economic migrants, playing protagonist, active roles. At the same time, throughout southern Europe policies aimed at reducing labour market rigidities and enhancing competitiveness have been introduced. This increases the eagerness of employers to hire undocumented workers, in a strongly gendered labour market that leaves few opportunities for women other than in the sex and 'entertainment' industries, and in feminized spheres of some services (tourism, nursing, domestic).

Cuts in social welfare or inadequate welfare provisions (Ferrera 1996) have resulted in increase in demand for undocumented cheap workers, such as for example, domestic services.[1] In Spain and in Greece domestic work is the largest area of employment for migrant women, while nearly a third of the work permits issued in Italy in 1995, were issued to domestic workers (Anderson and Phizacklea 1997).

An ageing population, changing family structures, changing lifestyles for women and a rudimentary welfare state unable to provide adequate care for people with special needs, the elderly, and children, make the demand for such services imperative. In Italy the demand for domestic workers – especially live-in domestics – can be traced back to the 1960s (Andall 1995: 10). Such demand, which in Spain and Greece until recently was met by local citizens, is nowadays met by migrant women.[2] It is important to study this recent growth in the demand for domestic workers in view of the possible legal, social and economic problems that increased migration may produce in the near future, for the migrant women living and working in these countries.

Domestic workers who come to work in southern Europe include a wide variety of nationalities, namely Moroccans, Eritreans and Ethiopians and Filipinas in Italy, women from the Dominican Republic, Morocco and Peru in Spain, women from Poland, Albania, Bulgaria, Ethiopia, Somalia and the Philippines in Greece. In Greece the Filipinas are the best organized; the Ethiopians, Albanians and Poles are highly visible. This chapter provides an analysis of the experiences of women migrant workers who come from the Philippines and Albania to live and work in a southern European country, Greece. As this chapter demonstrates, in the case of Greece a hierarchy of labour operates with domestic workers from the Philippines earning higher wages for shorter hours of work than the Albanians. Wages depend, of course, on the legal status of these women, on whether or not they have work permits, on the women's ethnic background and stereotypes attached to them.

Until the early 1990s, the literature on migrant labourers who came to work in Greece consisted of a few journalistic accounts, which rested on various anecdotes and examples culled in an unsystematic way (see for example, Gioulakis 1990: 80–6; Pierros 1990: 57–9). Recently, some articles on migration into Greece have been published, but with few exceptions (Lazaridis 1995; Lazaridis 1999a; Lazaridis 1999b; Psimmenos 1996; Lazaridis and Wickens 1999; Lazaridis and Psimmenos 1999), these are mainly based on secondary sources and are concerned primarily with male migrant workers (see for example, Petrinioti 1993;

Fakiolas 1995; Maratou-Alipranti 1994; Kontis and Balourdos 1994). There have been few attempts to collect primary data on samples of female migrants or to carry out ethnographic research on the way 'third-country migrants' perceive and interpret their experiences. With the exception of Lazaridis 1995; Anderson and Phizacklea 1997; Lazaridis 1999a and Psimmenos' paper in this volume, there has been no other investigation of migrant women from non-EU member states who live and work in Greece. Even national discourses on gender, which have rapidly expanded since the early 1980s, did not address migrant women. Moreover, domestic work per se is an occupation that in Greece remains largely unstudied. This chapter aims to overcome this omission.

The chapter focuses on the diversity of experiences of the Albanian and Filipino migrant female domestic workers and on the way in which the migration process per se, but also mechanisms of marginalization and exclusion, affect these two groups of women differently. It explores whether differences between the two ethnic groups under study can be explained solely on economic factors or whether other factors such as cultural differences and reputation rather than racial categorization (see Stone 1983) act as an additional constraint on these women's employment opportunities. The argument put forward here is tentative and exploratory, a first step towards a more detailed research that I plan to carry out in the immediate future. The comparative aspect of the paper is also of interest in that lessons can be drawn from the experiences of these two migrant groups that might be relevant to others.

Methods

The research, on which this chapter is based used mainly qualitative methods of investigation. A statistical compilation of data on general trends proved unfeasible. Many migrant domestic labourers are clandestine workers and escape official control, so they remain 'invisible' in official statistics. Official statistics in Greece exclusively focus on migrants who enter the country through legal channels.

The research concentrated on collecting primary data from samples of two groups of domestic helpers and cleaners, Filipinas and Albanians, in Corfu and Athens. The view taken was that totally unstructured qualitative research could make for unproductive use of time. To avoid this problem, questionnaires for gathering basic demographic information were designed and distributed to migrants. These were well received by the Filipinas but not by the Albanians. The latter were wary of formal setting with the researcher going through several questions, constantly taking notes or recording the answers. They found it difficult to give straight and honest answers to direct questions related to their work, reasons for migrating, point of entry into Greece, experiences in the host country, and so on. Their refusal to answer them was for fear, as they said, that such information might be used by the authorities and result in their deportation. I soon realized that answers would be obtainable only outside a structural format, in the course of informal conversations (Burgess 1989: 102).

As a result, a wide range of methods was used, including unstructured in-depth interviews and life histories for gaining useful information on the way migrant women perceive and interpret their experiences.[3] In addition, semi-structured interviews were used with key informants connected with them, group interviews with three or four women who made it clear that they felt uneasy with giving individual interviews, visits to key informants' areas and rallying-points, such as immigrant housing complexes, ethnic associations. Women were in the first instance approached through employers as well as through migrant community groups and their supporters. The latter provided an important source of information. As many migrant women were reluctant to participate, a 'snowballing' technique was used to obtain access to and select women for interview. It was intended to draw a random sample of migrant workers using lists from recruiting agents and churches (as many Albanians get baptized in Greece and Filipinas are dedicated Catholic churchgoers). However, this proved unfeasible because most migrants are illegal (they either enter the country illegally or become illegal when their visa expires). For ethical reasons, the identities of women who were interviewed were concealed. Additional information on domestic workers and migrants in other occupations came from employers themselves; it being understood that such comments share an inbuilt class bias and often lack knowledge of and sympathy with personal factors.

To conclude, I have been aware of my limitations as a white person with a stable job, seeking to understand fully the experiences of these women. At the same time, my background as a child of the Hellenic diaspora influenced my decision to research the lives of those women who experience multiple forms and degrees of exclusion. I entered this area of investigation having a mix of insider and outsider characteristics. I had been through a similar experience myself when, after having lived for most of my childhood in a Greek community in Africa my family migrated to Greece and had experienced the emotional tensions created in migrants by the uncertainty about the cultural meanings of one's own words and actions, and the insecurity and loneliness that come with it; I had an understanding of what it is to live as an 'outsider' in a community and the efforts it requires to try to get progressively more 'on the inside of it'. There are some moral ambiguities characterizing this research method. As Barnes (cited by Akeroyd 1990) has argued,

> There is no immaculate praxis of fieldwork. Whatever choice we make we are unlikely to be completely happy with it . . . The competent fieldworker is he or she who learns to live with an uneasy conscience but continues to be worried by it.

The sexist myopia of migration theories

> Population movements on a grand scale have become a prominent feature of contemporary society, but there have been as yet relatively few attempts to look beneath the surface of the mass movements of people and to disentangle the specific experiences of women (Buijs 1993: 1).

In early literature on migration women are absent; a considerable number of studies on migration have used exclusively male samples and hence, migration appears as a male affair only, even in contexts where the sex ratio in the migratory movements was in favour of females (see also Phizacklea 1983). As Morokvasic (1983: 13–14) argues: 'this deliberate exclusion of women is usually justified by the lack of research funds and by women's supposedly minor economic role'.

If one feature of the early literature on migration is its relative neglect of female migrants, another feature is that, whenever women were not neglected, they were mentioned within the framework of the family, in relation to children. This literature relies on stereotypes of migrant women as migrants' wives or mothers, isolated, maybe illiterate, secluded from the outside world and the bearers of many children. In the usual expression 'migrant and their families', 'families' are understood to be composed of dependent members – women and children – while the 'migrant' is considered to be a male breadwinner (see for example the work of Valabregne 1973).

For the first time around the mid-1970s researchers acknowledged the inadequacy and 'sexist myopia' that ran through previous approaches (Morokvasic 1974; Hoffman-Nowotny 1985, to mention two) and a radical shift of focus from the family to other issues, such as the migrant women's role as wage workers took place. From then onwards the fact that gender divisions are central to understanding the social placement of ethnic minority groups within the host society became widely accepted. While, however, female migrants became assessed as workers, female migration failed to be related to the migratory movements of labour and their determinants. As a consequence, migrant women were assessed as individuals whose behaviour was above all determined by their psychology and 'culture'. In other words, their migration was determined by individual motivation and their condition analysed within a perspective of adaptation to the host society.

Early attempts to explain the position of migrant women in economic relations tended to be economistic. For example, it was argued that women generally (Beechey 1977), and married women in particular together with migrants constitute a reserve army of labour, to be brought in and thrown out of wage labour according to the needs of capital (Castles and Kosack 1973; Castells 1975). However, as Anthias (1993: 167) argues, 'the unstated assumption in these positions is a homogeneous migrant labour category, whose embodiment is male'. She goes on to state that the postulate of *migrants* as a reserve of cheap labour is 'jeopardised by the existence of a segmented labour market or dual labour market that relegates migrants to a subordinate sphere' and the postulate of *women* as a reserve and cheap labour 'failed . . . to provide a satisfactory explanation of women's position in the labour market' (Anthias 1993).

Back in the early 1980s, Phizacklea (1983: 95–112) argued that, in terms of occupational distribution, migrant women originating from Third World countries occupy a subordinate position within the British, French and West German labour markets, as they are concentrated within the manual sectors of 'women's work'. As this paper and other papers in this volume show, this is also true nowadays for migrant women in southern Europe in general and in Greece in particular. Furthermore, since the late 1970s, both indigenous and migrant women have been shifting from manufacturing into the tertiary or service sector. But whereas indigenous women were moving in ever greater numbers into more 'desirable' low pay 'white blouse' jobs, migrant women have been moving from one form of low pay manual job to another, or to the lowest ranks of non-manual work. As this volume shows, this is also true nowadays for a large number of women who migrated into southern Europe and concentrate on domestic work, tourist-related activities and the 'entertainment' and sex industries. Migrant labour is also perceived by the labour in the host society to pose a threat to hard-won gains, and this works to keep women in gender specific and low paid sectors of work (Phizacklea 1983).

This chapter examines the varied and complex responses of women to migration, whether they were forced to migrate by political circumstances, as in the case of Albanians, or driven by the need to escape poverty and destitution, as happened with most of the Filipinas I interviewed. The aim of this chapter is twofold: first, to highlight the way in which women from these two different ethnic minority groups are positioned differently in relation to each other and to their Greek counterparts;[4] second, to examine the way in which the social and economic position of Albanians and Filipinas is determined by gender relations within the host society and the specific cultures of these two different migrant groups. As will be seen the latter interact with racialization processes that relate differently to Albanian and to Filipinas respectively, resulting in these women clustering in particular niches within the labour market of the Greek parallel economy.[5] The reduction of racism to colour racism cannot be used for connecting differentially racialized groups such as the Albanian and Filipina domestic workers with a specific economic positioning. As argued elsewhere (see Lazaridis and Wickens 1999), colour racism cannot act as an adequate explanation for the differential treatment of Albanians vis-à-vis other ethnic minority groups. Other aspects are much more important in Greece such as religion – Filipinas are Catholic, whereas Albanians are Muslims – which ties with ideas about the racialization of Islam in Europe. For reasons explained in Lazaridis 1999b, Albanians are constructed as 'the enemy at the doorstep', whereas, as this paper demonstrates, the Filipinas are constructed as 'the nice Catholic girls that one can place his/her trust with'. Racism as an ideology cuts across colour and connects racialized groups with specific economic positions (Anthias 1993) irrespective of their colour of skin and other phenotypic characteristics. The economic disadvantage experienced by these women is not solely the effect of racism, but is also the effect of a range of exclusionary practices in Greek society in general and in the Greek racist and sexist labour markets in particular, which affect differently different categories of the racialized population. Here I will try to consider ways in which race and gender ideologies and practices intersect in producing certain exclusionary outcomes. The argument put forward is that racist and racialized exclusions intersect with sexist relations within Greek society and the ethnic communities under study; this interplay of these processes operates differently within these two ethnic minority groups of women to produce different outcomes (see Anthias 1993 in relation to gendered ethnicities in the British labour market). In other words, as shown below, although these groups of women face similar (but not identical) economic and social disadvantages, one cannot characterize them as a homogeneous social category; a recognition of difference and diversity is necessary.

Paid Domestic Work: Why the Need?

Domestic work is now widespread in Greece. It is 'a form of production in which the goods and services produced are for the exclusive use of the domestic unit, are produced within that unit, and are exchanged for wages' (Cock 1980: 314). Many households employ domestic workers on a full-time or part-time basis. Until recently, most of the domestic workers employed were working-class Greeks originating from rural areas. Gradually, with an increase in living standards, reduction in flows from rural areas to urban centres and the acquisition of higher education, Greek women employed in this highly stigmatized sector slowly abandoned this type of work. In Greece, as in Italy, migrant domestic workers 'were not perceived as competitors in the employment market as they were occupying a sector which bore a considerable degree of social stigma and which was increasingly shunned by [local] women' (Andall 1995: 209).

There are a number of reasons for the increasing demand for domestic workers in Greece. First, the changing structure of Greek population with declining fertility rates from 2.28 in 1960 to 1.39 in 1992 (Eurostat 1994). Second, changes in family formation, and third, demographic ageing due also to increasing longevity (the over-60s and the over-80s represent 20.2 per cent and 3.2 per cent respectively of the population of Greece (Eurostat 1993)). This rise in the proportion of economically inactive elderly persons coupled with increased levels of dependency are not, however, met by the provisions made by Greece's welfare state. In the typologies of welfare developed by experts on comparative social policy, a distinction has been drawn between countries with a generous universal form of welfare provision at the one end of the continuum and those with a less generous or 'residual' or 'rudimentary' provision on the other (Esping-Andersen 1990; Leibfried 1992). Greece, along with other southern European states (Ferrera 1996), falls under the 'rudimentary' approach, characterized by 'underdeveloped social services, entitlements related to the employment and contribution record and an emphasis on the role of the family as the core unit of social care' (Katrougalos 1996: 41). Families and particularly women occupy a central position in provision of care for elderly, children and people with special needs.

The position of Greek women has changed over the last 30 years, as has the composition of the Greek family (Papadopoulos 1998). Urbanization and emigration in the 1960s and 1970s have weakened the traditional family relationships and related inter-generational reciprocal arrangements (Lazaridis 1992). With elderly parents staying behind in the rural setting, some siblings emigrating to 'guest worker' countries and others moving into large urban centres, traditional family structures with three or four generations started giving way to the smaller nuclear family unit. This has had implications for the care of dependants, which now falls under the responsibility of the nuclear family and in particular of women (mothers and daughters) who now lack the extended family networks and mechanisms of support these can provide. It has been the expected norm that the sacrifices the parents have made in educating their children and/or providing them with a dwelling and other means that enable them to ensure financial independence, will be reciprocated by providing personal care for the elderly. Solidarity within the family, is the motto. 'If not, [the woman] runs the risk of being severely criticised as "self-interested" (*egoistria*) and "ungrateful" (*aharisti*) towards her parents or in-laws, and consequently developing feelings of guilt which are reinforced by the [society's] intolerance towards such behaviour' (Lazaridis 1992: 349). The care has been provided on an unpaid basis, although the retirement pension of the older person/s is a contribution to the family budget.

Since the late 1960s women's social and economic role outside the household started changing. As shown below, these changes do not mean that these women's sense of obligation has weakened or that they care less for their relatives, but changing economic circumstances have started shaping and transforming patterns of practical support. As the Greek family remains firmly patriarchal in its structure, duties and obligations are still there, but are now dealt with differently. To paraphrase Dalley (1990: 12) it is now permissible for the woman to pay for the care to be brought in, provided that the setting within which the provision of care may take place is provided for. Instead of sacrificing herself, she is now sacrificing her purse.

A relatively large number of women have come into employment. For example, the number of female employees increased by 10 per cent between 1983 and 1991 (Lazaridis and Syngellakis 1995: 99). A large proportion of this employment is in the agricultural sector (23.9 per cent in 1995) and in services (62.2 per cent) (Papadopoulos 1998: 55–6; Vaiou 1996). The rapid growth of the informal sector, increasing flexible work patterns and technological change impact on women's employment (Lazaridis and Syngellakis: 1995: 100). Fear of loosing a stable job[6] often means that women often have no other option but to buy in help. The patriarchal family, which is one of the most important traditional institutions in Greece, has been retained, as have traditional values; despite the need for a dual family income, the wife's role is still centred on domestic affairs. Women are now faced with the double burden of having to work and to look after the domestic domain. But women's occupational and professional responsibilities do not permit this double role to be carried out effectively. New models of gender identity are therefore gradually emerging for Greek women, where the importance of women's paid employment is viewed as equally important as her essential family role. Women are still expected to perform the household chores, while supplementing the family budget via paid employment (Lazaridis and Syngellakis 1995: 102). As Papageorgiou (1993: 13) writes, 'the state, controlled by clientelistic arrangements, was rather indifferent to the needs of these women and to their demands and failed to make [appropriate] provisions', and as a result the burden of care falls overwhelmingly on the woman's shoulders, while in a society where sexist values and attitudes are deeply entrenched, men are expected to be the main breadwinners and women's labour to be expropriated within the household. Thus many women, who cannot rely on other family members, try to cope with this 'double presence' by hiring home help. In an article on Italian women, Franca Bimbi (1993: 140) writes: 'The concept of "double presence" has . . . been used to indicate a new model of gender identity which is no longer exclusively bound up with a woman's role in the family, but rather aims to establish a new equilibrium between public and private life'. Andall (1995: 206) maintains that 'it is this conflict between . . . women's desire to achieve some form of "equilibrium" and the attempted subjugation of their paid work role to the needs of the family which has contributed both to the specific economic niche within which . . . [migrant] women are predominantly concentrated and the "anomalous" role of migrant women that this engenders'.

The factors mentioned above have created a caring gap which, as stated above, was not met by changes in state provisions for childcare and care for the elderly. At present there are 1,300 public crèches and some 1,000 private, which are not covering demand (Balaska 1993: 18). Childcare provision for children under three years of age is very low, as it covers only 3 per cent of these children (Papadopoulos 1998: 49). As a result, women have to develop strategies that will facilitate their employment; they have to make their own arrangements and the best way around this is often to farm out house work and to make their own private arrangements for the care of elderly, children, or members of the family with special needs. Without underestimating the 'push' factors involved in the migratory process and the global aspects of migration outlined by Castles and Miller (1993) in their book *The Age of Migration*, one may argue that the demand in Greece may motivate female chain emigration. As Andall (1995: 209) writes in an article on migrant women in the Italian context, 'domestic service is one sphere where there is an acknowledged demand-based migration'; this enables local women to meet their caring responsibilities and may also buy them time for leisure, time for spending with their family, time for 'self' and access to a particular lifestyle that would otherwise be unsustainable. In other words, they are hired to rid the lifestyles of those who fall under the group which, in Bourdieu's (1990) terms, is a group whose consumption patterns score highly in the culture of extravagant excess and/or in cultural performance activities. Moreover, as Anderson and Phizacklea (1997: 10) maintain,

> the availability of a large pool of cheap and flexible labour willing to work for very low wages on the one hand, and significant numbers of families with large disposable incomes on the other may "create" a demand in itself, particularly if employing a domestic worker is regarded not simply as socially acceptable, but as a status symbol.

Filipina and Albanian women in Athens and Corfu

Domestic workers are amongst the most exploited groups in a society like Greece, which is marked with inequality. They are moving into a country with minimal public provision and where potential sources of informal care by families have, as mentioned earlier, been diminished. They are extremely insecure, lack fundamental workers' rights and often work long hours at very low wages. In order to establish that Albanian and Filipina migrant domestic workers are among the most exploited occupational groups in Greece, several aspects of their situation will be described: their wages, working hours, level of job satisfaction, their rights as workers, their social lives, their status in the community, and their relationship with their employers.

Prior to analysing these women's working conditions, I will briefly look at the motives for emigration as these differ between the two groups. Filipinas[7] are the fourth largest migrant group (were estimated at 40,000 in 1993) in Greece after Albanians, Egyptians and Poles

(Petrinioti 1993: 18). The Filipinas emigrate primarily for economic reasons, most in order to provide better opportunities for their children (this point will be taken up further down). As Campani (1993: 198–199) in her study of Filipina women in Italy maintains, the percentage of unemployed Filipinas is 65 per cent of the total Filipina population in Italy and even those who have graduated end up being unemployed or taking up low-paid jobs. Of those employed,

> even regular jobs (such as teacher, secretary, nurse, policeman or bank-clerk) and self-employment (for example butcher, veterinary) do not assure a sufficient standard of living, for example the ability to pay for the schooling of their children . . . [moreover] in the Philippines, women's wages are officially and legally lower than men's wages.

The wages these women earn in the host country are therefore an important part of the economy of the household back in the Philippines. In other words, sheer economic necessity forces these individuals to leave their country and seek new employment opportunities overseas; they play active protagonist roles in the migration process; they are what one would call, 'active women and on the move'. Other reasons for migrating are the wish for 'a better life' and the infiltration through education and the mass media of American culture and values, values related to acquired consumption patterns and habits[8] (Campani 1993: 200). The majority of women who migrated are unaccompanied; they are not part of what Chell (paper in this volume) calls 'a male thing', but must be considered as social and economic actors in their own right. Their situation is similar to that of 'distressed gentlewomen' in Victorian England who, in the late nineteenth century and early twentieth century, for reasons described by Swaisland (1993: 163), migrated as domestic servants to South Africa; the more educated ones became domestic workers with all the incongruence of status that entails.

The Albanians, on the other hand, are driven to migration not only because of economic necessity, but also for a number of political reasons associated with years of repression experienced by those of Greek ethnic origin in particular (for a detailed discussion of this see Mesimeris 1978; Hyfantis 1993; Lazaridis 1999b). Unlike the Filipinas, almost all Albanian women are accompanied by, or accompany, their men. Unlike the Filipinas, most Albanians, not all, are protagonists in migration flows from Albania, which can be said to be a 'male thing'. Albanians have not surpassed the role of dependent family member; within the Albanian community itself, they are still referred to as the wives, the mothers, the sisters, the daughters. On the rare occasions when they arrive without the male partner, this is not because of choice, but because the man did not manage to enter the borders or was captured en route and sent back home. Although the Filipinas enter the country legally (with tourist visas or working permits), the Albanians enter the country illegally; they either swim over to Corfu and are, as the locals say, 'being fished' during the night, or cross the borders by foot, through the mountains, aided by organized smugglers. The average price for smuggling someone from Albania to Greece is around 100,000 drachmas (around £200). Unlike the Filipinas, the presence of the Albanians in Greece was not until recently (1998) governed by bureaucratic procedures centred on the acquisition of residence and work permits. They came in illegally and they stayed illegal. Now, however, this is in the process of changing with the new efforts made by the Greek government to regularize illegal migrants. The effect of this process, which will determine their right to live as legal migrants with social citizenship rights, remains to be seen. It will certainly afford some security to those who manage to regularize themselves (for the hurdles encountered in the quest to legitimize their status see Lazaridis and Poyago-Theotoky 1997) in that they will no longer live under the fear of immediate deportation.

Arrivals of Filipinas can be traced back to the 1970s. Networks and agencies are important in the distribution of Filipina women around the world.[9] They migrate alone and later on some are united with their husbands. The extended family back in the Philippines plays an important role in enabling these women to migrate; parents' and grandparents' willingness to take care of the children back home,[10] and the willingness of the husband to stay back and 'invest' the remittances, plays an important role in decision processes. 'I had no choice, I had to emigrate in order to send back money for the education of the children', said a Filipina in her early thirties. Another woman, married with two children under ten, added: 'I had to come. I am sending back money, which my husband uses, for building our family house. I will return when he has finished the house.' The decision to migrate is undertaken for the good of the close-knit family unit and often challenges the traditional distribution of economic roles within the domestic unit. Yet another woman said: 'All I wanted was to escape . . . to escape the poverty, the battering, a life with no future . . . I wanted to change my life . . . to be happy . . .' For some women migration is not only a means for the financial improvement of those left behind, but also an avenue towards the fulfilment of unfulfilled dreams. Although the word Filipina has become synonymous with 'maid' in Greece in that the expression *eho Filipineza*, ('I have a Filipina') means 'I have a maid', there is no specialization in the work they do; they can also be found in the sex industry, in tourist related activities and unlike Italy, in nursing.[11] There is of course diversity in the lives these women have left behind, in the obligations they brought with them, their individual desires and expectations from the migratory project, their different experiences in the host country.

The mode of recruitment also differs between the two groups of women. Filipina domestic workers are obtained in two main ways: first, via agents based in the Philippines and having a representative in Greece and second, via recommendation by a friend of the employer, a previous worker, or Caritas (an international organization linked to the Catholic church; Caritas Hellas has branches all over Greece) or their local association (see below). Albanians, on the other hand, either find a job via informal networks through word of mouth, or often come to an employer's doorstep asking for work. Both groups rely heavily on support networks, which facilitate their insertion into the host country's labour force. Without the existence of such networks, migration would have involved much higher risks and costs than it does now. Until 1991, Filipina women were often high school or college or even university graduates, brought to Greece under the so called 'nursing aid permit'; this was a permit granted under the pretence of being employed as a nursing aid by a specific employer. As a woman said to me: 'I really thought that I was going to work as a nurse. I ended up working as a maid.' Most women although able to perform the duties of a recognized professional occupation, that of a nurse, are experiencing de-skilling and loss of occupational status. The Filipina worker cannot enter into the country legally unless she has a visa and has obtained a contract of employment through an agency bureau, which charges a high fee for the service it provides. 'It costs the domestic between 20,000 and 100,000 drachmas to find work through an agency, and the employer pays 50,000 to 60,000' (Anderson and Phizacklea 1997: 29). No such contract may be valid for more than two-years, although it may be renewed. This ensures the worker's vulnerability, in that if she chooses to break the contract and leave the job or if she gets fired, she has to leave the country. Others decide to overstay. This places them in a weak bargaining position, forcing them to accept poor working conditions, since it means that many domestic workers after the end of the two-year period become illegal. Some choose to become illegal whereas others remain in employment and endure a system of 'forced labour'. This system ensures the extreme exploitation of migrant labour. Indeed, some employers in Corfu admitted that they kept their employee's passport and other documents, 'for security reasons', as they put it. As a Filipina said:

> I am overworked. They treat me as a slave, but I can't leave; they have my passport locked somewhere in the house. Once I tried to explain that I wanted to leave but they said that they paid the agency a lot of money for me and that they will give me back the passport when the two year contract ends. A friend of mine, in a similar position, just left . . .

The wages that the two groups of women receive slightly vary. The wages of the Albanian domestic workers ranged from 1,000 drachmas per hour for the first five hours worked, but if they work more, they receive a lump sum of 6,000 drachmas (around £12) for the whole day's work. That is, even if they work ten hours or more (and many, in fact, do), with a few exceptions, at the end of the day they receive a lump sum of 6,000 drachmas. The remuneration of the Filipinas is slightly better, in that they are paid between 1,000 and 1,200 drachmas per hour; no upper limit is put on the daily wage. This difference can be explained in terms of the legal entry of the Filipinas and their 'good' reputation (see below). Both groups of women also received payment in kind (such as food), which are, however, difficult to calculate. Because domestic workers receive both payment in kind and wages, Callinicos (1975: 61) has suggested that the domestic worker has a 'quasi-feudal' relationship with her employer. The Filipinas justified their better remuneration in terms of their work being of superior quality to that of the Albanians and also in terms of the fact that they can be trusted. 'People know that they can trust us', a woman said. 'We are not like the Albanians. They are not good in what they are doing, one can't trust them, they are not as clean as we are: this is why people prefer us to them', another woman added. For those who are employed by the day there is seldom any bargaining over wages, apart from when the domestic worker is initially employed. The Albanians, however, seem to have less bargaining power over their wages than the Filipinas; in most cases these are settled by the employer. In this respect, the Albanian domestic workers are in a similar position to domestics in South Africa, where, as (Cock 1980: 31) writes, 'the employer states the terms and the employee accepts them without attempting to negotiate'. This also reflects the vulnerability and almost total powerlessness of the Albanian women *vis-à-vis* their employer and their main rivals in the market, that is the Filipinas. The association of the Albanians with various criminal acts reported in the media and their racialization by the media (see also Karydis 1992: 97–103; Lazaridis and Wickens 1999), has resulted in many employers expecting their employees to cheat and steal and has left these workers with little choice of alternative employment. The argument put forward by the employers for justifying this lower remuneration offered to the Albanian women is the risk they take in employing them of loosing all their household items. As one employer explained,

> my sister-in-law came back one day and all the silverware was missing; her Albanian maid had asked for a two day leave to visit her ill mother in Albania. When she returned, she confessed that she stole the items and promised to bring them back if she did not lose her job; a week later, she brought them all back

In stealing, some Albanians reinforce the employers' image of themselves as inferior people, and have reinforced crude racist stereotypes such as 'untrustworthy', 'cunning', 'thieves', 'criminals', (Lazaridis 1996) which, in turn, are the grounds on which the employers justify the Albanians' lower remuneration rates and their clear preference for Filipinas. Overt preferences are often made to recruiting agencies and/or networks.

The Filipinas on the other hand are the 'good Catholic girls', who can be relied on. Religion is one factor that may contribute to the social construction of Albanians as 'dangerous others'. The Catholic Filipinas are Christians and thus, despite their difference in terms of colour and physical appearance, are closer to 'us' the Greeks than the Albanians, the Muslims, the 'others'. This awareness of religious ties seems to bind Catholics and Orthodox together. As one employer put it: 'Filipinas are good girls, they are Christians, like us'. The Muslim religion of most Albanians, one the other hand, can be said to create a psychological distance between Albanians and Greeks. Orthodox Christianity has been historically tied up to ethnicity, to Greekness, it is viewed as a sustainer of ethnicity, as an element of Greek identity. Faith is used as a factor separate from theology in such a way as to proclaim non-conformity to 'otherness'. Orthodoxy has become a noble cause for opposition to Western influences as well as influences from the east. Emphatic anti-Muslim cries are strong in the media, amongst right-wing groups (for example Chrysi Avghi) proclaiming ethnic purity and among some members of the Greek church. According to Metropolitan Meletios for example, 'Greeks who forget the foundations of Orthodoxy . . . cease to be Greeks . . . and Greek Muslims never existed . . . those who became Muslim . . . entered another nation'. On the other hand, religious differentiation from the Catholics is not so great; after all, Catholics are Christians too, not at all like the 'others', the Muslims. Since the ideological and political division of Europe disappeared with the end of the Cold War, the cultural division between Orthodox Christianity and Islam has re-emerged even stronger. This dividing line can be said now to be uniting the Protestants and Catholics with the Orthodox against the Muslim; this fosters a mentality breeding intolerance to difference and the misuse of religion in making judgements about people and fostering racialization of the non-Orthodox, the non-Christian, and in particular of the Muslim. According to Fakiolas (1995: 39), 'all those of non-Orthodox Christian denominations are literally interpreted by some Orthodox [in Greece] as heretics, i.e., those who do not abide to the rule of God and do not accept the truth'. As a young mother said when asked why she hired a Filipina and not an Albanian woman: 'I will never have an Albanian bringing up my children. The children are very young, they have to be brought up with proper values. I have hired a Filipina; she will bring up the children with good Christian values'. Another woman said: 'I do not want my children to be brought up by a Muslim; their values, their beliefs, are different'.

Unlike the Albanians, Filipinas are not only paid higher wages, but are also live-in maids, in what seems to have become a relatively segregated domestic service labour market; in this case they receive food – some employers reported difficulties on the part of the Filipinas in eating Greek food and their preference for 'boiled rice' – lodging and a salary which in the mid-1990s ranged between 80,000 drachmas (approx. £160) to 150,000 drachmas (around £300) a month depending on the employer's goodwill – and sometimes clothing. Other forms of cash payment are rare; there were, however, two employers who mentioned that they give 5,000 drachmas pocket money to their domestic worker at weekends, whereas others (three) pay extra when they have guests for dinner and as a result the domestic worker stays up late. This salary does not increase regularly every year. The majority receive irregular increases in their salary, and at the time when the interviews took place no one knew how much it would be increased by the next year. They have a half-day off during the week (usually on Thursday afternoon) and the whole Sunday. Although the Filipinas go out and entertain themselves, the Albanians prefer to stay in. As an Albanian woman said:

> In Albania, we women were locked up in the house . . . Of course I can go out with my husband for a cup of coffee. But my husband was caught up by the police in a 'sweeping operation', as they call it, and was sent

off back to Albania . . . he will come back, I am sure . . . The Filipinas go out more than we do; every Sunday they dress up and go out with their friends – they meet in the Church.

The negotiated hours of work for live-in maids are 8 but they sometimes work for many more hours, depending on whether, in addition to the house work they perform, they are also looking after small children. The live-in domestic worker is considered available to give a hand whenever she is needed. Most start working at seven o'clock in the morning and never retire to their room before 10. I remember once visiting an employer, I stayed in the house until 12 o'clock in the evening, and until about 1 o'clock the domestic worker (a Filipina in her mid-thirties) was asked to bring refreshments, drinks and the like. They are seldom paid overtime for such work.

There is no job description. As in other parts of Europe, employers in Greece prefer the flexibility of not stipulating an employment contract (Andall 1998). The kind of work they are expected to perform differs from household to household, depending on the household's size, wealth and particular needs. Some ask for simple cleaning work; as one Albanian woman said:

> they treat you as if you are stupid; and they watch us, they think that we will steal; they treat us like animals; some employers insist that we have our own plates and mugs, as if we have a contagious disease . . . do you know that some Greeks turn their Albanian workers to the police after the job is finished so that they won't pay them?

Other employers are more demanding, requiring their domestic worker to perform more complicated tasks, such as looking after the incontinent elderly or cooking for a big party. So, the range of skills required by those who live in varies. The average size of the household was between three and four people, one-third included small children. Irrespective of their size, all the households were equipped with modern household appliances and employed just one worker.

Live-in work has some advantages. Most domestic workers who live in have the right to paid leave; every two years employers have to send their *Filipineza* home (to the Philippines) for a period of two months. In the case of day workers, they have no right to paid leave. Most illegal migrants, however, do not take advantage of this, because they are afraid that they will not be able to return to Greece.

Domestic workers are not protected by legislation stipulating minimum wages, hours of work, and the like. Nor are they covered by unemployment insurance, paid sick leave, or pensions; they are treated as disposable nappies. They are therefore an extremely insecure group of workers, open to exploitation. They usually have no access to medical insurance. For those who live in, medical expenses are covered by the employer. As Cock (1980: 37) writes in her book on domestic workers in South Africa, 'this is a beneficial aspect of the paternalistic nature of the relationship between workers and employers within the institution of domestic service'. Those who work on a daily basis, must take care of themselves, but in the case of the Albanians in Corfu, the Red Cross gives medicines to those who are ill and the local hospital treats them free of change 'for humanitarian reasons', as a local doctor informed me.

All the domestic workers in the sample had people dependent on their earnings (for example children, elderly parents). In the case of the Filipinas, as mentioned above, they were often the sole bread-winners and supporters of their families. They were forced to migrate in order to be able to send money back home to pay for the children's education and clothing. Their hopes for the future focus on their children's education and a better life. Life in Greece is seen as a sacrifice for the sake of the children. The price they pay is disruption of their marital relationship; as one woman told me, 'my husband left me for another woman; I can't blame him; he hadn't seen me for five years – my children now stay with my parents'. Many also expressed anxiety and sadness about not seeing their children growing up. This limitation on their family life is not unique to the Filipinas. Although, for example, the Albanians, work to supplement their husbands' income (most men are contract workers in the construction industry or work as casual workers in agricultural related activities and in the dockyards) and all the Albanians interviewed live with their husbands, some have left their children back home, because, as they said, they had no one to look after them and the Greek state child care units would not accept them because they were non-EU citizens. One Albanian woman who came to Greece with her husband and three children (aged eleven, four and two years) said: 'My eldest one is a very good student but we will keep him out of school next year; he has to stay at home to look after his brother and sister; I have to work, we need the money'. Anxiety was expressed by mothers as to who will look after the children when both parents work. 'We do not have anyone to leave our children with. We have no right to day care facilities for pre-school children', a migrant woman with two toddlers said.

As mentioned earlier, the Filipinas see their friends at weekends. They also belong to a Church. They form so-called 'friendship groups'

(Andall 1995: 203), that is woman centred groups that provide help and solidarity but also tips related to the job market and to finding accommodation. These informal networks are linked with formal associations and with the Catholic Church, all of which facilitate the migration to Greece and their economic inclusion into the Greek informal sector. Albanians, on the other hand, move almost exclusively in family networks. They generally have little time for leisure, less than the Filipinas do, and their potential for collective organization is constrained by their time-consuming labour. The accommodation migrants live in is bare. Eight or more Filipinas share a small flat, which is usually barely furnished, poorly decorated and damp. Some use it as a base for the days off; others use it as a permanent accommodation. It is there that they meet to share their problems and anxieties. So, in this respect, live-in domestic workers who have their own room experience a comparative advantage over those who do not enjoy such a luxury. Albanian families rent squalid flats. Unlike in Athens, there is no formation of ethnic 'ghettos' or neighbourhoods in Corfu. This has probably to do with the fact that there are no large complexes of flats or houses empty or dilapidated, where the migrants would have been able to settle. The flats and houses they live in are scattered all over the island.

With reference to a question regarding job satisfaction, none of the domestic workers said that they enjoyed their work. Many, especially the Albanians, informed me that they felt lucky to have a job, nevertheless none said that they derived any satisfaction from it. The Filipinas were especially critical of those, 'nouveau rich people who do not know how to behave'. As a Filipina domestic worker said to me:

> the nouveau rich are the worst of all. They have no education, many have had less formal education than we have – for example, I used to work as a secretary back home, but the money was not enough, so here I am – especially the ladies, they have married someone with money and they have moved to the suburbs. They have no manners; they boss us too much, treat us like animals just because we need to work. They are the worse . . . But they are not all like that. Some ladies are nice.

Domestic workers do not see the work as a means for learning something useful; their skills go down the kitchen sink. They rather see it as one of the least prestigious occupations, but as a Filipina domestic worker said, 'one should not be ashamed of the work one does for earning a living'. A number of factors contributing to the low status of domestic work are mentioned in Burnett's (1977: 172) work on domestic servants in nineteenth-century Britain:

Material disadvantages were no doubt important – the limited opportunities for promotion, the large degree of mechanical repetition in the
work, the length and irregularity of working hours, the lack of free time
... Yet it was the social disabilities which ultimately weighed more
heavily: the isolation of the servant, both from his employer and from
the community outside, the virtual absence of a private life, the degree
of control exercised by the employer ...

Some put emphasis on the extreme vulnerability and powerlessness
that they experience due to their illegal status and the subsequent
control that many employers try to exercise on them as a result of
that. This makes their bargaining position extremely weak, and it was
further weakened by the influx of other eastern and central Europeans
in the early 1990s. Since then, from what the migrants themselves
say, the level of unemployment among them seems to be relatively
high (although there is no data on this). For example, Filipinas complain openly that the influx of the Albanians from 1991 onwards has
spoiled the market balance because the latter work harder for less
money. Often lack of employment alternatives propel them into
prostitution.

Many women stressed that the worse thing about their job is the
insecurity that comes with it. Illegal migrant workers are in an especially vulnerable position; they are deprived of rights as a worker,
especially the right to negotiate wages, the right to collective bargaining and the right to legal protection. They are in what Cock (1980:
73) calls, 'a legal vacuum'. Laws stipulating minimum wages, hours
of work, paid holidays and the like do not apply to them. The minimum wage of the EC Social Charter, which Greece has signed, and
the Social Chapter of the Maastricht Treaty, do not cover these workers,
because of their illegal status. Only the few Filipinas that hold a
working permit have a contract. Breaking of the contract means that
the migrant has to return to her country of origin. Many refuse to
obey this and enter the world of illegality and insecurity.

Surprisingly, many of those women who see migration as a temporary phase in their lives and do not have any right to the benefits
mentioned above, stated that they prefer not to; 'I prefer to be given
the money that goes towards social security benefits; I am very poor,
I cannot afford the contributions', one Filipina said. They are caught
in a cycle of poverty, with lack of alternative employment opportunities. Like the South African domestic workers studied by Meer
(1975: 38), the Filipinas and the Albanians have been 'pushed into
the occupation because of their poverty-stricken backgrounds'. Those

who are not trapped in it because of their poor educational qualifications may gradually move into other occupations. It remains to be seen in years to come whether this occupational mobility is going to take place and what form it will take.

Going back to the issue of job satisfaction, the only weapon for a dissatisfied Albanian domestic worker who finds her job intolerable is to withdraw her labour and try to find another job; this is not easy, especially in small places like Corfu, because many jobs are found through personal contact, through a connection of kinship or friendship, or from word of mouth, one employer recommending her domestic worker's friend to another. The Filipinas on the other hand, through their association, have managed to cater for solving problems between employers and employees. The president of their association in Corfu is often mediating between the employer and the employee. She said:

> Often, a girl comes to me crying because she has been mistreated by her employer. I try to calm her down, I ask her to be patient, because she needs her job. If, however, things get worse, I mediate. I go and see the employer, I mention to her the fact that the girl is dissatisfied and I urge them to sit down and talk out their differences. It often works. If it does not, then the girl has to leave her job. If she is under contract, she cannot, because as soon as she leaves, and the employer reports this to the authorities, she has to leave the country. The contract is normally not transferable to another employer. She has therefore to leave 'at night', get a flight to Athens, and disappear there among the masses; it is easier in Athens to be illegal than in a small place like Corfu, where everyone knows you. Some leave behind their passports and other documents – if the employer refuses, because she is angry and vindictive, to hand them back to the girl.

Among the reasons for wanting to leave a job is sexual harassment. Live-in domestic workers are especially subject to sexual harassment by men for whom they work. As a Filipina said: 'Greek men, employ us as domestic workers in their houses, and they expect to have the service [she means sex] for free'. This is an illustration of Walby's (1990: 52) argument that contrary to J. Mitchell's (1975) approach (that sexuality has little to do with paid work) 'patriarchal sexual practices do have an effect on gender patterns of employment'. Such behaviour on the part of the employer has an adverse effect on the woman's working conditions. Nevertheless, it largely remains unreported because of fear that they will lose the case and be asked to leave the country. In such cases most just look for another job; this sometimes means breaking their contract (if they have one) and becoming illegal. The Filipina association in Corfu has also a matron, a Greek woman, herself an employer, who nevertheless supervises and somehow 'protects' these women against 'unreasonable employers', as she put it. She has gradually developed a system of protected migration under which her proteges are counselled, housed in a hostel in Corfu, and placed in employment on arrival in the host country. The association has also contributed in the development of a 'sisterhood' amongst the Filipinas. It has brought women together, who form mutual friendships, discuss their problems and support each other. Once a year they also hold a party where they invite their employers and give them national food and flowers in the name of 'good relationships amongst human beings'. Unfortunately, as the 'matron' informed me, not many employers attend these meetings.

The situation with the Albanians differs. Unlike the Filipinas, they did not want to organise themselves into any association or union. 'We are so scattered and widespread; we have no free time for things like this', an Albanian woman said. There is no sense of common purpose among them. Individualist values have replaced any sense of community feeling and solidarity they may have ever had. 'It is difficult to persuade such atomized workers to organize', a Catholic priest who works a lot for the migrants' rights said to me. And he continued: 'Because of the political restraints which were operating against them in Albania, these people will always be difficult to organize'. As a result and unlike the Filipinas, they have been unable to create a basis for collective action against external constraints (broad economic, political and ideological structures) these women are being subject to.

The evidence regarding these women's working conditions described above which involve 'deprivation of family and social life, lack of job satisfaction, low status in the community, and marginal position as a worker' supports Cock's (1980: 75) thesis that they are in a situation of 'ultra-exploitation'. They are given privileges but not rights. Their relationship with their employers is one of dependency on the part of the domestic worker. Often employers, using their clientelistic networks, help workers untangle themselves from the laws that bind their lives. Most relationships, however, have some degree of social distance, coloured by the different living standards between the two people and which is reinforced by gifts in the form of second-hand clothes, pocket money and so on, which promote feelings of gratitude, loyalty and faithfulness (see Mauss 1970). This aspect will be the subject of future research.

Concluding Remarks

In an attempt to analyse the constraints that operate on female migrant labour in Greece, and to document the injustice and exploitation that surrounds them, this study has drawn on a variety of insights from different disciplines and intellectual traditions. Taking into account the structural and interactional aspects of the domestic worker's life, it has been shown how female migrant workers are trapped in a condition of inferiority, immobility and ultra-exploitation. Like migrant men, they are disadvantaged through their legal and economic position, and through specific forms of racialization of their ethnic group; these intersect with sexist relations and practices within Greek society where partiarchal relations are deeply embedded in people's attitudes and behaviour. In the case of Filipinas it seems that cultural rules are of course transformed as 'solo migration' is seen as an asset for the survival of the family. In the case of Albanians, relations within the home affect patterns of migration. As this paper has shown, ethnic minorities are not unitary; these two different groups are positioned differently in the Greek market for domestic services. Differences in pay, in working conditions and in treatment exist, depending on their religion, stereotypes developed by the media, the way they arrived in the country and the way they have been inserted into the host community. It is important to differentiate between those who enter with specific work permits and those who enter illegally. The latter have greater insecurity under present immigration law and practice. In addition, although sexism disadvantages both groups of women, the effects of racism are more apparent in relation to live-in workers who tend to work for more unsociable hours than others and are more exposed to sexual harassment. So one cannot bunch all domestic workers in one category of disadvantaged women as this category may conceal the differences that exist in relation to legality/illegality, ethnicity, type of work performed, and the like. As different modes of sexist and racist ideologies and practices intersect, women from different ethnic backgrounds come to experience different forms of exclusion and discrimination, depending on their skill and conditions of entry into the host country; we cannot, therefore treat them as a homogeneous labour category.

Recognition of differences must not preclude organization and coalition-building across different ethnic groups. Organization must be set up with not only a social, but also a political function. As this paper shows, difference and diversity cannot obscure the material inequalities these women share. Recognition of difference must unite these women rather than divide them; alliances must be built, resources must be mobilized, to carve out spaces of control and to restructure the disadvantages and multiple forms of exclusion experienced in the host country.

But how can efforts be directed to protect these women? It is critical for women to receive accurate information concerning employment conditions in the host country. Women must be encouraged to build up support networks and associations, and make efforts to build a cohesive community in the host country. Such activities wherever they emerge (as is the case of Filipinas in Corfu, for example) must be strengthened and empowered so that the women are able to network actively and cooperate with non-governmental organizations in the sending countries that are actively involved in the protection of migrant women. Finally, cooperation with organizations set up by other ethnic minority groups and with government agencies must be encouraged; such cooperation may encourage the regulation of recruit-ment agencies in Greece and lead to programmes geared towards the active social and economic integration of migrant women.

Acknowledgements

Many thanks to Dave Mallion and Joanna Poyago-Theotoky for con-structive comments.

Notes

1. Relatively little work has been done in this regard (Ricca 1984), which is unfortunate, because it has lead to a situation where women play a central role in migratory flows into southern Europe, yet they are neglected in the sphere of policy.

2. With regard to female migration in Greece, two types can be defined: the first comprises women who arrived as part of the labour force, mostly maids, nurses and women working in the sex industry. The second comprises women who arrived with their husband and children and subsequently developed a strategy for getting incorporated in the local informal labour market.

3. The interviewees are mainly domestic workers, some with stable employ-ment, others not. These women live in the island of Corfu and in Athens, and work in relatively affluent locations. The decision as to which geographical locations to concentrate on was taken on the basis of the following criteria: due to its proximity with Albania (the distance between the two locations is

around two or three nautic miles), Corfu is the place where migrants from Albanian arrive. In addition, contacts had already been made during a previous visit in the island. Most, after spending a few years in Corfu, move on to Athens. The findings of this research derive from interviews carried out with 20 Filipina women and 18 women from Albania. The majority of the women interviewed, were aged between 24 and 46 and all had at least one child. Most of the women (90 per cent) were married. The length of the interview varied from one to three hours. Some of the interviews were conducted in the employers' premises; in few occasions, the employers seemed apprehensive about the interview and after one hour interrupted the meeting suggesting that 'it is time for the girl to go back to work.' The conversation was left to follow a 'natural' course, leaving the informants to express themselves freely and bring up in the conversation whichever themes were important in their opinion, without input from me. This approach resulted in a vast amount of data as well as in data on unexpected areas. Sometimes, informants offered to arrange meetings with other migrants; these gatherings proved very useful, because they provided an opportunity for them to cover themes that were important to them for me to hear. Albanians were eager to provide me with information on matters related to the political changes that took place in the country in the early 1990s, whereas the Filipinas were eager to convey to me the importance of remittances to those left behind. Some of these meetings have been taped, whereas others were not – some informants said they felt 'uneasy' and asked me to turn the recorder off. The reason given was almost always that they did not speak fluent Greek and did not want others to hear their 'bad Greek accents'. I discovered that having no tape recorder paid off in that the informants were less reluctant and more willing to disclose information. Others bluntly announced that 'immigration' is a 'politically sensitive issue' and refused to give any information. To overcome this, I approached different individuals who had access to the same material and the negotiations started once more. As Burgess (1989) writes

> there are multiple points of entry which require a continuous process of negotiation and re negotiation throughout the research. Research access is not merely granted or withheld at one particular point in time but is ongoing with the research.

4. The centrality of the double set of sexist relations (those internal to the ethnic group and those of the dominant group in the host society) that are implicated for ethnic minority women were first analysed by Anthias (1993) in relation to ways in which gender, class, ethnicity and race intersect in the British labour market.

5. In relation to the British society, Anthias (1993) suggests that migrant women are inserted into two sets of social relations: those of their own ethnic group and those of the dominant group within British society. She argues that these two sets interact with racialization processes to produce particular economic outcomes.

6. The unemployment rate for women (13.8 per cent) is significantly higher than that for men (6.2 per cent) (Papadopoulos 1998: 56).

7. Emigration from the Philippines began in the mid-1960s, when Marcos was still in power, and has steadily increased since. 'The election of Corazon Aquino did not stop migration: on the contrary, the new government encouraged it as a means of obtaining hard currency remittances necessary to cover the huge national debt. Between 1982 and 1986 alone, the remittances have totalled $3.8 billion' (Campani 1993: 195).

8. For example, Campani (1993: 200) mentions that this Americanization is so important that 'there is a flourishing traffic in American products' like make-up products, perfumes, gadgets, from the American base at Camp Darby in Pisa.

9. As Campani (1993: 196) writes, 'Filipinas migrate to Hong Kong, Singapore, Japan, the Gulf countries, the United states, Canada, Spain . . . Italy' and of course Greece.

10. The 'replacement migration', which is occurring in Italy (see Chell's paper in this book) whereby older migrant women retire, return to the Philippines to care for the family and are replaced by their daughters, is not yet evident in Greece.

11. In Italy there are no Filipina nurses because the Italian law has until recently limited access to employment as nurses to the Italians.

References

Akeroyd, A.V. (1990), 'Ethics in relation to informants, the profession and governments'. In R.F. Ellen (ed.), *Ethnographic Research: a Guide to General Conduct*, London: Academic Press.

Andall, J. (1995), 'Migrant women and gender role definition in the Italian context', in *Journal of Area Studies*, Vol. 6, pp. 203–15.

Andall, J. (1998), 'Catholic and state constructions of domestic workers: the case of Cape Verdean women in Rome in the 1970s', in K. Koser and H. Lutz (eds), *The new migration in Europe*, Basingstoke: Macmillan.

Anderson, B. and Phizacklea, A. (1997), *Migrant Domestic Workers: a European Perspective*, research paper: University of Leicester and Equal Opportunities Unit, DGV.

Anthias, F. (1993) 'Gendered ethnicities in the British labour market', in H. Rudolf and M. Morokvasic (eds), *Bridging States and Markets: international migration in the early 1990s*, Berlin: Sigma.

Anthias, F. and Lazaridis, G. (eds) (1999), *Into the Margins: Migration and Exclusion in Southern Europe*. Aldershot: Ashgate.

Balaska, J. (1993), 'Gender roles in the Greek family', in *E.N.W.S. Newsletter*, No. 9, October.

Beechey, V. (1977), 'Some notes on female wage labour in capitalist production', in *Capital and Class*, Vol. 3, pp. 45–66.

Bimbi, F. (1993), 'Gender, 'gift relationship' and welfare state cultures in Italy', in J. Lewis (ed.), *Women and social policies in Europe*, Aldershot: Ashgate.

Burgess, R.G. (1989), *In the field*, London: Unwin Hyman.

Bourdieu, P. (1990), *In other words*, Cambridge: Polity.

Burnett, J. (1977) *Useful Toil. Autobiographies of working People from the 1820s to the 1920s*. Harmondsworth: Penguin.

Buijs, G. (ed.) (1993), *Migrant Women. Crossing Boundaries and Changing Identities*. Oxford: Berg.

Callinicos, L. (1975), 'Domesticating Workers', in *South African Labour Bulletin*, Vol. 2, No. 4.

Campani, G. (1993), 'Labour markets and family networks: Filipina women in Italy', in H. Rudolf and M. Morokvasic (eds), *Bridging States and Markets: International Migration in the Early 1990s*, Berlin: Sigma.

Castells, M. (1975), 'Immigrant Workers and Class Struggles in Advanced Capitalism: the Western European Experience', in *Politics and Society*, Vol. 5, pp. 33–66.

Castles, S. and Kosack, G. (1973), *Immigrant Workers in the Class Structure in Western Europe*, Oxford.

Castles, S. and Miller, M.J. (1993) *The Age of Migration*. London: Macmillan.

Cock, J, (1980) *Maids and Madams: a Study in the Politics of Exploitation*, Johannesburg: Ravan Press.

Dalley, G. (1990), *Ideologies of Caring*, London: Macmillan.

Esping-Andersen, G. (1990), *The Three Worlds of Welfare Capitalism*, New York: Polity Press.

Eurostat (1993), *Rapid Reports: Population and Social Conditions, 1993/1*. Brussels: Eurostat.

Eurostat (1994), *Rapid Reports: Population and Social Conditions, 1994/7*. Brussels: Eurostat.

Fakiolas, R. (1995), *Preventing Racism at the Workplace: Greece*, Working paper WP/95/45/EN, European Foundation for the Improvement of Living and Working Conditions.

Ferrera, M. (1996), 'The southern model of welfare in social Europe', in *Journal of European Social Policy*, Vol. 6, No. 1, pp. 17–37.

Fielding, A. (1993), 'Mass Migration and Economic Restructuring', in R. King (ed.) *Mass Migration in Europe*. London: Belhaven. 1984.

Gioulakis, G. (1990), 'Six thousand dollars per head', in *Tachydromos*, Vol. 50, pp. 80–6.

Hoffman-Nowotny, H.J. (1985), 'Switzerland', in T. Hammar (ed.), *European immigration policy: a comparative study*, Cambridge: Cambridge University Press.

Hyfandis, N. (1993), *Northern Epirus yesterday and today.* Ioannina: Idryma Vorioepirotikon Erevnon.

Karydis, V. (1992), 'The fear of crime in Athens and the Construction of the 'dangerous Albanian stereotype', in *Chroniques*, Vol. 5. pp. 97–193.

Katrougalos, G. (1996), 'The southern welfare model: the Greek welfare state', in *Journal of European Social Policy*, Vol. 6, No. 1, pp. 39–61.

King, R. and Black, R. (eds) (1997), *Southern Europe and New Immigrations*, Brighton; Sussex Academic Press.

Kontis, A. and Balourdos, D. (1994) *Migration into Greece*. Athens: EKEM.

Lazaridis, G. (1992), *Agriculture, Handicrafts and Women's Associations in Two Villages in Western Crete*, Ph.D Thesis, University of Bristol, UK.

Lazaridis, G. (1995), 'Immigrant women in Greece: the case of domestic labourers', in European Forum for Leftist Women (ed.) *Nationalism, Racism, Gender*, Salonika: Paratiritis, pp. 47–75.

Lazaridis, G. (1996), Immigration to Greece: a critical evaluation of Greek policy, in *New Community*, Vol. 22, No. 2, pp. 335–348.

Lazaridis, G. (1999a), 'Of prostitutes and pimps: trafficking of women in Greece', paper presented at the ESA conference, August 1999, Amsterdam, Netherlands.

Lazaridis, G. (1999b), 'The Helots of the new millennium: ethnic-Greek Albanians and 'other' Albanians in Greece', in F. Anthias and G. Lazaridis (eds), *Into the Margins: Migration and Exclusion in Southern Europe*. Aldershot: Ashgate.

Lazaridis, G. and Syngellakis, A. (1995), 'Women's status and employment in contemporary Greece', in *Journal of Area Studies*, Vol. 6, pp. 96–107.

Lazaridis, G. and Psimmenos, I. (1999), 'Migrant flows from Albania to Greece: economic, social and spatial exclusion' in R. King, G. Lazaridis and C. Tsardanidis (eds), *Eldorado or Fortress? Migration in Southern Europe*, Basingstoke: Macmillan.

Lazaridis, G. and Wickens, E. (1999), 'Us and the Others: the experiences of different ethnic minorities in Greece', *Annals of Tourism Research*, Vol. 26, No. 3, pp. 632–655.

Lazaridis, G. and Poyago-Theotoky, J. (1997), 'Illegal Migration: issues of regularisation'. Paper presenter at the conference Central and Eastern Europe – new migration space, Pultusk Poland, 11–13 December, and published in International Migration Quarterly Review 1999, Vol. 37, No. 4, pp. 715–740.

Leibfried, S. (1992), 'Towards a European welfare state', in Z. Ferge and J.E. Kolberg (eds), *Social policy in a changing Europe*, London: Westview Press.

Mitchell, J. (1975), *Psychoanalysis and Feminism*. Harmondsworth: Penguin.

Maratou-Alipranti, L. (1994), 'Foreign labour force: tendencies for and problems of social integration', in EKKE (ed.) *Social Exclusion in Greece*. Report for the European Social Fund, Vol. 11, Athens.

Mauss, M. (1970), *The Gift*. Harmondsworth: Penguin.

Meer, F. (ed.) (1975), *Black Women, Durban 1975*. Durban: University of Natal.

Mesimeris, S. (1978), *The rights of Greeks and the Silent Tragedy of Northern Loannina:* H Foni tis Vorias Epirou.

Morokvasic, M. (1974), 'Les femmes Immigrees au Travail'. Paper presented at the CEE Conference on Migration Problems. Louvain-Ia-Neuve.

Morokvasic, M. (1983) 'Women in migration beyond the reductionist outlook', in A. Phizacklea, (ed.), *One Way Ticket: Migration and Female Labour,* London: Routledge & Kegan Paul.

Papadopoulos, T. (1998), 'Greek family policy from a comparative perspective', in E. Drew, R. Emerek and E. Mahon (eds), *Women, Work and the Family in Europe*, London: Routledge.

Papageorgiou, Y. (1993), 'The role of woman within the Greek family', in *E.N.W.S. Newsletter*, No. 9, October.

Petrinioti, X. (1993), *Immigration into Greece*. Athens: Odysseas.

Pierros, F. (1990), Towards a common policy for the migrants. *Ikonomikos Tachydromos*, Vol. 52, pp. 57–59.

Phizacklea, A. (ed.) (1983), *One Way Ticket: Migration and Female Labour.* London: Routledge & Kegan Paul.

Phizacklea, A. (1998) 'Migration and globalization: a feminist perspective', in K. Koser and H. Lutz (eds), *The new migration in Europe*, Basingstoke: Macmillan.

Psimmenos, I. (1996), 'The making of periphractic spaces; the case of Albanian undocumented immigrants in Athens City', ERCOMER conference 1996, Utrecht, Netherlands.

Ricca, S. (1984), 'Administering migrant workers in an irregular situation in Greece, Italy and Spain'. Working paper, Geneva: ILO.

Stone, K, (1983), 'Motherhood and Waged Work: West Indian, Asian and White Mothers Compared', in A. Phizacklea (ed.) *One Way Ticket: Migration and Female Labour.* London: Routledge & Kegan Paul.

Swaisland, C. (1993), 'Female Migration and Social Mobility: British Female Domestic Servants to South Africa', 1860–1914, in G. Buijs (ed.), *Migrant Women: Crossing Boundaries and Changing Identities.* Oxford: Berg.

Valabregue, C. (1973), *L'Homme Deracine',* Paris: Mercure de France.

Vaiou, D. (1996), 'Women's work and everyday life in Southern Europe in the context of European integration', in M.D. Garcia-Ramon and J. Monk (eds), *Women of the European Union: the Politics of Work and Daily Life,* London: Routledge.

Walby, S. (1990), *Theorizing Patriarchy.* London: Basil Blackwell.

four

The Making of Periphractic Spaces: The Case of Albanian Undocumented Female Migrants in the Sex Industry of Athens[1]

IORDANIS PSIMMENOS

The present study is about women migrants who work in the sex industry, as part of a *'human landscape'* which is constructed out of global economic interdependencies and out of the *racialization* of labour in Athens. This *human landscape,* as Sibley (1997: ix) argues, can be 'read as a landscape of exclusion' and also as a landscape that takes shape within a particular *context* and *social space*, and derives its sociological meaning out of the juxtaposition of the two in relation to women. The *human landscape* that is analysed here relates to the transfer of women across borders, to their work in providing sexual services, their placement in exclusionary spatial settings, and networks that reproduce and culturally maintain those settings. These processes both *interconnect* female migration across borders and at the same time *'fragment'* their identities and cultural presence in the particular social environment. This chapter is based on field research of Albanian undocumented migrants in Athens and in particular of economic migrants, who arrived during the period 1991–5, as part of cross-border interconnections and as part of the global–local expansion of the service sector and in particular of domestic and 'entertainment services'.

Contrary to what is believed by many scholars, the flow of Albanian migrants, and especially female Albanians (1991) did not start at a time when southern European countries changed from major 'exporters' of cheap labour force, to major 'importers' of economically destitute people. The region historically has always experienced migratory flows of different magnitude, and Greece, particularly Athens and Salonica (the two largest cities in the country), has always attracted labourers or traders from the Balkans or refugees from Asia Minor, Cyprus and the Middle-Eastern countries. In fact one could argue that migration and displacement constitute the contemporary history of Greece if one includes the migratory flows that took place during the Ottoman Empire, the two world wars, the civil war and the contemporary flow of migrants and political refugees from Egypt (1957), Cyprus (1974), Kurdistan (1980s) as well from Pontos (1980s, late 1980–1990s).

According to estimates, Greece has the largest (in comparison to other south European countries) number of undocumented migrants from Albania, Bulgaria, and Poland (OECD 1997). According to the Ministries of Labour and of Public Order (1996–7) more than 400,000 migrant workers live and work in the country. This figure fluctuates by 10 to 15 per cent during the months of harvesting and of seasonal tourism (Fakiolas 1997). Some 50,000 to 70,000 workers have come from the ex-USSR, the Far East, and the Maghreb countries, whereas Albanians constitute almost 80 per cent of the total undocumented population in the country (Lianos 1995; Psimmenos 1997). There are no official estimations of undocumented female migrants working in the sex industry. However, in relation to official estimates, (based on deportation figures) 200 under-age migrants and almost 1,000 adult female migrants were repatriated forcefully to the country of origin (Ministry of Social Security 1996).

The context for explaining migration to Athens must give attention to the collapse of the socialist economic and political system, and the emergence of a single European frontier (Schengen). But most important is the emergence of a global political and economic reorganization, where female migration constitutes part of the chain towards greater profitability and labour flexibility. Such migration is constituted by the imposition of global policies on the management of labour, and of global labour networks (such as the sex industry and in the trafficking in women). In this chapter, emphasis is placed on the processes and experiences that dictate and shape the pivotal socio-economic spaces of undocumented female migrants in Athens.

In particular, this chapter explores, through the analytical use of the concept of globalization, the social processes that produce and reproduce the somatic and social exploitation of Albanian female migrants caught in the web of the Athenian sex industry. The processes that are central to the above condition are not only responsible for the contemporary marginalization of women and for the development of periphractic (fenced off) social spaces, but also for the structuration of a new type of labour categorization and a new type of labouring force. Both are linked to the rapid growth of trafficking in women around Europe, especially from the ex-socialist countries (both the ex-USSR and the Balkan countries); the rise in deregulated labour activities; and the rise in the provision of personalized services (for example domestic labour, street-hawking, prostitution).

The Global Economy and Flexible Labour

The rise of global networks of economic and political life have had a profound effect on structures and relationships within the European Union (EU). Profound changes have taken place regarding work and in relation to the flexibility of labour. It could be argued that a new flexible and cheap labour force in Europe is reflecting a dynamic relationship between *global* and *local realities* (Cardoso 1974; Dunn 1989). The rise of global economic networks has bonded together divert communities and affected the nature of their development, but it has also produced global networks of people through global labour migration (Amin and Thrift 1995a). The collapse of local economies in ex-socialist Europe, as well as the continuous economic shifts in the EU, have impelled such migratory labouring flows. This chapter will discuss the mechanisms employed to produce and maintain the marginal status of female Albanians in Greece.

The dynamic and contradictory characteristics of the global economic formation are reflected through the presence of both *harmonization* and *liberalization* principles of socio-economic activity in the EU and through the political realm that the processes of integration and deregulation/re-regulation facilitate (Larrain 1994; Psimmenos 1997). Both seem to have unleashed new tendencies in the organization and experiences that stem from labouring spaces. Through the centralization of decision-making procedures and the unification of socio-economic structures, an entire new schema has unfolded. This is centered around a globalized system of work, that 'despotically exalts the corporate powerlessness of Labour' (Rustin 1989) and undermines its collective identity.

On the other hand, the drive for greater flexibility and the re-emergence of Victorian values concerning labour relations, have unleashed further fragmentation and the collapse of both labour markets and social rights (Psimmenos 1995; Phizacklea 1995). The emergence of a globalized socio-economic activity involves the parallel production of both peripheralized labour activity globally (Frobel *et al.* 1980), as well as in the transfer and creation of a peripheralized labour force in core societies (Murray 1990). The latter is reflected in the rise of informal/illicit economic activities and in the rapid devaluation of social standards and life chances, especially for women, ethnic minorities, and migrants (Mingione and Magatti 1994). The migrant is 'pushed' into a situation of social exclusion (Miles 1993; Albrow and Eade 1992) that is limited by *periphractic spaces* (fenced-off spaces) and defined by the loss of identity and the power to be included in society (Zukin 1992; Goldberg 1993). In such spaces a contemporary 'slave' labour force is created that exists in the margins, and is *ephemeral* and *flexible* (Murray 1990; Cohen 1994).

The labouring spaces of a migrant's life today are characterized by both integration and deregulation leading, on the one hand, to a further centralization of decision-making powers, and on the other hand to the fragmentation of both work procedures and power representations. Central however to the maintenance of those labouring spaces is the ideological projection of *global flexibility*. The term itself implies many things at the same time and certainly its meaning differs slightly from case to case. However, in the case of the female migrant worker it is certainly the understanding of the ideological content of *flexibility* and of the occupying space of the *flexible worker* that holds together both the margins of the migrant, and the local–global politics of labour racialization and economic restructuring. There are four main key words that characterize flexibility: *transferability, ephemerality, servitude, diffusion*. Transferability: to be transferred across places or labour procedures, according to market necessities; ephemerality: to be involved with projects of short duration, fragmented, and directly consumed; servitude: to be involved with tasks that necessitate the further decentring of identity and work and to be used as an auxiliary to the main economic activity; diffusion: not to hold any attachments or loyalties that may impede the completion of the labour process.

Female Migration and the Sex Industry

Examining female migration and its relationship to the sex industry, one has to analyse the dominant global work processes and tendencies, as well of the specific nature and patterns present in this specific type of work activity. According to Campani (1997) the increasing phenomenon of the feminization of migration is contextualized in terms of changes in the position of women in both sending and receiving countries.

In the sending countries, gender roles are changing deeply in the family, the networks, the society. 'In many underdeveloped countries of origin, emigration is one aspect of the social crisis which accompanies integration into the world market and modernization' (Castles and Miller 1993: 3) . . . In the receiving countries, changes in the labour market and in production system have affected the labour demand, which is growing in the tertiary sector and is reduced in the industrial sector . . . In this new landscape, the demand for female labour force in services, including services to private persons has increased. In the countries of Southern Europe, the growing demand of services is combined with the traditional presence of a large informal sector . . . This changing labour market is also strongly gendered. The feminization of migration corresponds precisely to the growing of the demand in "female" jobs (for example: maids, nurses, entertainers) (Campani 1997: 1).

Against a global context of female migration, the sex and/or entertaining industry is growing, involving greater numbers of women especially from the ex-socialist countries:

while women from many parts of South-East Asia and Africa have been deceived and "trafficked" by the sex industry, now women from Eastern Europe and former Soviet Union are part of this lucrative trade. The traffic in women is largely illegal and undocumented. Many women are recruited as entertainers, but when they arrive in the migration setting they realise that the only entertainment they are expected to provide is sex. Others indebted in their home country may be trafficked as bonded labour . . . (Phizacklea 1997: 6).

According to a recent report by the International Labour Office (1997), there has been a rapid growth of trafficking in women in Europe, especially from the ex-socialist countries. This is mainly attributed to the rapid increase in both poverty and unemployment levels, especially amongst women, as well as the development of agencies and networks in the leisure industry. Both seem to be responsible for the recruitment of women in the sex industry, as well as for their transfer to countries other than in their place of origin:

Trafficking in women and children for sexual exploitation is becoming an increasingly grave problem within the European Union. Other than from Central and Eastern European Countries, women and children are being trafficked from developing countries in Latin America, Africa and Southeast Asia. The phenomenon of female international migrants involved in prostitution also appears to be growing in other parts of the world. Some women migrate precisely for this purpose, others drift into prostitution because it is the only occupation open to them, and others are tricked or forced by unscrupulous recruiters and crime syndicates (Lim 1997: 10).

Acknowledging however both the push and pull factors affecting women's migration and in particular their involvement with the sex industry, is only one aspect. Questions about the nature of the sex industry and the work activity itself, as well as women's life experiences of marginalized social spaces, are left unanswered. The analysis of female migration seems to stop at the 'borders', as if their role and relationship with the indigenous population of the receiving countries matters less than the information and explanation provided for the initial reasons that pushed them into the sex industry.

Indeed, the globalization of the world economy cannot be reduced to a listing of population flows or into a theoretical modelling of migration patterns without an explanation of the processes involved in the making of global periphractic social spaces. Residence and work experiences, together with the social effects they have for the production and reproduction of gendered life formations, constitute the centre of scholarly debate on female global migration. It is therefore the intention of this chapter to present an example of this within the Athenian spatial context.

Some Methodological concerns

In order to present a discussion of Albanian migrants in the sex industry of Athens, it is important to consider a number of theoretical and methodological questions. Works that situate their subjects against the social context of the urban environment stress the importance of the particular environment upon the marginalization of the female migrant (Vaiou and Chatzimichalis 1997; Wacquant 1996). They also emphasize the role of the economic geography of the urban space, especially in relation to the international division of labour and the rise of the tertiary sector (Amin 1995b; Sassen 1995). The female migrant is thus contextualized within the division of labour and the local economy. This stresses factors such as the casualization of labour, patriarchal relations in the process of marginalization. This becomes more evident in the depiction of the role played by local informal economies, in the geographical distribution of migrant labour, and female and child labour (Mingione 1996; King 1997; Fakiolas 1997). There are also scholarly debates on the rise of the city-place as a *crimogenic* environment, where prostitution and violence against women dominate (Lea 1997; Mooney 1997), and studies on the rise of women's trafficking that emphasize the rise of the industry in the urban space as a global criminal industry (Marangopoulos Foundation 1996; IOM 1995).

According to such work, the city place is central to the analysis of female migration and prostitution, and to the process of marginalization. This is more true if one considers the city place as the *command point* between the global economy and the local environment. In this interconnection, economic activity becomes internationalized and migrants constitute the new marginalized group of people of the urban order (Sassen 1994). This research is based on the analysis of inner-Athens housing and work areas, and the interviews draw information on the urban construction of marginality, and how this marginality is reflected in the self-presentations of women in prostitution. But their marginality did not start in Athens, or for that reason, in any other specific place. In other words, marginality did not begin with the politics of the place, as it is elegantly put by many academic scholars. 'Place', and for that reason Athens, has been the filter of a more widespread process of marginalization that synchronically has affected women in Albania and has produced the necessary economic and moral spaces for their location in exploitative casual labour in Athens. Thus, prostitution is here understood as a result of a series of marginalizations that have taken place. These are all generated by processes that distance women from economic alternatives to prostitution and from political and cultural representations of their *'voice'*. These processes, although reflected in the local environment, certainly take shape in the global sphere. This is responsible for: economic and social welfare, migration into the EU, and the rise or transfer of particular employment for a particular labour force. Thus, Albanian women in prostitution have indirectly or directly gone through a series of exclusions prior to their 'arrival' in the Athenian sex industry. Poverty, displacement (in the case of forced migration), the destruction of social networks (as in the case of family relations in Albania), and the rise of informal service activity are all being brought together in the new social spaces that Albanian women find themselves.

This takes us through to the question of the role *female voices* play or should play in our research. Prior to the design of the research for this chapter, there were two important methodological questions that had to be answered. The first related to the categorization and actual representation of female voices in the study of Albanian migrant women, whilst the second was related to the relationship between the external structural conditions that push migrant women to prostitution and the internal response towards these conditions.

The research design was careful to avoid placing at the centre *binary oppositions*, such as Albanian/Greek women. As argued by Bradley

(1996) in response to the theoretical understandings of Haraway (1990):

> the very act of naming something or somebody (even oneself) brings exclusions. Categories also construct one essentialized set of people as 'the other' . . . whose experience is defined against that of the dominant group and often pathologized, seen as 'deviant' or inferior. These oppressive categories need deconstructing if a different 'reality' is to be built allowing individuals to think in different and freer ways . . . (Bradley 1996: 101).

The emphasis in the research design was mostly placed upon the social and political status that at the time characterized the majority of people from Albania, and at the same time defined much of their social location in the Athens area. The *undocumented* marginal and temporal work of *Albanian* people was related at the time to the immigration and economic policies dominant in the EU. The use of the term 'undocumented Albanian' serves to denote both the exclusionary status of this group as well as the diversity of experiences that may be present (as in the case of those identified with the Greek/Christian tradition) and between different ethnic groups of migrants (Anthias and Yuval Davis 1993). The analytical framework of the Albanian 'voices' necessitates some further clarification. Certainly the question of sociological presentation of both the structural inequalities women face (as part of migratory and work experiences) and their active response, is not new. Indeed, one could trace the issue of the relationship between what most now recognize as the structure-agency debate as far back as the Aristotelian concept of *teleological action* between the actor and a world of existing states of affairs. These issues relate to the way one uses those Albanian 'voices' sociologically.

There is much scepticism today concerning whether we can afford, in our analytical journeys, to 'ignore' the role(s) played by the subject we sociologically analyse. This is true for post-structuralist theorists as well for radical feminists or post-Fordist critics of labouring spaces. It is therefore not so much the issue of whether the subject is playing a role in the phenomena one is analysing, but rather what kind of a role and how it should be analysed. In the case of women's experience of inequality Bradley (1996) suggests that:

> his ideas (Giddens) hold potential for a more satisfactory theory of gendered power. It is possible to identify a number of dimensions of power in terms of access and control of different resources and investigate how these are deployed in specific empirical cases. For example, we might distinguish economic resources . . . positional resources . . .

symbolic resources . . . domestic resources . . . sexual resources . . . and personal resources. Although historically men have appropriated more of the first three of these, women's control of sexual domestic and personal resources has often allowed them to exercise power especially in personal relationships or in the home . . . (Bradley 1996: 105).

In a similar way in relation to migration, Phizacklea (1997) suggests that:

migratory flows do not simply represent an enforced response to economic hardship, but also represent a recognition on the part of gendered individual actors that migration provides the best opportunity of escaping a repressive environment. Another example would be the mail-order bride who has calculated that marriage will be the easiest and possibly only legal route of gaining employment commensurate with education and qualifications. It is within this analytical context that I am beginning to explore the supply and demand for migrant women in the sex, marriage and maid industries . . . (Phizacklea 1997: 5).

The emphasis on the role played by the subject and the duality of meaning this role may represent for our sociological explanation are central to the investigation of the *voices* of women in the sex industry of Athens. However, one should note that in the case of the sex industry probably the opposite is true from what Bradley (1996) is suggesting. Sexual pleasure in prostitution has more to do with the loss of sexual and personal control rather than the opposite. In any case, one should actually ask whether the actor has any alternative. One should also not ignore the historical and cultural context within which this sexual exchange takes place. In the case of Albanian female migrants in the sex industry, the design of the interviews allowed women to tell their story, on how matters are 'working' or not 'working' for them. It is important to recognize the role(s) the actor may play, but more important to understand the *lifeworld* within which the actor is *playing a role* (Habermas 1995).

The research design of the larger study concentrated upon the spatial organization of both accommodation/communal housing and work activities of female and male Albanian migrants in Athens. The sample of almost five hundred Albanians was randomly selected amongst ten representative (in relation to age, sex, ethnicity, years of stay in Athens) housing/collective accommodation sites. In addition to the ten sites (i.e. hotels) the research took place in almost all high-concentration locations available within the region of the Athenian centre (such as Omonoia, Vathis Squares). These locations included spaces of work and cultural activity. The interviews were originally designed to reflect demographic accommodation and labour organization issues. However, due to female adult and child prostitution in the area, it was necessary to include in the original design a separate semi-structured interview concentrating on the somatic and economic exploitation of Albanian female migrants (n = 30). This forms the basis of this chapter.

In relation to demographic issues, the undocumented migrants were asked questions concerning four main themes: the documentation of family-educational networks in the home country; the reasons for and forms of migration; flows of communication between home and receiving country; and social networks amongst Albanians in Athens. In relation to housing/accommodation issues, the questions were oriented towards the following themes: reasons for selecting communal type of accommodation and the particular region in Athens; organization of life conditions within the hotels (amenities, room-sharing, food consumption levels); and issues concerning the social networks that developed between occupants.

As was indicated above, the interview concerning the work activity of undocumented Albanians in Athens was separated into two sections. The first section, which this paper will concentrate on, was concerned with Albanian adult and child prostitution, whereas the second section was oriented towards the provision of information about work activity/conditions that prevailed amongst the adult population, not involved in illicit economic activities. The first section concentrated on relations with parents and friends, cultural expressions (fashion, type of entertainment, educational interests) and upon conditions of housing and of work (avoiding any reference to moralistic judgements). The whole orientation of this section was upon comparisons between life standards in Albania and in Athens, and upon experiences of alienation by the minors.

Periphractic Spaces of Collective Living

The study of undocumented Albanian migrants in Athens concentrated on an area of approximately four square miles, where during 1991–5 almost 3,000 Albanians were living. Almost half of them were residents in ten major third class hotels. The same residential neighbourhoods were used to accommodate the first wave of migrant labour from rural Greece (1920–1930s), the refugees of Asia Minor (1922–) and the American high-ranking military personnel (1950–67) in the nearby American bases. During the 1970s, due to low-cost housing, the decline in entrepreneurial activity, and the outward flow of city dwellers, the area of Vathis and Omonoia was officially used by the then governments as a shelter for war and political refugees. The area was systematically used for the provision of temporary accommodation for Greek-Cypriot (1974–75), Kurdish, Iranian and Iraqi political refugees. The majority of these people were in the same third class hotels (which our study concentrated on for the analysis of Albanian migrants), whilst later they were rehoused in more permanent types of accommodation. The official policy, in relation to the first wave of migration, was the provision of collective temporary shelter to families in need, prior to any UN and governmental final decision on the reallocation of migrants. The same policy line was followed in the case of the second and third flows of migration that were connected with the Iran–Iraq war and the Israel–Palestinian conflict, respectively. The policy of first assistance, based on the idea of collective sheltering prior to the transfer of populations to a more permanent type of accommodation, began to be obfuscated with the arrival of the first wave of economic migrants. The increasing demand for a cheap labour force in the area, the ever-increasing flow of economic migrants due to the collapse of local economies, and the rise in informal employment have all played a crucial role in the formulation of a new social policy towards the area. The areas of Vathis and central Omonoia began to be transformed into a ghetto of social exclusion, serving the needs of a temporary, undocumented and 'ready to be economically exploited' labour force. The policy of first assistance was to be transformed into a policy of institutionalized exclusion, which indirectly or directly produced and reproduced collective spaces for a temporary labour force.

According to the major findings from the study on undocumented Albanians, the spaces of collective accommodation in the area were nothing but a mere extension in the social sphere of what Albanians in the economic sphere 'enjoyed' in Athens. The processes identified that produced and reproduced such periphractic spaces were: the development of a flexible and informal service economy; the ideological racialization of the new labour force; the criminalization of the collective living spaces; and the destruction of private space amongst the population. In this research, the majority of Albanian respondents stated that they came to central Athens because of a growth in the informal labour market. In fact, the majority stated that the flow of migration was indirectly regulated by village-group networks, and by employers in Athens. The development of such a labour market was also responsible for the economic inability of Albanians to move towards another type or area of settlement.

Secondly, according to the experiences of the Albanian respondents, communal third-class accommodation was in reality the only choice the undocumented migrants had. Nationalism and the moral values that stigmatized the distinctive jobs Albanians took meant that the Albanians were systematically portrayed by social and government agencies as illegal, dirty, lazy, piratic and, most of all, criminal (Lazaridis and Rowaniszyn 1996). The social stigma reproduced the ideological necessity to construct social spaces fenced off from others. Social impoverishment and homelessness were seen as 'necessary' policies for people who 'deserved nothing better' and for people who were not part of the Athenian community. The policies of social exclusion were in fact welcomed even by social scientists as steps towards curbing migration (Petrinioti 1994). On the other hand, the negative images attached to the Albanian labour force, made it extremely difficult to leave the area, as no one would rent a flat to an Albanian because of the above stigmatization (Lazaridis and Rowaniszyn 1996).

Thirdly, frequent arrests in the streets of Athens and the use of the riot police for mass deportations have all played a crucial role in the production of a social space where the Albanian is to be found in hiding away from the 'public eye'. Those third-class hotels were mostly considered as shelters from the police force. Only inside these could Albanian migrants protect one another from mass expulsions and public abuse in the streets.

Lastly, the study of the Albanian population showed a severe and absolute destruction of the latter's private space, which in turn produced social environments of temporal use and of exclusion. Throughout the study, the destruction of private space, even at third-class hotels, had resulted in an *amorphous environment*, full of physical and moral humiliation, and unable to care for the physical, spiritual and emotional needs of the population. As Arendt has argued, adequate housing with safe private spaces is not only a humanitarian necessity but also an essential tool for free polities, community and social life itself (Arendt 1989). In the case of the Albanians, social spaces were turned into *risk spaces*, due to fear of deportation and continuous reminders of who they are not, and where they should not be.

In those periphractic spaces, life amongst the Albanian population was mostly centred around day-to-day survival, which more or less reflected mid-Victorian Britain in terms of rights and amenities. Up to 20 people were living together in most of the hotel rooms, in self-made wooden constructions, one on top of the other, whilst families usually had to negotiate with others to occupy one bedroom by themselves. They shared everything: beds, clothes, food (to combat starvation, the migrants had established common kitchens) but most of all they organized their life around their common village-group network. People of the same village or place of origin often occupied the same hotel or the same room, protecting one another against crime and the police, and establishing in that way a human linkage with the families left behind. That was possible by sending goods and exchanging mail between families and migrants whenever someone visited Albania or arrived in Athens. The rest of life was organized mostly in safe places like cinemas or the underground station in Omonoia where they could sell goods or seek employment.

In relation to female migrants involved in prostitution, the study shows a rather different picture. Firstly, all the interviewees mentioned shared accommodation, characterized by restricted communication with the surrounding community and its temporary character. In most cases, women and children lived in places that were also used as 'work-places', or were in total isolation from any direct contact with the local population (with the exception of clients). They changed their accommodation frequently, for security but also for marketing reasons. Thus, one can argue that living spaces often follow the flow of the prostitution trade, and the areas of accommodation change according to age, experience and the type of prostitution of Albanian female migrants. Secondly, in most cases, accommodation was provided on the basis of profit making. Thus, the females that were not 'successful', or were not in a financial position to bargain for better housing were mostly concentrated in crowded, downgraded third-class hotel accommodation. Homelessness, coupled with restrictive accommodation, produced a spatial network of residence for women and children in prostitution that explicitly rested upon the marginal status of the above people. Social, cultural and political interactions were strictly prohibited, whilst at the same time any relation with commuters and the neighbouring population was strictly profit oriented and negotiated on the basis of personal services.

Furthermore, the general characteristics of accommodation seem to follow not so much a pattern of *geographical restrictiveness*, associated with either a particular place (as in the case of red districts) or a single type of accommodation (such as hotels). Instead the social exclusion of female migrants who work in the so-called sex industry or entertainment business seem to be most identified with *power restrictiveness* and to be characterised by a set of relations (economic and racial) that establish three major *zones* of housing or accommodation '*services*' for women. All three *zones* seem to meet specific needs that are analogous to the type of services provided by women, their ethnicity and the networks responsible for their trafficking in southern Europe and Greece. Zone A, is centered around female migrants who work in entertainment and/or the provision of sexual services, and is mostly located around highly visible semi-legal businesses that act as in-between agencies for the provision of sexual services (for example clubs, massage parlours, and strip places). This shared type of accommodation is regulated by the economic flow of business and the housing distribution of women usually follows a seasonal pattern according to '*cash flow*' and demand by clients for different services. The most common form of accommodation is in hotels where entry and exit is controlled through the business or entertainment schedule and through the form of services provided to clients by female '*entertainers*'. The essence of such zones of accommodation is that they usually act as housing *enclaves* for the management of sexual services within a semi-legal or legal place and for the complete control of female subjects.

Zone B is usually a zone of accommodation for female migrants who are not dependent upon one type or form of business and are usually at the lowest end of either ethnic categorization and/or cash flow. Albanian women who work in direct prostitution are found to belong to this zone of accommodation. Their housing distribution does not follow the flow of prostitution, but of social *networking* in different areas of Athens or Greece. In this sense, there is a collective type of accommodation in less saturated (in terms of client availability) areas, usually hotels or rented apartments, and there is a new form of accommodation of rented housing sites which include both collective work places and living quarters, all in one spatial location. The latter are places of low visibility and act as work places, '*safe-houses*' for the residential isolation of women from the public gaze and especially immigration control officers, and as labour markets for the recruitment of new women in the prostitution business. This takes place through published 'job vacancies' in the local post, and usually, according to the interviews collected, attract many teenagers or undocumented female migrants who happen to have no other way to be independent of the '*ex-impressarios*'.

The last zone (zone C), seems to be centred around forced or child prostitution and this is a special zone, since it is characterised by *hypersegregation* accommodation. The social exclusion of women or children seems to serve almost one purpose and that is the enforcement of prostitution. Collective or otherwise, accommodation seems to function as a sad reminder of an *asylum*, where the practice and maintenance of absolute control regarding physical mobility, eating and sleeping patterns, the maintenance of silence, and control over communication with the outside world all produce a nightmarish social environment.

Periphractic Work Spaces

This study in a sense reaffirmed what Moore and Pinderhuges (1993) have proposed, that the new type of migration is central not only to European national economies, but also to the life and the restructuring of present cities. This is found in the provision of a continuous flow of cheap and socially restricted labour force. In this sense, in Athens we have a relative continuation of the 'guest-worker' philosophy of the 1950s, although, as will be shown, the differences are immense.

In Vathis and Omonoia squares, the study unravelled two important new categories of work activity and three main mechanisms through which we have the production/reproduction of a cheap and ephemeral labour force in Athens. During the period of the study (1991–5) the entire schema of work activity between the Albanian and the Athenian Greek community was unfolding in the area of personal 'pleasure' services. In the first category belong the ensemble of sexual services that were mostly provided through prostitution, although there were services like pornography and strip-teasing in night clubs. The majority of prostitution services were offered by under-age Albanian boys and girls. The interviews with respondents listed a number of major social problems. According to under-age (twelve to fourteen years of age) Albanians, one of the biggest problems that they experienced was that of the physical and psychological abuse within the prostitution networks. Some were forced to succumb to prostitution through being deprived of water and sanitation restrictions or being humiliated through sexual and verbal abuse. It should be noted that at the time of the research, especially in the third-rate hotels of central Athens, most Albanian prostitutes were deprived of control of the body and its necessities. However, in the cases we examined, the symbolism of such loss of control reminded one of the real nature of the sex industry and its relation to the migrant female Albanian population. There was a racialized categorization of Albanian migrants that, in addition to male domination, subjugated women to ethnic humiliation as well. Albanian women were often named as *dirty, cheap* or *useless* for anything other than providing cheap sexual services. In contrast, Polish or Russian prostitutes in Athens were often categorized as *highly priced, educated, clean* and *mature*. This can be seen in different advertisements for call girls or maid services that appeared, in local newspapers. Albanian women were often referred as *submissive, cheap, not minding being told how to perform* certain services, and so on.

Low-esteem and the strong criminal networks did not allow them to visit parents or friends. A fourteen-year-old prostitute in central Athens states that:

> If I return home, for certain, my father or brother (now that they have a knowledge of my doings here), this is the moral code back in Albania, will kill me with the axe . . . There is no way to return home . . . (Psimmenos, 1995: 164).

Another young Albanian migrant (seventeen years old) says:

> I do not have the means to return home. First of all I do not even have my passport, . . . nor I am certain that I can look straight at my parents . . . If I manage to save enough money, I may open my own beauty centre . . . I may go to Ioannina, the people are friendly there, and when I am rich enough, then my parents could visit me in Greece or I will visit them in Albania . . . (Psimmenos 1995: 164).

Initial entry into Greece constitutes the beginning of the loss of identity and citizenship. These children and women enter the country without a visa or even a passport and any other legal documents are usually stolen and destroyed by criminal networks in Athens. Family networks in Albania consider prostitution as a moral crime and both the victim and perpetrators are likely to be blamed for it. Almost the same conditions prevail amongst the Greek law-enforcing agents who would normally arrest the Albanian minors and either prosecute or deport them. Under such conditions children in prostitution become easy targets of exploitation. They constitute a new category of people without the ability either to return home or to stay in the country.

The fragile nature of their social situation in Athens is reflected in the short-lived nature of the sexual services they provide, for their 'economic value' starts to decline between the ages of seventeen to twenty. One consequence of this was their relocation to rural environments outside Athens, and another was their promotion into drug trafficking or other illicit activities.

It is important to note that the economic organization of sexual services varies according to age, place and ethnic categorization. The *socio-spatial economics* of prostitution is reflected in both migratory flows and networks that are responsible for women's trafficking, as well in the working context of women. Female trafficking from Albania was organized mostly around agencies that were responsible for promoting the hiring of maids and farm labourers. In contrast, women from Russia or the Balkan countries were usually hired by home entertaining agencies or by Greek 'impresarios' that were responsible for their promotion into the sex industry. In the first case migration is a way out of poverty or the repressive socio-cultural home environment. In the second case, migration is by design, where involvement with the sex industry and a particular section of it (such as strip-teasing, or massage parlours) is for a limited period of time-only.

According to Ilena, a fourteen year old Albanian girl in prostitution, life inside the social spaces of the Athenian sex industry involves both a progressive loss of self-esteem and status, as well the development of 'social ties' that prohibit the possibility of an exit route from prostitution.

> I was born at Berat in Albania . . . I have never worked before because I was at school. My mother and father own few acres of land which they use for grazing . . . when I was at school, I learned both Spanish and Italian . . . I liked to listen to Rock and Soul . . . to watch detective stories . . . when I was in Albania I wanted to become a poet . . . I look cheap, dirty you can even smell my clothes . . . Just before you came I was remembering something from the days at school. I remembered my schoolteacher who once kept me [at school] two more hours examining me . . . She was telling me that I'll never succeed at school. Afterwards I went back home and the next day I went at school and placed a live snake at her desk . . . Athens is a beautiful city but if I was in Albania I would not advise any of my girlfriends to come [over here] especially now . . . I don't know what to do with myself, I cannot stay anymore here, but I cannot also go back . . . (Psimmenos 1995 p. 171).

Ilena has been violently cut off from social spaces that enable one to relate freely with others, to self-identify and orient themselves according to one's personal choices. Somatic experiences and body language have become tools of commercial exchange, where one learns to separate oneself from past experiences, memories and identities. Indeed, in most cases, the interviews showed that work in the sex industry (especially amongst under-age Albanians) presented bodily functions and identity issues as a mosaic of incomprehensible, dissart-iculated events in the history and presence of the individual in a particular place. Pain, pleasure, the recollection of memories, together with the encounter of new things, were all presented in an amorphous, flat, autonomous way. In this way, the subject is being objectified, responding in the same way as if nothing makes sense, and most of all as if being in Athens and working in the sex industry is separate from the person that occupies this space and is occupied in this type of work.

Conclusion

The 1993 hunger-strike protest for human rights by an Albanian migrant in Greece has reminded the Greek community that a new period of political and economic life is present in the country. In this paper, we have offered only a *brief exposure* of the new life for migrants, and in particular of women migrants in the Athenian sex industry, paying attention to the general and particular processes and mechanisms responsible for the establishment of periphrastic spaces. These processes and mechanisms have been attached to three key issues: *globalization*, the *feminization of migration;* and *marginality and the politics of social exclusion*. These three issues are presented here as articulating effects of major movements of capital towards the restructuring of economic and political pathways, working on a three-level analysis: the construction of the economics of sexual services; the construction of power relations; and the meaning(s) attached to these.

Firstly, our analysis has placed women's sexual and political exploitation by the sex industry within the context of global restructuring. Economic life for Albanian female migrants in the sex industry of Athens is seen as a continuation of a range of economic forms of exploitation and marginalization that women have suffered prior to their arrival in Athens city. The re-ordering of economic activity, across territories and cultural spaces, has resulted in the production of degenerative spaces, which women are pushed into. One such degenerative space is the case of the entertainment business and in particular of the sex industry. In the second place women have been placed at the margins through a number of *economic mutations* in their local society. The involvement of women from Albania in the sex industry of Athens is seen as a continuation of women's lack of power to represent their interests and to seek viable economic alternatives. Women migrants in the service sector constitute a new *substitute-casual labour force*. The production and organization of the consumption of services produced by such a labour force rests upon the creation and maintenance of workspaces where power is further transferred and dispersed away from the actual workers. In this case women's position in Athenian society has been further dislocated from both their relations with collective networks of representation, and from their relation towards past memories, and mostly their bodies.

The *rules of residence*, *layout of housing* and the *use* (by the Albanian women) of the *local place* (in terms of relation networks) remind one of both their ephemerality and restricted existence in Athens. They are spaces of limited social visibility, where subjects are induced into self-shame and are socially controlled. Like in a *panopticon*, the living spaces of Albanian women rest upon their isolation and individuation and the total control of their everyday activities. In the case of work spaces, the economic activity of sexual services is based upon an ethnic categorization of women, international networking, and a labour market that is profiting out of the inability of women to integrate with the home or receiving society. Ethnicity, age, and status (in this case undocumented) synthesize the new *cartography* of labour economics, where Albanian women seem to occupy to lowest stratum in the business of prostitution.

Acknowledgement

I would like to thank Professor Floya Anthias and Gabriella Lazaridis for their help in preparing this chapter for publication.

References

Albrow, M. (1997), *The Impact of Globalization on Sociological concepts*, London: Routledge.

Amin, A. and Thrift, N. (1995a), *Globalization, Institutions, and Regional Development in Europe,* Oxford: Oxford University Press.

Amin, A. and Thrift, N. (1995b), 'Globalization Institutional Thickness and the local Economy' in Healey, P. et al (eds), *Managing cities: The New urban context*, Sussex: Wiley, pp. 91–109.

Anthias, F. and Yuval-Davis, N (1993), *Racialized Boundaries*, London: Routledge.

Arendt, H. (1989), *The Human Condition,* Chicago: University of Chicago Press.

Beck, U. (1992), *Risk Society*, London: Sage.

Berger, J. and Mohr, J. (1975), *A Seventh Man: The Story of a Migrant Worker in Europe*, Penguin: Harmondsworth.

Bradley, H. (1996), *Fractured Identities: changing patterns of inequality*, Cambridge MA: Blackwell.

Campani, G. (1997), 'Immigrant women in Southern Europe: Social Exclusion and Gender', paper presented at the Conference 'Migration in S. Europe' organised by *IIER and Regional Network on Southern European Societies*, 19–21 Sept., Santorini, Greece.

Cardoso, F. (1974), 'The Industrial Elite in Latin America' in H. Bernstein (ed.), *Underdevelopment and Development*, Penguin Books; Middlesex, pp. 191–205.

Cohen, R. (1994), *Frontiers of Identity*, Harlow: Longman.

Dunn, C. (1989), *Global Formation, structures of the World Economy*, Oxford: Basil Blackwell.

Eade, J. (ed.) (1997), *Living the Global: City, Globalization as local Process*, London: Routledge.

Fakiolas, R. (1997), 'Recent Efforts to regularise undocumented immigrants in Greece', unpublished, Athens.

Frobel, F., Heinrichs, J. and Kreye, O. (1980), *The New International Division of Labour*, Cambridge: Cambridge University Press.

Habermas, J. (1995), *The Theory of Communicative Action: Reason and the Rationalization of Society*, Volume One, Cambridge: Polity Press.

Goldberg, D. (1993), *Racist Cultures*, Oxford, Blackwell.

I.O.M. (1995), *Trafficking and Prostitution: the Growing exploitation of migrant Women from Center and Eastern Europe*, Geneva: IOM.

King, R. (1997), 'Southern Europe in the changing Global map and Typology of Migration,' paper presented at the Conference 'Migration in S. Europe' organised by, *I.I.E.R./Regional Network on Southern European Societies*, Santorini, Greece.

Lazaridis, G. and Romaniszyn, K. (1996), 'Albanian and Polish Undocumented Workers in Greece: A comparative Analysis', *European Social Policy Journal*, Vol. 8, No. 1, pp. 1–22.

Lea, J. (1997), 'Post-Fordism and criminality' in N. Jewson and MacGregor, S. (eds), *Transforming cities: contested Governance and new spatial divisions*, London: Routledge, pp. 42–56.

Lianos, T. (1995), 'The Impact of Immigration on Local Labour Markets, The case of Northern Greece', paper presented at *CEPR* workshop, Halkidiki.

Lim, L. (1997), 'Flexible Labour Markets in a Globalizing World: The implications of International Female Migrants', *International Labour Office Report*, ILO, Geneva.

Marangopoulos Foundation (1996), *Women trafficking*, paper presented at Conference organised by Panteio University, Athens.

Miles, R. (1982), *Racism and Migrant Labour*, London: Routledge.

Miles, R. (1993), 'Migration and the New Europe', *Ethnic and Racial Studies*, Vol. 16, No. 3, pp. 459–67.

Mingione E. and Magatti, M. (1994), *The Informal Sector*, Brussels: European Commission.

Mingione, E. (1996), *Urban Poverty and the Underclass*, Oxford: Blackwell.

Mingione, E. (1997), 'The insertion of immigrants in the underground Economy in Italy', paper presented at the Conference 'Migration in S. Europe' organised by *IIER and Regional Network on Southern European Societies*, 19–21 Sept., Santorini, Greece.

Ministry of Social Security (1996), 'Interview of the state of Services', SKAI channel TV, Athens.

Moore, J. and Pinderhughes, R. (1996), *In the Barrios, Latinos and the Underclass debate*, New York: Russel Sage.

Murray, C. (1990), *The Emerging British Underclass*, London: Institute of Economic Affairs.

Petrinioti, X. (1994), *The Immigration towards Greece*, Athens: Odisseas.

Psimmenos, I. (1995), Metanastefsi apo ta Balkania: Koinonikos Apoklismos stin Athina, Athens: Papazisis – Glory Book.

Psimmenos, I. (1997), *Globalization and Employee Participation*, Avebury.

Phizacklea, A. (1997), 'Sex, Marriage and Maids: paper,' paper presented at the Conference 'Migration in S. Europe' organised by *IIER and Regional Network on Southern European Societies*, 19–21 September, Santorini, Greece.

Phizacklea, A. (1995), 'Gender, Race and Migration', paper presented in the workshop *Praxis International* May, 4–6, Athens.

Ross, R. and Trachte, K. (1983), 'Global cities and Global classes: The Peripheralisation of Labor in New York City', *Review*, Vol. 6, No. 3.

Rustin, M. (1989), 'The Trouble with New Times', in S. Hall and M. Jacques (eds), *New Times*, London: Lawrence & Wishart, London, pp. 303–32.

Sassen, S. (1994), *Cities in a World Economy*, Pine Forge, California.

Sibley, D. (1997), *Geographies of Exclusion*, London: Routledge.

Smith, M.P. and Feagin, J.R (1987), *The Capitalist City*, Oxford: Basil Blackwell.

Vaiou, D. and Chatzimichalis, K. (1997), '*Me tin raptomixani stin kouzina kai tous Polonous stous Agrous*' Athens: Exantas.

Wacquant, L. (1996), 'Red Belt, Black Belt; Racial Division, class Inequality and the state in the French Urban Periphery and the American Ghetto', in E. Mingione (ed.), *Urban Poverty and the Underclass*, Oxford: Blackwell, pp. 234–75.

Zukin, S. (1992), *Landscapes of Power*, Berkeley: University of California.

five

Female Migrants in Italy: Coping in a Country of New Immigration

VICTORIA CHELL-ROBINSON

Introduction

As growing numbers of women are likely to opt for international migration as a means of improving their life chances, it seems particularly important that we consider how these women cope with their new lives and how the countries, where they arrive, receive them. The context for this study is the migration 'about-face' that has occurred in southern Europe since the early 1980s. Over the past two decades, southern Europe, and specifically for this study Italy, changed from being areas of net emigration to areas of net immigration, most importantly with significant immigrations from the 'south'. This study focuses not so much on this well-documented turnaround,[1] but on the effect on women of international migration to a country of new immigration and on their economic and non-economic activities. Key findings of the data include altered power and status relationships between the sexes and across generations. This is exemplified in the spatial arrangements constructed within the migrant's new environment. The investigation is also a response to the general need for a better understanding of the role of women in international migration, concluding with the observation that these women are pivotal members of their communities in allowing them access to new forms of production.

To investigate the issue of women's participation in international migration this study relates the experience of two female migrant groups arriving in Italy at a tumultuous time in Italy's immigration history, Filipinas and Somalian women. Initially, female migration to

Italy tended to be fairly limited, concerning only a few women from a handful of nationalities: mainly women from the Cape Verde Islands, the Philippines and Eritrea who were employed as domestics. Today the number of female migrants has increased sharply with a greater range of nationalities represented, yet still remaining confined to the service sector. The findings presented in this chapter are based on my doctoral research completed in 1994. At that time, Filipinas were a regular sight in most Italian cities; they had provided unskilled labour for Italy since the early 1970s and were beginning to exhibit signs of a maturing migrant community – family reunification and diversification into new professions. However, the second migrant group at the centre of this study, Somalian women, are a more recent phenomenon, still at the initial stages of a migration process initiated by civil unrest.[2]

Female migrants have arrived in Italy from various countries and with different migration projects, exemplified in the two groups concerned here. Indeed this study intends to show that although there are few generalizations to be made concerning the migration of women to Italy and its impact, these women are playing an active and pro-tagonist role in contemporary international migrations, contrary to reductionist stances that portray female migrants as dependants (Morokvasic 1984). These women are illustrative of the need to reassess the traditional treatment of migration in gender-blind terms. There are marked gender and occupational selectivities in migration streams, a difference that deserves special consideration.

New Migrations to Italy

This section concentrates on the emergence of Italy as a country of immigration since the 1970s, drawing attention to the fact that the economic and social isolation of this study's participants are a by-product of naïve and ineffective reception policies. International migrations to Europe have grown in size in recent years, their compositions and directions substantially altering (King 1993a; Campani 1990; Pugliese 1991). Significant among these alterations is the emergence of southern Europe as a destination in the new pattern of migration flows to the EU (see Table 5.1),[3] and the equally important recognition of non-EU females as economic migrants within these flows. The rapidity of Italy's transformation, in a little over twenty years, from a country of emigration to one of immigration has been achieved through a combination of return migration, and the influx of new (largely non-EU) migrants (King 1993a).

Table 5.1: Estimates of foreign population stocks (in thousands) for southern Europe

	1970	1980	1990
Portugal	23.4	49.3	107.8
Spain	148.4	182.0	277.0
Italy	147.0	298.7	781.1
Greece	93.0	182.0	229.0

Sources: National Statistical Yearbooks: SOPEMI reports; as reported by Hall and White (1995:163)

The existence of immigration in a traditional country of emigration like Italy may seem paradoxical (King 1985: 172), but it can be explained when several corresponding factors are considered in combination. One factor is the diversion effects of measures taken in the main receiving nations. In 1973 strict immigration controls were imposed throughout the EU, enforced through border controls and national regulations. This led to a reduction in the number of clandestine migrants in the main receiving countries and their diversion to southern European countries, added to which there may have been migrants expelled from the main receiving countries finding alternate destinations. Some observers termed this 'the development of a "buffer state" situation' (Collinson 1994; Barsotti and Lechini 1995) in which migrants were absorbed without being transmitted further north (Hall and White 1995: 165).

The fundamental role of the 'underground economy' in Italy is another factor. In economic terms, Italy's fortunes have profoundly altered. The country once considered as an economic backwater to western Europe has blossomed at a time when the highly fragmented and segmented nature of southern European, and especially Italian, labour markets created a sectoral shift away from heavy manufacturing to high technology and service industries (King 1993a). Consolidated niches have developed that demand specific labour characteristics, typified in the case of migrant workers by a thirst for 'inexpensive and flexible' labour in 'marginal' areas of employment. The concentration of such employment in cities such as Rome, Bari, and Milan only consolidates the effects of this precarious employment, with the migrants' poor conditions at work replicated by bad housing and living conditions (Salt and Johnson 1992: 67). 'Immigration to Italy has become a model case because of the power of the informal economy

... this informal economy (and its flexibility) needs an unorganized labour force that is willing to accept any kind of working conditions, and migrants can provide this' (Campani 1990: 307). The 'secondary labour force' employed in this underground economy consists mainly of young women and retired Italians and foreigners. Significant among this group are the irregular migrants employed in mainly service sector jobs, jobs that are hard, dirty, unattractive and sometimes dangerous. It would be wrong, however, to make the assumption that the migration phenomenon in Italy consists almost entirely of non-EU migrants. Four out of the ten largest migrant groups in Italy are from West European countries and the US.

Italy is attractive to non-EU migrants for a number of economic reasons: it is also relatively easy to enter and moreover is geographically proximate to North Africa. The country is still very open to entry with a tourist visa[4] and the geographical proximity of Africa and Tunisia in particular, makes Sicily and the Mediterranean ports easy to enter. Cultural proximity through a colonial heritage has also attracted particular national groups such as Eritreans and Somalians, with many people in north African nations having some knowledge of the Italian language. Also important is that Italy is the centre of the Catholic faith, with missions from Italy to Africa and Asia (relevant particularly to the Philippines) acting as a means of forming interest in Italy and extending the information networks that facilitate migration. However, besides those flows originating in Africa and Asia, the political developments in eastern Europe have created a potential new source of migrants that have also found Italy easy to enter.

Yet another factor explaining the influx of migrants into Italy is its uncertain national immigration policies. For some time it has been suggested that southern European nations have not been prepared to deal with large-scale immigration and that national legislation is inadequate (see Table 5.2). Perhaps it can also be speculated that immigration is far behind in political urgency in a country that has other problems and issues to address, and this can, to a degree, explain the non-intervention of the government. When crises have occurred, these nations have not been ready to deal fully with the situation; they have instead resorted to *ad hoc* policies (Andall 1992). For decades, these southern European countries have had to deal only with emigration and adopt policies that protected these emigrants' rights. Yet today, they are forced to adopt similar policies to those of the former countries of immigration. This has meant confronting clandestine immigration; a difficult task when there are political and moral contra-

Table 5.2: Summarised Italian Immigration Legislation (1986–1992)[5]

Law no. 943, 30/12 1986 (renewed through Act no. 81, 1988)	This law, the first Italian law on immigration, proposed an amnesty for the undocumented aliens residing in Italy, and laid down provisions for subsequent immigration. It also attempted to foster integration through provision for Italian lessons for foreigners whilst also ensuring the protection of ethnic identities.[7] This regulation aimed at regularizing the situation of migrants, not limiting the inflow of new migrants.
Law no. 39, 28/2 1990 (from a decree of 30/12 1989) 'The Martelli Law'	In conformity with the Geneva Convention, the Martelli Law abolished the special territorial limitations whilst making visas compulsory for those coming from 'high emigration risk areas'. It also introduced a minimum income level for those residing in Italian territory. Nationals and EU citizens were given priority in the right to work.
Act no. 390, 24/4 1992[6]	A new status of asylum, 'asylum for humanitarian reasons' was invented, which was more flexible than the status of political refugee, specifically designed for those coming from the former Yugoslavia.
The New Nationality Law, Act no. 91 5/2 1992	Raised the period of residence required for non-EU citizens from five to ten years, reduced to four for EU persons, and three for people of Italian origin.

dictions to be overcome and at a time when the political and economic situation of Italy is very different from that the northern European countries were faced with in the 1970s.

Political ambiguity in relation to immigration matters and the difficulty of finding a way forward may explain the reluctance to impose European immigration reforms, which until the Schengen agreement of 1989 remained implicit rather than explicit. The result to date has been residual gaps in the national legislation that allow individuals to slip through the net and into the underground economy. Because of its physical location, a thriving 'underground' market, and the insufficiency of legislation governing the inflow of migrants, Italy earns its reputation as an unguarded and unpredictable backdoor to the rest of Europe. It is a predicament compounded by the transitory nature of many migrant flows to southern Europe.

Female Migrants in Italy

How can one explain the concentrated presence of non-EU female domestic workers in Rome? In the early stages of immigration during the late 1970s the tertiarization of the Italian economy generated mainly white-collar, female-typed jobs filled by Italian women who, with a heightened feminist consciousness, have preferred them. The incoming migrants, particularly the female migrants, have satisfied a demand for work that comes not from the productive system, but the redistribution of income where families from the 'middle-classes' have rediscovered a function for migrant labour not readily available from Italian nationals.[8] This development would seem to indicate a similar experience to the northern European countries' past demand for migrants through industrialization and changing labour relations, yet Italy's employment demand is configured in a significantly different manner. The functions of labour migrations have altered, with a preponderance of female migrants confined to the service sectors. These immigration flows are no longer for quantitative rebalancing of labour markets where there is a need to supplement the shortfalls in native labour, but there are qualitative rebalances, required to ensure flexibility of the labour market in areas where particular duties and qualifications experience a shortfall. Meanwhile, structural unemployment in countries such as the Philippines created a surplus population, which finally migrated in the desire for income and a better standard of living. The immigration of Somalian women was for distinctly different reasons. The onset of their move from Somalia coincided with the outbreak of civil war in their country. However, the move also coincided with the introduction in Italy of the Martelli Law in early 1990 (see Table 5.2). Respondents stated that the regularization opportunities presented in this law, the fact that Somalia was once an Italian colony, coupled with the economic opportunities available in Italy, were together strong incentives for choosing Italy to go to. Indeed, it is fair to say that the exile itself was caused by civil unrest, but that the prolonged stay in Italy, even after the unrest had abated, was due to the need for economic security in the wake of hardship incurred in exile.

Such economic determinism only goes part of the way to explaining why it is that, in a country such as Italy where the supply of domestics is larger than the demand, more women still migrate. I suggest that in addition to the economic attractiveness of Italy, both the existence of 'facilitating conditions' in Italy (intermediaries such as the Catholic church and strong personal networks) and a 'culture of migration' within certain migrant groups have continued to facilitate the migration of female migrants to Italy. I would also suggest that the over-representation of women in the domestic care niche is perpetuated because of sexist and racist stereotypes. Indeed, 'Filipina' and 'domestic help' are synonymous to many. (As indicated by Lazaridis in her chapter in this volume, the synonymy of 'Filipina' and 'domestic help' is also widely encountered in other southern European countries such as Greece). The Italian employers interviewed in this study supported this hypothesis, going so far as to state that in the hierarchy of domestics available, Filipinas were the 'domestic of preference'.

The migration of women to Italy is also being fuelled by a new occupational demand. Evidence from this study revealed that the domestic 'home help' phenomenon is now itself being transcended due to a shift in Italy's demographic profile. The Italian fertility rate is well below the 2.1 rate which assures replacement of the population. Italy's 1.27 fertility rate is the lowest in Europe. The percentage of the population in the over-65 group in 1991 was 14.8 per cent and by 2011 will have reached 20.8 per cent. An indicator of the significance of this for the labour force is shown in the ratio of under-15s to over-65s. In 1991 it was 91.2 elderly for every 100 under-15, but by 2011 this will be 151.7 (Bonifazi 1993). An increase in the number of aged has future implications for the demand for those female migrants who perform 'home help' tasks, using formal qualifications in the medical professions that they are not legally allowed to perform in Italy. Those medically qualified migrants move from the cooking and cleaning to the more lucrative and professionally rewarding business of providing basic health supervision for the elderly.

The female respondents in this study are anything but a homogeneous group: they have different experiences, different cultural origins and references, personal and specific histories, and individual desires and expectations. There are those who leave voluntarily in hope of economic gain and for family reunification; there are also those who were forced to leave their homes – they are refugees or have no hope of surviving in a country like Somalia, where civil war combines with ecological disaster. There are those women who have arrived from the large and cosmopolitan cities of Africa and Asia, and there are those that have left directly from rural villages and life in the country. There is also diversity in the lives that these women have left behind. Beside those women who have been economically active there are the housewives and those who belong to Muslim groups.

Filipino migration to Italy began in the late 1970s, accelerating during the 1980s. By 1981 there were already an estimated 15,000 Filipinos in Italy, which grew to over 35,000 by 1990. The accelerated growth of the group can be attributed not only to the burgeoning Italian economy which was undoubtedly attracting more migrants into its tertiary sector, but also the movement of Filipinos from the Gulf States, which experienced a recession during this period. Throughout the first half of the 1990s, this number grew to 40,000 and more, fuelled by the promises of the new Martelli law. The Somalian community, by contrast, is relatively new. The group's numbers were swollen in the early 1990s by refugees, adding to the modest number of diplomats and students already present in Rome, accounting for some 17,000 individuals by 1995. Despite this numerical difference, the group exhibits a few similarities with the Filipinas. Female migrants dominate both, and both concentrate in Rome. For the Filipino group, the abundance of domestic work from the wealthy middle-classes during the 1980s created a strong pull. Rome as the centre of the Catholic faith, was also a strong factor of attraction. In contrast, the Somalian women were not drawn to the Italian economy so much, as to facilities provided by the Italian government for those in exile. These basic differences in reasons for migrating and residing in Rome are central in understanding why these women hold different positions in the same economic activity. The majority of both groups were employed in domestic work, however the Somalian women's primary intention in migration from home was flight as refugees, not as economic migrants. Consequentially, they have found their recourse to domestic work a necessity, not a goal. The Filipinas by contrast, experience a 'top of the pile' situation. They have made a career out of domestic service, and are able to command the highest wages. (As one can see from the chapter by Lazaridis in this volume, this is not unique to the Filipinas residing in Italy). The income gap is also attributable to the greater experience of the Filipinas, and the preference of Italian employers for Filipinas as domestics. For both groups, migration was seen not only as a means to short-term financial gain for the migrant, and above all for her family, but also as a long-term fulfilment of goals and dreams. That the migrant women would have to endure hardships and considerable sacrifice was seen as unavoidable, but a worthwhile price to pay. Amongst both groups residing in Rome, future economic aspirations were *prevalent* but *not exclusive*: migration is understood and experienced both in relation to economic settlement and in relation to personal and family achievement, and for some this included a cautious movement towards self-determination and autonomy.

Means of Coping

The information gathered during the study goes some way toward an explanation of how the women's ability to 'cope' is a direct product of the support networks that they develop on their arrival. In a general sense, the evidence leads to recognition that the insertion of these women into a domestic work setting, coupled with the separation from family, has immediately created a barrier to negotiating integration in their new setting. The unskilled migrant faces a complex and problematic situation on arrival in a country such as Italy: how to rebuild the familiar in order to be able to cope with the unfamiliar? This study moves toward the general conclusion that although migration has the potential to improve the status of women through economic wealth, this is often at great personal and familial cost with individuals preoccupied with ideas of dislocation and loss. The relationships that are then formed in their new host country are central in the women's ability to 'cope' and move towards a hopeful future. These wider relationships provide sustenance and refuge but may also reinforce traditional gender relations. Such social dependence can hinder the potential for liberation that economic independence might bring. These relationships have also quickly marked the position of women within their new environments. Paradoxically, the 'Western' environment itself may perpetuate and exaggerate the image of the women as 'home makers', consigning them to 'traditional' economic roles within the service sector.

The consequences of migration are many. There are numerous

indications of the relative social isolation of these two groups of women working in Italy, yet female migrants are more than isolated women. If the assistance that the church and voluntary agencies supply and the personal networks were to be excluded, female migrants would have had to learn to fit into Italian society themselves. Indeed, there is a pervasive assumption that these women, who are earning a wage and supporting themselves, are gaining independence. Yet the moral obligation to provide support for the household is rooted strongly, and the individual finds herself to be a vital member of the household, more so abroad than at home, remitting most of the earnings from her employment. Such economic exile is vital to fulfilling the expectations made of them.

How to cope with this uprooting is a dilemma the unskilled female migrant is faced with in a country such as Italy, which has largely failed to provide adequate legislation or social provisions for new migrants. It is worth commenting that while the re-conceptualization of Italy as a country of immigration has been recognized in academic terms, critically the Italian government at the time of this study (early 1990s) had failed to make adequate provisions for the application of legislation such as the Martelli law (see Table 5.2). As a result, not only is the economic integration of foreign workers difficult in the labour market, but other forms of reception from voluntary organizations, such as the Caritas, are the only means of recourse for new migrants. The Martelli law, introduced in February 1990, required the establishment of reception centres for new migrants and refugees; however, three years later only two municipal reception centres existed in Rome. As many of this study's respondents pointed out, it is now too late for initial reception facilities. For many migrants the situation has developed further. A housing solution is now required. The policy implications of this are essential. Official immigration, reception and housing programmes are necessary, measures that should fundamentally incorporate the initiatives of migrant populations and groups such as Caritas and Saint' Egidio, ideas which may not conform to the ideas of policy makers. A good example is the Caritas migrant community programmes. The centre provides health care and shelter specifically designed for women and children, and unaccompanied children, a regrettable but growing phenomenon of non-EU migration to Italy. Such targeted social programmes should extend into many other areas of migrant assistance, a move in which the migrants themselves should be involved, so that they can be relevant to the needs of all migrants. One such means is to support migrants' information networks.

The Advantage of Personal and Social Networks in Coping: Extending the Domestic Unit

Throughout the study that this chapter is based on, the role of personal networks in the migration process was established. These networks influence the direction, content and timing of migration flows, provide initial social and housing requirements, and also allow the individual to build a support system that may alleviate some of the loneliness and hardship of family separation.

Both the Filipino and Somalian female migrant workers operate within social networks that have been described in terms of concentric spheres, the inner core consisting of close relatives, to which there are binding obligations. Around this there are graduated spheres, one of more distant relatives, one of fellow countrymen and friends, and one of persons who are not specifically obligated to the individual but who may be called on for their services (migrant traffickers, religious organizations, the state). These relationships are the focus of support both before and after migration. The network acts as an organizing force, perpetuating the migration flow and assisting in subsequent adaptation to life in a host country. It is the crux of an individual's ability to 'cope'. If women are involved in their country of origin with activities outside the domestic unit, the situation is manageable; this is because there is a set of domestic relations that cushion the effect on the women in these extra-domestic activities. But this is far more problematic when the individual leaves that local environment in search of waged employment, and where the reciprocity of help and services are absent on initial migration. The major problem facing these new migrants, therefore, is how to reconstruct this support network; there are strong obligations to home in the country of origin, which sometimes make it difficult to generate independent networks abroad.

> The migrant is a fragile thing, she is unsure and a scared creature, with an initial reaction to group together for security in the hope of finding a sort of ethnic identity, before attempting to be subsumed into the host society so that she has a degree of self assurity and confidence. Encompassed in this is the need to merely find a job, to achieve what they came here for, to send money home, in effect just to survive in the host nation. There are few thoughts of actually recognising themselves as a woman and a woman with rights etc. or displaying those feminine instincts that would be expressed in their own country. There is little thought of an education process or independence. (Interview with Graziano Tassello)[9]

The extent, to which a woman is 'successful' in her migration and retains her sanity, depends on the extent to which she can balance these conflicting demands. In the case of refugees from Somalia and migrants from the Philippines, social networks were the main source of accommodation and assistance in finding employment. In a country such as Italy, with a problematic housing situation and no effort being made for placing migrants on waiting lists for public housing, the recourse to friends and family is a necessity, not an option.

The strength of these personal and social networks also plays a decisive role in the impact of migration on the adaptation and status of migrant women. Not all the outcomes from this support are necessarily positive, however. Not only is little independence gained because of the economic obligations to remit money home, but also the strong social networks encountered on arrival in Italy leave little chance for encountering other lifestyles. In the case of the Filipinos, the Catholic Church is the dominant form of assistance. However, provisions from the Church have followed the Catholic tenet of assistance and charity. Such intervention is not conducive to self help but encourages the continued reliance on charitable assistance for the mental, physical, social and economic health of the individual.

> The Catholic organisations are more concerned with being there to act as their salvation, as their crutch, and through this there is nothing given back in return (from the migrants), and the migrants get used to having everything done for her/him, and of living within this false institutionalised structure. Through this there may also be abuse of the system. It is a sort of control through which the migrant is not exposed to any kind of independence, and then is reliant on the church (Anne-Marie Dupré 1992)[10].

By migrating and working abroad, the Filipino migrant women at the centre of this study became the main source of income for their families, yet it is questionable whether there has been a corresponding shift in economic control. In fact, the slight asymmetry of economic roles between men and women in the household, in favour of the women, does not seem to have produced the same change in their political and social ability to make decisions for the family unit. Similarly, the Somalian women were almost exclusively the only wage earners for their household, yet decisions over the use of that income are relinquished to male members of the household. The strength of personal and social networks, coupled with a desire to be close to the social norms of the community from which they derive all kinds of support seem to be partly responsible for this outcome. There were other indications of the social isolation of the women. Most of the women interviewed had no Italian friends or friends from other national groups.

These social networks have yet another aspect to them. Not only do they initiate migration and support the migrant in her migration – they also encourage further migrations. This migration of non-EU women, primarily stimulated by the rapid growth of the Italian economy, is fuelled by it's own momentum. It is a process that is already so prevalent that it has, through information networks, generated its own mythology and oral traditions. Indeed, migrants are often depicted as wide-eyed, naïve newcomers, arriving at a large city overwhelmed by the unfamiliar nature of their destination. In fact, the majority of those who move are following a well-worn path previously travelled by family and friends. The fundamental role of these networks is to reduce the risks associated with migration and assist in the individual's efforts to 'cope' away from home. There are other ways in which these women rebuild a form of security similar to that available through networks. Many of the women involved in this study were able to build a new form of security and express in spatial terms their challenge or reaffirmation of gender and occupational roles.

Building Place and Identity

How do you cope in an unfamiliar built environment? You build an environment that is familiar. We are born into relationships and an identity that are always based in place; there are indications however, that these migrant women consciously and unconsciously display the dialectical process of reconstructing and rebuilding 'new' female identities through the use of place. Space becomes not only a physical territory, but has a social and psychological dimension.

Examining the interplay between social relations in the household and the workplace mediated through space is an important way of understanding migrant women's resistance to unequal gender and social relations. For many migrants, security and peace of mind are obtained through a continual investment in an idealized perception of the country of origin; for those who are refugees, culture becomes a symbol of what has been lost and sacrificed. Music, religion, ritualized daily routines and places of meeting are means of retaining a collective identity, whilst the reception of this spatial display from Italian society may reinforce stereotypical images of the migrant phenomenon. This situation is further complicated when relationships of age, gender and ethnicities are introduced. This perception is particularly valuable when these relationships are contextualized within the already spatially defined 'us' and 'them' association a migrant has with the state.[11]

Different spaces have been used to confront the changes which migration has brought to otherwise familiar lifestyles in the absence of adequate Italian reception and housing policies. Most public spaces in Rome have a spatial definition that incorporates ethnic demarcation (the separation of different national migrant groups), gender demarcation (women in one area and men in another, whilst in the same public space), and a more subtle spatial demarcation built around distinctions between areas of origin (the Philippines or Somalia). The distinctions between these areas are not always rigid, especially if the population in a public space at any one time is small, then there may be some mixing, but when there are many people in one area, such as a Sunday or Thursday afternoon at Termini,[12] these distinctions become clear.[13] These spaces have become social maps.

Termini, the piazzas and Eur station[14] are all public spaces where transport routes converge, and as such there is maximum accessibility for the migrants. In general these public spaces are used because of a lack of provision from the 'Commune di Roma'[15] of any meeting or leisure facilities for migrant groups. So what does this mean for the women? With specific reference to the Filipina group, the need for places to meet other than such public areas, is necessary to mask the divisions and negative aspects within the community, largely accelerated through the continual arrival of Filipino men. When I asked the current labour attaché to the Philippines in Rome *What are the main problems you feel the community in Rome is facing?'* he replied:

> The main thing is that there is nowhere for them to meet [the Filipinos] constructively, for them to use their time well. There are just areas like Termini and that are not good, they can't spend their time productively and then they get into trouble. They lack a Filipino club with space, where they can gather and exchange ideas, where they can play sport, play videos and hold parties. This is a great need.[16]

Public spaces in the eyes of the community leaders and the Church are accruing negative images for the community as a group, through their association not only on Sundays as areas where large community groups meet, but also because of what is seen daily as the preponderance of male migrants. The men, it is said, give the rest of the community a bad name through their drinking, their gambling and womanizing. However, it is due to the social constraints exercised at the church that not only the men, but also the women, go to such areas. Here they are away from the watchful eye of the priests and sisters where 'the lighter side of life' can be enjoyed, and relationships can be formed that may be frowned upon in the Church areas.

This distorted image of the migrant phenomenon as largely male is compounded by the specific employment opportunities available for migrant women in Rome. An unemployed mass of migrant men is created who have largely joined these women, and who, through gathering at public spaces such as Termini and the piazzas, are perpetuating an image of the migrant phenomenon in Rome. As such, the use of public space is increasing the complex set of assumptions and attitudes used in reference to migrant women, due to this image of the migrant phenomenon as male, non-white, unproductive and uncontrolled. These are images unlikely to lead to the adjustment of migrant and national groups, or acceptance by Italian society, as frictions with the host society are likely to increase. Through the examination of space and gender, it is shown that although place is often the way in which gender and power relations are defined, it is also through the lack of alternative space that public areas are used for this expression. Secondly, intolerance and racism are developing in part due to the absence in the Italian public mind of any visible state control of migration to Italy. The consequences of this in the recent political climate are strong anti-migrant policies towards both economic migrants and refugees. It is this local confusion of reactions, of who these women are, what their function is, and how they can best be assisted in their adjustment to life in Italy, which is both the result of this distorted image of the visible male migrant as the economic actor and of the misconception that the invisibility of women may mean that they need no help in adjusting. Both groups of women, Somalian and Filipino, indicated that local government organizations, trade unions and voluntary organizations, were little able to attend to or recognize the specific concerns of these women (issues such as domestic violence, pregnancy and hospitalization, counselling for the emotional distress caused by migration and for Somalian women the issue of infibulation).

The absence of large numbers of Somalian women in public areas is in fact due to their concentration in private accommodation. The drastic changes that have occurred in their lives as a result of their exodus from a civil war, combined with the feelings of being uprooted, may have instigated a search for tradition and an attempt to reconstruct familiar lifestyles within the private space. In this sense, the women themselves do gain power in the gender relations, as they themselves become a source of continuity and comfort for the rest of the community. Such strategies to cope may, however, leave a patri-archal system intact, although this may paradoxically be a source of support for the women in the absence of a certain future.

What the Future Holds

The aim of this study thus far, has been to identify and explore women in international migration and how they are able to cope with the changes that these migrations bring to their lives. It seems fitting to conclude by considering how, what is an undoubtedly fluid situation, may develop.

Return migration is an important aspect of international migration, because it may be said to represent the last stage of the migration process and the attainment of the ultimate migration goal. Data from this study suggests that a migrant's return is not necessarily the end of the migration phenomenon for either herself or her household. The obligation to financially support a household may continue beyond the initial migration. Findings gathered from the Filipinos clearly suggest that the nature of Filipino migration is changing. Besides a process of family formation, what I have termed an 'inter-generational, sequential migration' is occurring. Lack of desire on the part of early Filipino migrants to unite their family in Italy but a high degree of importance placed on the income generated for the family through remittances has created a new pattern of family migration. The Filipina who has been a migrant for up to twenty years and is now in her fifties or sixties will have supported her family in the Philippines through remittances, allowing her children to finish school. As the family has not been united in Italy and as the mother has reached her time for retirement, her daughter enters Italy to replace her mother as the main provider of a family income. As such, there is a replace-ment of migrants, which is likely to continue sequentially in the future, unless the Philippine economy becomes more prosperous or Italian immigration restrictions are strengthened. Given the higher ages and longer history of migration from the Philippines, this replacement phenomenon is confined to the Philippines. This cross-generational migration is being accelerated by the falling average age of the Filipinos migrating to Italy. During the 1970s, when the first large wave of Filipinos arrived in Italy, many of the women were in their 30s or 40s. Since about 1985, unemployment and economic deterioration in the Philippines have pushed younger women, including those graduating from college and university, into migrating. It used to be that it was the mother who migrated leaving her children behind.

Now, the children convince the mother to retire in the Philippines whilst the grown-up children themselves migrate. This turn-around has meant that, unlike their mothers, who had children before they migrated, these women are migrating early in their reproductive life, delaying a family. This might indeed have great significance for future generations as the phenomenon could carry on indefinitely across future generations.

Emerging Employment Patterns

Men are increasingly joining the female members of their households in Italy. For the Filipino men, this is due to the reduction in economic opportunities in the Gulf States where many of them have previously migrated. The Somalian men are moving from the exile locations they had held proximate to Somalia (often in Ethiopia or Kenya), and on to Europe, having become disenchanted with the prospect of return to a war-torn Mogadishu. Charmed by news of a burgeoning economy in Italy, these men expect to find opportunities awaiting them in Rome. This is not the case. Domestic service is distinctively biased towards the employment of women only. The women are then the only means of access these men have into the productive economy. One Filipino (Josie) described how this new migration has proved profitable for the Filipino men and begun a new economic trend:

> Many of the men who come here have a technique of getting a job. They have to find a girlfriend to find a job; this is why so many marriages are in trouble in the Philippines. If a man spends some time with his girlfriend whilst she is doing her job the employers get to trust him, and then after a while the girlfriend leaves for another job. He will then take over the job. This is a way of getting around the reluctance of the Italians to employ men in the domestic sphere.

Finally, as previously suggested, some Filipinos in Rome are renegotiating their economic position in the Italian labour market. The domestic work sector is not only poorly paid, it is also an unskilled sector of the economy in which you find many highly qualified women. Given the opportunity, therefore, those individuals who are frustrated with such a situation are moving into an area of employment not satisfied by national labour supply, an area of employment that allows the use of their skills and qualifications as health workers, nurses and doctors. Some Filipinos (termed *assistensas*) who were employed as domestics are taking charge of the care for sick and elderly members of a household instead of the normal domestic work tasks. However, these *assistensas* are often administering medicine and undertaking medical procedures without the required authorization from Italian authorities, and, as such, are putting themselves at risk legally. This process is a vital step in the adaptation of the group. Although the women may remain in social isolation, not yet managing to achieve emancipation and integration into the host society, their economic activities have begun to exhibit signs of maturing through a movement into areas other than domestic work. There is also evidence of stratification within the group. Legally resident, longer established and better-qualified Filipinos move up into the *assistensa* category, creating space at the lower end of the domestic sector for other groups. Recently arrived Filipinos, Filipino men, arrivals from countries not traditionally associated with the domestic service market, such as Somalia and Poland, all compete to fill this vacant spot. The main effect of this has been to reduce the overall cost of domestic work and produce a hierarchy of domestic labourers (see also Lazaridis in this volume).

The recognition of *assistensa* activities as well as the recognition of a demand for them, must be of priority in future Philippine and Italian negotiations of bilateral agreements. Not only may these new activities be important in the stabilization of the Philippine community in Italy, but they may also be the key to one area of Italian social services that has shown a demand for qualified medical staff. As such, the provision of educational training that supplies the women with the necessary linguistic abilities to exercise their skills within the social services sector would release a latent pool of labour.

Conclusion

This study evolved out of an interest in female migrants, their objectives, their dreams and their means of coping. A few concluding points sum up this exploration. It was recognized that these women, when acknowledged, had usually been relegated to consideration as 'dependants' or else studied as 'the women left behind', I have pursued a movement towards refuting this 'invisibility'; the women are focal members of their economic household. Meanwhile, in studying female migration, it has been common to emphasize that the problems faced by migrant women are compounded by being women, migrants, and often racially distinct from the national population. In the course of this study, the context of Italy as a new country of immigration with delayed legislative formation has been shown to exacerbate these factors with the effect that female migrants are overlooked in the scant reception facilities that exist in urban Italy. Indeed it has been suggested that what remains is a situation whereby female migrants are faced with dilemmas of coping on their own. Personal and social networks are of prime importance in enabling these strategies of adaptation, whilst the built environment provides migrants with the arena for change. Beyond this, the recency of immigration has had both retrospective and prospective aspects. This is a complex inter-dependent relationship only touched upon, but which opens discussion into the impact of international migration on female migrants. Of course, it is also recognized that not all the changes deriving from migration, especially into a country of new immigration, would necessarily be positive changes for the status of the women involved.

To conclude: from the moment one delves into the field of female international migration, one begins to realize the paucity of research focusing exclusively on female migrants and the complexity of the phenomenon. The recency of immigration to Italy is interesting given the emerging recognition of female international migration and the presence of some migrant flows in Italy that are almost exclusively female. Such an opportune moment provides an almost perfect situation in which to examine the effects that gender-specific migration has on female migrants, especially amongst those who are still at the initial stages of the adaptation process.

Notes

1. For further reading on the development of southern Europe as a region of immigration see Bonifazi 1993; King 1984.

2. The information for this study comes from my doctoral thesis completed in 1995. The data come from three main sources: national statistical data; self-completion questionnaires filled out by 100 Filipinos and 60 Somalian women; and in-depth interviews with 14 Filipinos and 10 Somalians. These sources were supplemented by interviews with Italian government officials and representatives of the Philippines and Somalia; interviews with officials from the NGOs concerned with the two groups; and information drawn from diaries kept by chosen individuals.

3. Source: Council of Europe report 1995: net population flows to selected European countries.

4. Policy measures within the framework of the EU will eventually change.

5. This legislation is only that pertinent to the time of the study. There have been developments since (see paper by Orsini-Jones and Francesca Gattullo in this volume).

6. Bonetti, P. 1993 La Condizione giuridica del cittadino comunitario, Rimini: Maggioli editore.

7. There was no money laid aside for these provisions and so they became known as the 'paper rights'.

8. United Nations Expert Group Meeting on International Migration Policies and the Status of Female Migrants – A comparison of male and female migration strategies; the case of African and Filipino migrants in Italy. Italy, March 1990.

9. Conversation with Graziano Tassello, the then Director of the Centro Studi Emigrazione Roma, Italy, 10 December 1992.

10. Taken from an interview conducted with Anne-Marie Dupré who is the political co-ordinator for the 'Federazione delle Chiese Evangeliche in Italia e Servizio Rifugiati e Migranti' (FCEI).

11. For example, the restricted access of migrants to public housing, property ownership, and the restrictions that work and residence permits impose on national and international travel.

12. Termini, is the railway for central Rome. The forecourt is approximately one acre in size.

13. Termini forecourt displays spatial relationships between two Philippine provinces, each polarised to the extremes of the space available, an arrangement which surely would not exist in the Philippines.

14. Eur station, is located in an urban area built during the fascist era in Italy, a highly planned environment with distinctions laid between leisure, business, and residential areas, and where many public offices are located. As a result there are many domestics living in this area as their employers work in these public and administrative buildings. The station is where the metro (underground) connects Eur to central Rome, and the Ciampino airport.

15. The *commune di Roma*, is the local government for the Rome (urban and suburban) area, within the larger Lazio region.

16. Gil Y. Macaad is the current labour attaché to the Philippines in Rome.

References

Andall, J. (1992), 'Women migrant workers in Italy', in *Women's Studies International Forum*, Vol. 15, No. 1, pp. 41–48.

Barsotti, O. and Lecchini, L. (1995), *The Experience of Filipino Female Migrants in Italy,* United Nations Expert Group Meeting on International Migration Policies and the Status of Female Migrants. San Miniato, Italy, March 1990.

Bonifazi, C. (1993), 'From the Third World to Italy: the experiences of a new immigration country, between growth of push factors and containment policies'. Presented at the General Conference of the International Union for the Scientific Study on Population, Montreal.

Campani, G. (1990), 'Il Lavoro delle donne migranti tra autonomia e professionalitá' in G. Favaro, G. and M. Tognetti Bordogna (eds), *Donne del Mondo*. Rome: Angelli.

Collinson, S. (1994), *Europe and International Migration*, London: Pinter.

Hall, R. and White, P. (eds) (1995), *Europe's Population: Towards the Next Century*, London: UCL Press.

King, R. (1985), 'Italian migration: the clotting of the hemorrhage', in *Geography*, 70, pp. 307–324.

King, R. (1993a), 'Southern Europe and the International Division of Labour; from emigration to immigration'. Paper presented to the IBG Annual Conference, London.

King, R. (1993b), *Mass migration in Europe: the legacy and the future*, London: Belhaven.

Morokvasic, M. (1984), 'Birds of Passage are also Women', *International Migration Review*, Vol. 18, No. 4.

Pugliese, E. (1991), 'La Portata del fenomeno e il mercato del lavoro', in, M. Macioti and E. Pugliese (eds), *Gli Immigrati in Italia*.

Salt, J. and Johnson, J. (1992), *Population Migration.* From the series, *Aspects in Geography*. Walton-on-Thames: Thomas Nelson & Sons Publishers.

Migrant Women in Italy: National Trends and Local Perspectives

MARINA ORSINI-JONES AND FRANCESCA GATTULLO

Introduction

For the first hundred years of its existence as a unified nation state, Italy was a country of emigration, not immigration. Many hundreds of thousands of Italians migrated to north and south America and to other countries of Western Europe, such as France, Germany and Belgium, in search of greater economic wellbeing. To these migrations abroad was added, in the years that followed the Second World War, the phenomenon of internal migration. Thousands more moved from southern Italy to work in the factories of the northern 'industrial triangle' – roughly the area delimited by the three cities of Genoa, Turin and Milan – during the boom years of the 1950s and 1960s.

These internal migrations, however, were often seen as short term. Young men led the way, leaving the family behind, at least temporarily. The distance was not so great, it was still the same country and the same language. Any needs to be met were those of young men, either single or with a family to be sent money and visited whenever possible.

In Western Europe, in the post-war period, the archetypal situation has been that of the young male pioneer, hoping to send for his family once he has established himself financially (or perhaps to find himself a wife later from his country of origin). Meeting the needs of immigrants therefore has meant primarily meeting the needs of young males, who often did not establish families in the new country until they themselves were able to provide for them, financially at least. The needs of migrant women were often overlooked completely.

This chapter, on the other hand, looks specifically at the experience of migrant women in Italy in the years since 1970. It examines the situation in two large Italian cities, Bologna and Florence, by looking at the experiences of migrant women in these cities, and at the efforts of the local authorities to provide support for them. It also aims to show how the local reality of individual cities/regions matters as much, if not more than the national one in Italy and how it can shape migrant women's experience. The chapter will focus upon the experience of Third World non-EU migrant women in Bologna and compare it to that of Third World non-EU migrant women in Florence.

An Outline of National Migration Trends in Italy

Italy became a country of immigration in the 1970s when it became a privileged destination for migrants, after the introduction of restrictions on immigration in the European countries traditionally associated with it. However, it was only in the 1980s that Italians in general and politicians in particular become aware of the issue (Favaro and Bordogna 1989).

Between 1970 and 1985 the number of migrants in Italy nearly tripled. There was a great increase in immigration from non-EU countries in general and from the Third World in particular between 1989 and 1995, and in January 1997 the number of documented migrants from outside the EU came to 852,558[1].

The total number of migrants does not at all justify Italian fears of an 'invasion' (Gattullo, Hoskyns and Orsini-Jones 1994). In 1997 Italy still had fewer migrants than any of the other major industrialized countries in the EU. According to the Italian Ministry of the Interior, in 1997 the number of documented migrants came to 1.9 per cent of the total population in Italy. This means that at a rough estimate the total presence of documented and undocumented migrants might come to something between 3.5 per cent and 4 per cent of the Italian population, since it has been estimated that in Italy the proportion of undocumented to documented migrants is 1:1 (Besia 1992: 248). The 1997 statistics confirm that Italy attracts migrants from a great variety of countries, the first three of which are Morocco, Albania and the Philippines. Non-EU migrant women come mainly from Cape Verde, the Philippines and Brazil. The sudden increase in the population of immigrants made indigenous Italians realize that they were racist (Balbo and Manconi 1992) even if they were not prepared to admit it (Riotta 1995).

In comparison with the 1970s, documented migrants – both men and women – are nowadays more evenly distributed throughout Italy, albeit with a stronger presence in the north and in the centre. This has had a positive impact on their visibility, compared with previous years. In the years between 1965 and 1985, the Italian migrant population (unlike that of other European countries) was characterized by a high presence of women (Campani 1989). Roughly 50 per cent of migrants in Italy were women, mainly single women arriving to work as domestic servants. Many of them had a Christian (usually Catholic) background and came from countries where the Christian religion is predominant, such as the Philippines and El Salvador. Many others came thanks to special bilateral agreements between Italy and their own country (for example Ethiopia, Cape Verde). Their motives for migrating was by and large economic, but there were also asylum seekers from Eritrea.

Between 1986 and 1992 the proportion of men rose to 61 per cent of the total migrant population in Italy. This increase was due to several factors: the economic crisis in many African countries (which led to the arrival of unskilled workers from those countries), the lack of border controls in Italy compared with those of other EU countries and the economic boom Italy enjoyed in the 1980s. All of these factors made Italy a popular destination amongst migrants.[2]

Once migrant women arrived in Italy they had a very similar migratory pattern: they first settled in big cities, and then, via friendships and relationships, moved to smaller towns and villages or suburbs of medium-sized cities (Campani 1989; Moruzzi and Fiorenza 1990: 11; Parmeggiani 1992). They all shared a condition of 'invisibility': they were mainly working as domestic helpers and this meant (and still means) being segregated in a house with very few hours of freedom. Still, despite their invisibility, they managed to create solid family networks and to set up associations with the support of the Church and the Church-related association *Caritas Diocesana*, local feminist groups within political parties, trade unions and local authorities.

Non-EU migrant women in Italy can be broadly classified as follows:

(1) *Domestic servants/maids*. It is mainly within this category that we encounter women, particularly Filipino and Eritrean, who have migrated on their own and have managed their own 'migration project' entirely.

(2) *Housewives*: women who have joined their husbands. They come mainly from the Maghreb area of north Africa and from Pakistan. The migration of these women was, until recently, seen as 'passive'. More recent research has shown that even if these women migrate

to join their partners they need a lot of initiative to do so and that they themselves do not perceive their migration project as passive (De Bernart, Di Pietrogiacemo and Michelini 1995).[3]

(3) *Professional women* (not working as domestic servants). These can be of any origin, though South American, Filipino and Eritrean women are strongly represented in this group.[4]

(4) *Prostitutes and pimps*. Prostitutes come from different backgrounds. Sometimes they have managed their own migration project; in other cases they have been unwittingly coerced into prostitution by international mafias. Most are part of the very sad 'slave trade' that is flourishing across Europe. In Italy such trade involves mainly Nigerians and East Europeans, particularly Albanians. More recently a new phenomenon has developed: migrant women acting as pimps. The prosecution figures for migrants for procuring provide the disturbing evidence that 21 per cent of the perpetrators are women, according to statistics from both *Caritas* and the Association *Parsec*, quoted in an article published in the Italian weekly magazine *L'Espresso*.[5]

Migrant Women's Invisibility Under the Law

The first Italian national immigration law – Law 943/86: 'Norms on the employment and treatment of non-EU migrant workers and against undocumented immigration' – was passed in 1986. It reflected the more humanitarian trends towards immigration in the EC in the 1980s (prior to the fall of the Berlin wall in 1989), and put Italy in line with the other EC member states (Favaro and Tognetti-Bordogna 1989). It aimed at defining the rights of migrants working in Italy, and devolved implementation to the local authorities, who were in effect left to cope on their own, without clear guidelines from the centre. As so often in Italy, the application of law 943/86 varied according to the way it was interpreted locally (Hoskyns and Orsini-Jones 1995).

Other national laws on immigration passed between 1989 and 1996 are:[6]

(1) Law 39/90 (also known as 'Martelli Law'): 'Urgent norms on political asylum, entry and residence permits for non-EU and stateless citizens already present on the national territory.'

(2) Decree-Law 187/93 (also known as 'Conso Decree'): 'New measures on penitentiary treatment and the expulsion of foreign citizens.'

(3) Decree-Law 489/95 (also known as 'Dini Decree'): 'Urgent measures on immigration policy for the control of entry and residence

permits on the national territory for non-EU citizens' (renewed as Decree-Law 376/96).

(4) Decree-Law 122/93 (also known as 'Mancini Law'): 'Measures against racist verbal and physical abuse.'

However none of these laws makes direct reference to the particular circumstances of migrant women. The aspect of immigration law that most directly affects women is legislation on family reunions. The laws used in this field are both EC ones (1612/68; 312/76) and Italian ones; mainly the above mentioned law 943/86. This states, in article 4, that workers who are legally resident in Italy can ask for family reunion with their husband/wife, their children or their parents, if they are financially dependent upon the worker in question. This is becoming the main channel for migrant women to enter Italy, which leads them to be seen mainly as 'appendages' to their husbands. With very few exceptions, such as the laws referring to the employment of domestic servants, the main national immigration laws ignore the issues relating to migrant women.

Italian governments tend to be short lived and therefore there is little cohesion and consistency in immigration policies. There is no long-term planning, and this results in a lack of housing and services for migrant men and women alike. In Spring 1997, the first left-wing coalition to govern Italy since 1948, headed by Romano Prodi, nearly collapsed as a consequence of the lack of proper laws on immigration and on political asylum after the crisis that followed the civil war in Albania.[7]

The Italian press gave ample coverage to the 1997 Albanian crisis, particularly when a ship bringing refugees to Italy sank in the Adriatic Sea. One of the most poignant articles about this crisis appeared in the financial newspaper *Il Sole-24 Ore*,[8] in which Massimo Livi Bacci (1996) wrote that the Italian government needed to give priority to the discussion and approval of a new law on immigration and political asylum, so as to clarify and control the ways in which migrants could enter and reside in Italy. According to Bacci (1996), a law was needed to help Italians to change their attitude towards migrants and enable them to see documented migrants who wanted to study, reside or work in Italy as good neighbours, rather than as 'unexploded mines' to be avoided or defused.

As for specific laws on women at work, up to 1997 in the EU there were only regulations on temporary work, dictated by the Schengen agreement. Such regulations were made for the temporary male migrant workforce and totally ignored the long-term needs of migrant women with children. It is in this context that our previous research high-lighted the fact that migrant women do not really benefit from Italian national immigration laws, but are more likely to benefit from EU laws relating to equal opportunities (Hoskyns and Orsini-Jones 1995). In the years 1993–5 the Italian Government passed laws which aimed at giving status to and protecting domestic work carried out by migrant women.

In Italy new laws are not always enforced, and in some cases the 'over-protection' of women can act to their disadvantage. This happened for instance after the introduction of the new EU directives on equal opportunities for Italian women in the 1980s. The great demand in the area of domestic work has kept alive the incoming flow of single women looking for a job in this field.[9] However, Italian women who work have become so protected by the law that in some cases employers either do not employ them at all or insert in their contract illegal 'waiver clauses', mainly referring to pregnancy, which can have an intimidating effect on the employees. This could be a significant factor in the increase in the number of undocumented migrant women in domestic service.

Case-study 1: Bologna, Emilia-Romagna

Bologna has long been actively involved in the promotion of human rights for asylum seekers (mainly from Chile, El Salvador and Eritrea in the past and the former Yugoslavia more recently). It also has a long-standing and active feminist culture and is currently the city in Italy with the greatest number of feminist associations.

According to data provided by the City Council, in Bologna in 1986 women amounted to 48 per cent of the total number of migrants, which was in line with the national balance in the mid-1980s. The city was an attractive destination for migrant women, because of its healthy job-market and its traditions of progressive welfare services, of popular participation in local affairs and of feminist and other associations (Orsini-Jones and Gattullo 1996).

The city council very quickly started to make moves towards under-standing new immigration issues. In the mid-late 1980s, groups com-posed of councillors, officers and social workers analysed immigration in other major industrialized countries in the EU to learn from the examples of best practice in this field. A typical example of this was the exchange of visits between Bologna and Birmingham and Coventry (in the West Midlands, UK) in the years between 1988 and 1990.[10] In the years between 1985 and 1992 there was a dramatic increase in the number of migrant men in the city, which had three major effects. First, it created an awareness of the presence of migrants amongst the Italian population. This in turn helped women to become more visible themselves. Second, it caused a series of institutional interventions, which appear to have been based on prejudice and on the assumption (or wishful thinking) that the migrants would eventually leave. The local authorities in Bologna in the years 1985–92 saw the arrival of male migrants as an 'emergency' and a 'problem' and dealt with it accordingly.[11] This meant that the city council mainly created services that would suit a male audience (Moruzzi and Fiorenza 1990; Moruzzi 1991; Hoskyns and Orsini-Jones 1995: 61). Third, it changed the pattern of traditional female migration to Italy; many of the new migrant women were now trying to reunite with partners, rather than coming on their own to work as domestic servants.

However in the years between 1994 and 1997 the situation changed again. The male influx slowed down and the number of women increased.[12] As a consequence migrant women's associations began to mushroom again and they gained a visibility of their own, rather than a secondary kind of visibility acquired via their male counterparts.

In Bologna, in 1996, there were significantly more migrant women than men originating from Philippines, Eritrea, Ethiopia, Somalia, Brazil and Peru (see Table 6.1),[13] whereas the numbers of men and women originating from former Yugoslavia, China and Nigeria were roughly equal (see Table 6.2).

An analysis of the age of migrant women in Bologna in 1996 shows that there is more diversity than in previous years in terms of age groups. The presence of single adult males is counterbalanced by the presence of women of various ages, by the presence of young men below the age of 25 and by the presence of male and female migrants over the age of 50 (six per cent of males and nine per cent of females). Compared with the situation in 1990/1991, the picture that emerges in the years between 1994 and 1997 is thus one of much greater fluidity and variety.

A full overview of what is available in terms of both services and associations for migrant men and women living in the city can be found in Intercultura a Bologna (Interculture in Bologna) (Traversi 1995), which lists a great wealth of new initiatives. Many of these are aimed specifically at women, who can rely upon a wide range of services.

The literature from the city council and related associations for the years between 1994 and 1997 shows that reciprocal understanding has improved in comparison with the literature written in the years

Table 6.1: National groups with a predominance of female migrants in Bologna in 1996

Country	M	F
Philippines	453	684
Eritrea	9	50
Ethiopia	87	195
Somalia	45	129
Brazil	35	106
Peru	43	117

Table 6.2: National groups with a balance between male and female migrants in Bologna in 1996

Country	M	F
Former Yugoslavia	268	240
China	388	361
Nigeria	31	34

between 1985 and 1992. First of all there is a very noticeable change in the vocabulary chosen by the city council to address the issues relating to immigration. In the introduction to the first number of *Osservatorio,* a publication launched by the city council in 1994, which deals with immigration issues (Bernadotti, Capecchi and Pinto 1994), the key words are *pluralismo* ('pluralism') and *multidimensionalità* ('multidimensionality'). Previously, in city council documents on immigration (Moruzzi and Fiorenza 1990; Moruzzi 1991) the key words were *problema* ('problem'), *fenomeno* ('phenomenon') and *integrazione* ('integration'). Moreover there is a real effort in 1994 to analyse the needs of both male and female migrants in order to understand their differences:

> The focus when dealing with this information was to keep a major point of reference in mind: that is to say to document the presence of migrant people bearing in mind the differences between men and women and between different nationalities. If we were to have aggregate statistics under the 'blanket' of the word *extracomunitari,*[14] without specifying

anything about sex or nationality, we would not face these issues properly and in their complexity in the Bolognese area (Bernadotti, Capecchi and Pinto 1994: 2, our translation).

The headings to the different chapters within the abovementioned *Osservatorio* try to present a picture of 'differences' and 'equal opportunities' too. They include *'I livelli di istruzione degli immigrati e delle immigrate'* – our stress – ('The levels of education of migrant men *and women'*, Bernadotti, Capecchi and Pinto 1994: 27). It would seem, therefore, that at least in theory women are enjoying more visibility and recognition than in previous official or semi-official city council literature. Moreover, it would appear that the city council is showing a greater awareness of the different facets presented by the migrant community in Bologna. Even in Bologna, however, migrant women find that there is often a discrepancy between ideology and reality, and that the city council could do more to help them in a practical way. The political instability affecting Italy at present is not a good omen and it reinforces the fear of racism and prejudice against migrants, as Italians brace themselves for a period of political uncertainty.[15]

The evidence collected shows that migrant women do not want outside assistance from the City Council any more, they want to participate directly in the creation of the bodies or associations that will help them to live in Bologna. The first written evidence of this new drive and determination is the *Manifesto* they wrote on the occasion of the *Primo Incontro Nazionale tra le Associazioni di Donne Immigrate* ('First National Meeting of Associations of Migrant Women') held in Rome on 15 June 1995. This document was the first one at national level in which migrant women were proposing their own 'agenda for change'.

The Bolognese association of migrant women *Donne in Movimento* (Women in Movement) took part, with many other associations from all over Italy, in the above meeting. It produced a manifesto that aims at raising awareness of the problems faced by migrant women in Italy today. In it migrant women outline the key issues they would like to see addressed by the Italian authorities:

(1) *Legal status*: women who migrate either on their own or to join their partner find it very difficult to obtain proper documentation. As a result of this they risk exploitation, abuse and ending up as prostitutes.

(2) *Social security*: this is already a serious issue for Italian women. Migrant women lack protection and security even more as they

are often the victims of a triple discrimination – they are women, they are migrants and they are mostly black or Asian.

(3) *Healthcare and pregnancy:* migrant women often cannot choose to keep their baby. They are forced to have an abortion because their work and their social status would not enable them to bring up their children. Often not enough support is offered in terms of healthcare. Moreover, undocumented women fear hospitals, as, in the event of termination of pregnancy, all details are handed to the local police stations (*questure*) and they might lose not only their privacy but also their freedom.

(4) *Family:* the migrant woman's family often disintegrates under the pressure caused by the condition of hardship shared by so many women. There are mothers who cannot be reunited with their children and others who work too much to see them. Children are often housed in foster families or in boarding schools supported by charities.

(5) *Violence:* immigrant women and their young children are an easy target for abuse of various kinds: moonlighting for long hours, underpay, sexual harassment, physical and psychological abuse, prostitution, slave trade both for prostitution and for arranged marriages.

(6) *Job market*: most migrant women are forced to accept jobs that are below their qualifications. This causes on the one hand their loss of intellectual life on the other the danger of not getting proper protection at work in terms of pension, national health contributions, etc.

Some positive evidence has been collected in Bologna about migrant women thanks to an initiative that will probably be of benefit to them, albeit indirectly. It is financed by EU funds and it is the *Coordinamento per il Monitoraggio degli Incidenti Razzisti a Bologna* (office that co-ordinates the monitoring of racists attacks in Bologna). The initial findings of its surveys show that women are not the prime target of racist attacks, unlike elsewhere in Italy (see the situation in Florence below) or in Europe (attacks on Turkish women in Germany, for example). An analysis by gender of the 54 reported cases of racist attacks between September 1996 and April 1997 shows that only five out of 54 (i.e. 9.25 per cent) were against women. The prime targets of racist attacks in Bologna are Moroccans (17 out of 54 of the reported attacks) and Senegalese (11 out of 54 of the reported attacks), both of which groups have a prevalence of males.[16]

We would like to conclude this section by saying that positive data have emerged in Bologna in 1997 compared with the situation between the years 1991 and 1993. Firstly, it would appear that the statement that migrant women 'have very little access to resources and that participation is just beginning' (Hoskyns and Orsini-Jones 1995: 73) does not hold anymore. Migrant women have set up many new associations, such as the abovementioned *Donne in Movimento* or the *Gruppo Autogestito di Donne Filippine* (Filipino Women's Self-Managed Group). Secondly, the debate about gender, the right to differ, real pluralism and multiculturalism as opposed to integration and assimilation, has filtered through to official city council literature.

As in the years between 1989 and 1993, migrant women have greatly benefited from equal opportunities initiatives aimed at promoting women in enterprise. These are mainly financed by the EU Social Fund. On the other hand, the gap between theory and practice is still proving difficult to bridge. There still is a lot of suspicion on both sides (city council and migrant women), and although collaboration between the two has increased, there are no migrant women – or men – occupying key posts within the city council, not even in relation to immigration policies. This means, of course, that they still find it difficult to accept that the city council is truly willing to understand their needs. Furthermore, a new aspect that is surfacing is conflicts of interest between different migrant women's groups.

Although much has been done, further initiatives are needed in order to create a more tolerant environment for migrant women in Bologna, improve basic services such as housing and welfare and set up opportunities for those migrant women who are still left out of participation and are still invisible. Nevertheless, the efforts of the local institutions in Bologna with regards to anti-racism, multiculturalism and acknowledgement of gender-related issues are quite impressive. It is not often the case in European cities of recent immigration that migrant women enjoy so much recognition in terms of policies and services. The local dimension of strong associationism has also helped the development of such trends amongst migrant women.

Case-study 2: Florence, Tuscany

Like Bologna, Florence too has a history of commitment against racism and inequality. However, as in Bologna (Hoskyns and Orsini-Jones 1995), there have been in the last ten years episodes of intolerance and unprovoked racist attacks. The reaction of the majority of Florentines to such attacks used to be one of solidarity towards migrants. For example, in 1990, when some Senegalese were beaten up in the streets by a group of right-wing Italians, a march against racism was organized by white and black people which obtained great support. In recent years, due to a changed attitude towards migrants and the subsequent decline in the tolerance level towards them, the right-wing parties have become more successful at sowing the seeds of racial hatred (Riotta 1995). Furthermore, as in Bologna, in the years of the great influx of migrant men (between 1990 and 1992), which also coincided with one of the greatest crises in post-war Italian politics, the support for migrants from the City Council faltered (Hoskyns and Orsini-Jones 1995).

The report *Confronting the Fortress*[17] (Hoskyns 1995: 180) highlighted the need for further research into the theme of migrant women in the Tuscany region, which was made more urgent by the following factors:

(1) There were more migrant women than men in Tuscany: 52.56 per cent of the residence permits in 1992 and around 51 per cent in 1995, according to data provided by the charity *Caritas*.
(2) There was a void in the analysis of matters relating to migrant women in Tuscany by the local authorities.[18]
(3) Some migrant women had made specific requests to start new initiatives in their favour and the local authorities had yet to respond to these requests (Hoskyns 1995: 9).

The researchers who compiled the report *Confronting the Fortress* found that there were very few women-only organizations. Moreover, except in rare cases, those that did exist had no permanent offices and were listed under a member's address. Very few of the organizations contacted were involved specifically with women's issues. The migrant communities were led by men and therefore women's issues were seen as having little relevance.

The situation in Florence therefore differed considerably from that in Bologna. The organizations contacted had little awareness of the EU literature on women's issues and equal opportunities. Racism and discrimination towards migrant women was apparently more virulent than against migrant men. The local authorities were not as aware of the gender issue as in Bologna, and there was less co-ordination amongst local associations. One similarity with Bologna, however, was the fact that 'health, maternity, housing, conditions of work and places to meet were highlighted as priorities' (Hoskyns 1995: 181).

It was not possible to obtain precise data for our research about the migrant women's population from the city council in Florence, as the Ufficio Immigrati (Immigration Office) only opened in 1996 and started collating data about immigration in Florence in 1997. From the few data available up until 1997, it appears that in terms of numbers of migrant women, Filipinas come first, then Chinese women, then, in this order: women from Poland, Brazil, Rumania, former Yugoslavia and Somalia. Data collated between 1997/99 by the Ufficio Immigrati confirm our findings and show that in Florence there is a bigger percentage of women from South America than in Bologna.

In fact, the situation of migrant women in Florence in 1995 closely resembled that of migrant women in Bologna at the beginning of the 1990s. Despite their good will, most indigenous women failed to recognize the real needs of migrant women. Misconceptions on both sides often marred the possibility of working together. Migrant women wanted to manage their own needs and were not impressed by ideological debate that did not lead to any practical improvement of their situation, such as better housing facilities. Furthermore, migrant women demanded diversification and the recognition of the differences between groups such as the Somalis, Arabs and Chinese.

The frustration of migrant women was made worse by the lack of sufficient services for them. There were not enough bilingual social workers to help in the implementation of proper care for migrant women. Even in 1997 although family planning clinics existed, their activities were not as structured and as successful as the Family Planning Clinic in Bologna (see Hoskyns and Orsini-Jones 1995 on the latter point). People working within them lamented a lack of support from the local institutions, despite the fact that they were the only service of real practical value for migrant women and their children, apart from those provided by voluntary Catholic associations.

In the cases in which it was possible to involve migrant women directly – as in some co-operatives or associations – it became apparent that they mistrusted not only the local institutions, but even the migrant men who in some instances were the representatives of their own associations. Furthermore, they have often been cheated by money brokers or employers, and will therefore only trust other women, as long as they belong to the same community. In Florence, migrant women still prefer to keep in touch via a network of informal contacts (extended families and friendships). These provide a support role for all daily activities, such as job swaps, solidarity, common resources, contacts, but do not fit within Italian institutions, which migrant women have learnt to suspect (Decimo 1996).[19] Unfortunately, there is also evidence of instances in which migrant women do not even trust other women from the same community. Such lack of trust can lead to the breaking-up of tightly-knit and long-standing solidarity networks.[20]

The analysis of migrant women in Florence provided in another report – *L'immigrazione al femminile in Toscana: primi risultati di una ricerca-azione* – (*Immigration in Tuscany, First Outcomes of an Action-Research*),[21] came to the same conclusion as the report *Confronting the Fortress*, that the region should first address the two issues of rights at work and rights concerning motherhood and the way they interact in the lives of migrant women. Most migrant women in Tuscany work, because a job, with some exceptions, is the main aim of their migration project. Most of these women also want to have children, but without the support of their families they cannot afford to have or to keep their children.

Due to the weaknesses of the Italian welfare system, the Italian institutions are failing to provide migrant women with basic support for their primary needs. If the state and the regions do not provide professional training, training leading to self-employment and dedicated infrastructures for the use of migrant mothers who work, the gloomy future scenario for many of these women will be that of permanent relegation to the two fields of illegal sexual or domestic work, or of remaining prisoners in their homes after reunion with their husbands. Thus priority needs to be given to legislation and services specifically targeted at migrant women, to help them emerge from invisibility.

On a more positive note, there is a new world of collaboration between indigenous and migrant women emerging in Florence, particularly with regard to equal opportunities. Migrant women are helping indigenous women to sharpen their focus on women's needs and to see the more practical side of the implementation of equal opportunities for women at work.

Conclusion

Our initial contention that the local reality tends to shape the migrant women's experience seems to be confirmed. In Bologna the strong feminist tradition has provided a fertile ground for the mushrooming of women-only migrant associations and has encouraged women's participation in local initiatives. Family networks exist, particularly for Chinese women, but are not as widespread as in Florence and in Naples. This could be due to the fact that there is a strong welfare infrastructure supported by the interaction of the local authorities and the local charities and associations.

On the other hand, in Florence local economic interests have been a hindrance to the reciprocal understanding between Florentine and migrant people. Furthermore, in Florence the lack of strong directives from the local authorities has caused a situation of greater 'invisibility' for migrant women, despite the fact that their numbers are higher than in Bologna.

Between 1994 and 1997 migrant women have become more assertive in their demand for services. They expect the Italian institutions – both at the national and local level – to respect their 'right to differ' and to provide them with effective services, such as vocational training initiatives built around their existing skills; literacy courses; linguistic support for the integration of their children at school, and housing services for single women with children.[22]

Another factor which has emerged in the 1990s is the worrying increase in the 'sex trade' of non EU migrant women, both black and white. This makes it even more urgent for the Italian government to provide effective laws at the national level to tackle the issue of undocumented migrant women in a serious way, otherwise the submerged world of abuse to which many 'invisible' migrant women are subjected will go unpunished.[23]

It is difficult to draw precise conclusions about a situation that is so fluid. The evidence collected seems to indicate that migrant women are more exposed to discrimination, exploitation and racism in Florence than in Bologna. As previously pointed out, in Bologna the city council has set up a new series of initiatives aimed at providing services for all migrants. At the same time it has accepted that migrant women are different from migrant men and need different services. In Florence the recognition of the latter point was still in its embryonic stage in 1997.

Although much has been done at the local level in Bologna and Florence for migrant women, more needs to be done in terms of initiatives of real practical use for them. Furthermore, as in our previous research, we found that not enough is done for migrant women at the national level: serious issues relating to immigration, particularly regarding gender, are still not addressed.

Notes

1. This is according to a dossier written by the most influential Italian charity, the *Caritas* in Rome. The dossier was prepared jointly by *Caritas*, the *Ministero degli Interni* (Ministry of the Interior) and the Italian Institute of Statistics *ISTAT*. The data can be obtained via Internet at http://www2.comune. bologna.it/bologna/immigra/. For those who do not have Internet access, information can be obtained from: *Comune di Bologna, Istituzione dei Servizi per l'Immigrazione, Via G. Petroni, 9, 40126 Bologna, Italy*. Fax: (00 39) 051 260066.

2. There is one peculiarity that must be pointed out: despite the traditional female predominance in the Filipino group of migrants, there has been an increase in Filipino migrant men (they are the second biggest male group after men arriving from the former Yugoslavia). The Filipino group is probably a unique example in European immigration in which migrant men come to a foreign country to reunite with their spouses/partners.

3. De Bernart, Pietrogiacomo and Michelini (1995) stressed the importance of Moroccan women in the role of preserving traditional Moroccan values within the Bolognese society, while at the same time acting as 'brokers' for their husbands and children in the adoption of new Western values, necessary for survival, in Bologna (De Bernardt, Pietrugiocouo and Michelini 1995: 45–50). For further information on North African women in relation to family links see also the bibliography about Algeria and Magreb with reference to women's issues at: http://soalinux.comune.firenze.it/cooperativadonne/alger/htm.

4. Although there have always been Eritrean women in Bologna who had good jobs, they were quite rare until recently. Our field work showed that the number of migrant women who are now working as translators and teachers, just to give two examples, has increased considerably in the years between 1994 and 1997. This is why we are now adding this new category to our previous classification (Hoskyns and Orsini-Jones 1995).

5. '*Sul marciapiede comanda Maman*' *L'Espresso*, (Benvenuti 1996: 67). Prostitution is probably one of the most difficult areas to investigate, as one of our Bolognese correspondents, Lara Parmeggiani confirmed to us, as she was nearly beaten up by pimps while trying to distribute leaflets about the family planning clinic to some migrant prostitutes in the outskirts of Bologna. The Region Emilia-Romagna is beginning to analyse the issue with a new project (which started on 25 April 1997): *Progetto Regionale Prostituzione*, which will deal with all prostitutes, both black and white. As for Florence, further information about the issue of migrant women's prostitution can be found at: http://www.isinet.it/PdD/num9/sommario.htm., which contains research data collated by Giovanna Campani of the University of Florence: *Il traffico delle donne immigrate per sfruttamento sessuale: aspetti e problemi*.

6. For an update on Italian legislation on immigration see the Bologna City Council's site '*Società Multietnica*': www2.comune.bologna.it/bologna/immigra

and the *'Ufficio immigrati'* Florence's City Council site: www.comune.firenze.it/ servizi_pubblici/stranieri/capitolo8.htm

7. It must be pointed out that this article was written before the war broke out in Kosovo.

8. *'Immigrazione, i motivi di una nuova legge'*, *Il Sole 24 Ore*, (Bacci 1996:1).

9. Many factors are at play in the choice of employing a domestic servant: the lack of a strong welfare system; the will to preserve the family unit by keeping the elderly and the ill at home; the legendary 'house pride' of Italian women (otherwise the neighbours will gossip); the lack of involvement of men in the sharing of the housechores.

10. We were involved in this exchange as advisers and interpreters and it was interesting to see the different points of view of the British and the Italian contingents. The Italians felt that in Britain the creation of specific spaces dedicated to migrant people created a 'ghetto' environment which they did not like. The British contingent, particularly migrant people, felt the Italians had a patronizing approach and did not understand that multiculturalism required dedicated spaces.

11. According to the *Osservatorio Comunale delle Immigrazioni* (City Council Observatory for Immigration), the numbers of documented migrants has not increased much after 1993 and it represents more or less the two per cent of the total population of the Province of Bologna (Bernardotti, Capecchi and Pinto 1994).

12. We have obtained most of the data provided by the Italian Ministry of the Interior – situation at 1 January 1997.

13. These tables have been elaborated from data provided from the City Council in Bologna and the Italian Ministry of the Interior dated 31 December 1996.

14. This is a neologism, the legal Italian translation of 'non-EU citizen'. It has acquired a negative connotation as it tends to be applied to black people only.

15. For a general survey on the Italian situation in recent years see Mark Gilbert, *The Italian Revolution* (Gilbert 1995).

16. The Project was set up by the local authorities with the help of European funding. The data quoted here are reported on pp. 2 and 4 of the report about racist attacks from September 1996 to April 1997.

17. The report is *Confronting the Fortress: Black and Migrant Women in the European Union,* commissioned by the European Women's Lobby and published by the European Parliament (Hoskyns 1995). The Italy country profile contains a case-study of Florence based upon research carried out by Giovanna Campani of the University of Florence and by field work by Deyanira Henriques Vargas, National Director of the *Comitato di Coordinamento per gli Immigrati* – Coordinating Committee for Migrants – of the left-wing trade union *CGIL* (*Confederazione Generale Italiana del Lavoro*). The main aim of the project was to increase the visibility of Third World non-EU migrant women both within the EU and within the Forum itself. Marina Orsini-Jones helped with its compilation.

18. This does not mean that there were no people who were researching the issue in Florence, as Giovanna Campani is based at this city's university and is a pioneer in the research of immigration and gender in Italy.

19. In this the situation in Florence resembles more that in Naples, than in Bologna. For more information about Somali women's networks in Naples see Francesca Decimo's article 'Reti di solidarietà e strategie economiche di donne somale immigrate a Napoli' (Solidarity networks and economic strategies of Somali migrant women in Naples), in Studi Emigrazione/Etudes Migrations, Centro Studi Emigrazione, Roma, 123/1996, pp. 473–93 (Decimo 1996). See also Vanessa Maher's Il potere della complicità (The power of complicity) (Mahler 1989).

20. In the Somali networks in Naples, in fact, migrant women tend to reproduce the same pattern of civil war between different clans that they had experienced in Somalia and this can be devastating for their networks (Decimo 1996). We were told by some of the migrant women we interviewed that they do not like to have women friends of their own nationality and prefer to watch television all day rather than mix with people from their own country. Others spoke openly of conflicts and jealousies caused by the new consumerist society they are now living in.

21. L'immigrazione al femminile in Toscana: primi risultati di una ricerca-azione ('Female immigration in Tuscany: first results of an action-research'). Florence: Regione Toscana, Giunta Regionale, n.5, May 1996 (Anon. 1996).

22. Even in progressive Bologna it took the City Council five years and a lot of determination from the women involved in the project to open a Casa per le Donne – House for Women – for migrant women. Furthermore the House is not what it was meant to be at the beginning: i.e. a focus for the promotion of enterprise skills of migrant women, but it is simply a refuge. The structure can house up to 15 non-EU migrant women single or single mothers. Four part-time worker work in the house, three of whom are migrant women themselves.

23. This has been very eloquently described in an article by Massimo Todisco published in the newspaper Il Manifesto (Todisco 1995), the title of which title tells us how much still needs to be done: Nessuno parla delle Immigrate – Nobody Talks about Migrant women.

References

Anon, A. (1996), L'immigrazione al femminile in Toscana: primi risultati di una ricerca-azione ('Female immigration in Tuscany: first results of an action-research'). Report. Florence: Regione Toscana, Giunta Regionale, n.5, May 1996.

Livi Bacci, M. (1996), 'Immigrazione, i motivi di una nuova legge', *Il Sole 24 Ore*, 10 May, p. 1.

Balbo, L. and Manconi, L. (1992), *I razzismi reali*, Milano: Feltrinelli.

Benvenuti, A. (1996), 'Sul marciapiede comanda Maman,' *L'Espresso*, 29 August, p. 67.

Bernardotti, A., Capecchi, V. and Pinto, P. (1994), 'L'Osservatorio delle Immigrazioni del Comune di Bologna: un servizio per chi vuole documentarsi e conoscere', in *Osservatorio*, 0, November, pp. 2–3.

Besia, F. (1992), 'L'immigrazione in Emilia-Romagna in una prospettiva storica', in S. Cifiello (ed.), *Non solo immigrato*, Bologna: Cappelli, pp. 246–50.

Campani, G. (1989), 'Donne immigrate in Italia', in G. Cocchi (ed.), *Stranieri in Italia: caratteri e tendenze dell'immigrazione dai paesi extracomunitari*, Bologna: Istituto Carlo Cattaneo/Misure, pp. 3–16.

De Bernart, M., Di Pietrogiacomo, L. and Michelini, L. (1995), *Migrazioni Femminili, Famiglia e reti sociali tra il Marocco e l'Italia*, Torino: L'Harmattan.

Decimo, F. (1996), 'Reti di solidarietà e strategie economiche di donne somale immigrate a Napoli', in: *Studi Emigrazione/Etudes Migrations*, Vol. XXXIII, No. 123, September, pp. 473–93.

Favaro, G. and Tognetti Bordogna, M. (1989), *Politiche sociali e immigrati stranieri*, Firenze: La Nuova Italia.

Gattullo, F., Hoskyns, C. and Orsini-Jones, M. (1994), 'Donne Immigrate a Bologna: temi e problemi', in *Tuttitalia*, Vol. 10, pp.17–34.

Gilbert, M. (1995), *The Italian Revolution*, Oxford: Westview Press.

Hoskyns, C. (ed.) (1995), *Confronting the Fortress: Black and Migrant Women in the European Union*, Brussels: European Parliament, Directorate General for Research.

Hoskyins, C. and Orsini-Jones, M. (1995), 'Migrant Women in Italy: Perspectives from Brussels to Bologna' *The European Journal of Women's Studies*, Vol. 2, No. 1, pp. 51–76.

Maher, V. (1989), *Il potere della complicità: conflitti e legami delle donne nordafricane*, Torino: Rosenberg & Sellier.

Moruzzi, M. and Fiorenza, A. (1990), *Progetto per l'Immigrazione*, Bologna: Comune di Bologna/Assessorato alle Politiche Sociali.

Moruzzi, M. (1991), *Nota sullo stato di attuazione del progetto immigrazione e proposte per il completamento della prima fase di intervento*, Bologna: Comune di Bologna.

Orsini-Jones, M. and Gattullo F. (1996), 'Visibility at a Price? Black Women in Red Bologna', in *Tuttitalia*, Vol. 14, pp. 24–38.

Parmeggiani, L. (1992), '*I diritti delle donne migranti*' in: *Parità e differenza:*

tesi del corso operatrici di parità, Bologna: Bromurodargento, pp. 77–102.

Riotta, G. (1995), '*Razzisti no, però* . . . – *Noi italiani, un popolo di intolleranti' Il Corriere della Sera*, 24 November.

Todisco, M., (1995), '*Nessuno parla delle immigrate' Il Manifesto*, 13 October.

Traversi, M., (ed) (1995), *Intercultura a Bologna*, Bologna: CD/LEI, 2 March.

References from the Internet

For further information about Bologna and national statistics, *Società Multietnica*: *http://www2.comune.bologna.it/bologna/immigra/*

For further information about immigration services in Florence, *Ufficio immigrati*: *www.comune.firenze.it/servizi_pubblici/stranieri/capitolo8.htm*

For further information about north African women in Italy, *Algeria e Maghreb*: *donneecultureaconfronto:http://soalinux.comune.firenze.it/cooperativadonne/alger/htm*

For further information about prostitution and migrant women, *Il traffico delle donne immigratepersfruttamentosessuale:http://www.isinet.it/PdD/num9/sommario.hm.*

Acknowledgements

We would like to thank the following people.

In Italy:
Bologna: Dott.ssa Caccialupi, *Centro per la salute delle donne straniere e dei loro bambini*, USL 28; Luisa Granzotto, *Servizio Immigrazione*, Comune di Bologna; Adriana Bernardotti, *Osservatorio delle Immigrazioni,* Comune di Bologna; Loretta Michelini, *Parsec;* Zita Argata Sabatini, *Associazione donne filippine;* Cecilia Urritria, *Donne in Movimento*; Lara Parmeggiani, *Centro per le Famiglie*; Marta Murotti, *FILEF*; Francesca Decimo – Ricerca sulle donne somale; Silvia Bartolotti, Centro Stranieri;
Firenze: Moreno Biagioni, *Ufficio Immigrati*, Comune di Firenze; Deyanira Henriques Vargas, C.G.I.L.; Giovanna Campani, Dipartimento di Scienze dell'Educazione, Università di Firenze.

In Britain
Catherine Hoskyns, David Jones and Rona Epstein, Coventry University.

Organizing Domestic Workers in Italy: The Challenge of Gender, Class and Ethnicity

Jacqueline Andall

Introduction

The employment of domestic workers has been a vexed question for feminists globally with writers such as Enloe (1989: 179) questioning whether the notion of a 'feminist domestic employer' was not in fact a contradiction. In contemporary Europe, the restructuring of the European welfare state (Cochrane 1993), combined with changing patterns of family organization within Europe, has encouraged both governments and individuals to consider domestic workers useful and necessary. The characteristics of paid domestic work in the southern European countries tend to validate Bakan and Stasiulis's (1995: 303) assertion that: 'the employment of domestic workers in private households is a crucial means through which asymmetrical race and class relations among women are structured'. Global examples relating to the US (Rollins 1985), Singapore (Tan and Devasahayan 1987), and Brazil (Pereira de Melo 1989) all indicate a problematic relationship between female employers and their domestic employees and the resurgence of domestic work in southern Europe is bringing these issues to the fore. Nakano Glenn's argument (1992: 3) that 'the racial division of reproductive labour . . . is a source of both hierarchy and interdependence among white women and women of colour' is thus beginning to have increasing resonance for the southern European context.

Despite the existence of patchy state welfare provision in some of the southern European countries (Leibfried 1993), as well as a familiaristic social structure, the issue of domestic work continues to be some-what misleadingly conceptualized as a relationship between women – female employers and female employees. This in part reflects the fact that an easy correlation can be made between southern European women's increased presence in the labour market (Vaiou 1995) and the employment of migrant women to replace them in the home. Women migrants to the southern European countries find themselves predominantly located in and restricted to the domestic work sector (Andall 1997; Escrivá 1997; Lazaridis in this volume). Italy is certainly no exception to this trend and the domestic work sector is now employing significant numbers of migrant women. Evidence of female single-sex migration to Italy for domestic work is prevalent in a range of migrant communities. Data for 1996 indicate that several commun-ities were largely female – Filipino (67%); Cape Verde (85%); Somalians 66%) (Caritas de Roma 1997) – and research documenting the character-istics of these groups have confirmed these women's restriction to the domestic work sector (Korsieporn 1991; Andall 1997; Chell 1997). Migrant domestic workers are concentrated in the major cities of Italy. In the early 1990s, Rome and Milan accounted for 48% of the total number of regularly employed domestic workers (ISMU 1996).

The existence of a national domestic workers' association in Italy makes it a particularly interesting case to study. The ACLI-COLF[1] was established in 1946, to organize domestic workers under Catholic rather than communist political influence. Its early history therefore needs to be understood in the context of the Cold War[2] and the desire within the Catholic sphere to develop a counter perspective to com-munist and socialist goals in terms of labour relations. The association has since been significantly affected by social and political change in post-war Italy, notably the radicalization of the worker's movement in the late 1960s and 1970s (Bedani 1995). When the ACLI-COLF was initially established, external migrants were not yet present in Italy and domestic workers came from the depressed regions and under-privileged classes of Italy. This meant that the association dealt princi-pally with issues of class between Italian women. It would be at a later stage that the presence of migrant women would force the ACLI-COLF to consider the relationship between gender, class and ethnicity. None the less, ahead of any feminist group, the ACLI-COLF had begun to acknowledge the presence of migrant domestic workers in the early 1970s and my discussion of the organization will be used to gauge possibilities for a politics of coalition between Italian women and migrant women at both a personal and associational level. The fundamental shifts that have taken place regarding both supply and demand within the domestic work sphere and the ACLI-COLF's long relationship with the sector certainly warrants closer observation. The research for the chapter is based largely on primary documentation consulted in the ACLI-COLF's national archives in Rome. This includes material produced at its national congresses, which have been held approximately every three to four years. The material sheds light on the structural constraints that first Italian women and then migrant women would encounter working within the sector. I shall be arguing that the ACLI-COLF's change in ideological direction in the 1970s – from a clerical to a radical class approach – appeared particularly conducive to an integrative approach to migrant women. By the mid/late 1980s, however, the gradual adoption of a gender focus to interpret domestic work was unlikely to prove as beneficial to migrant women as the earlier class-based perspective had been.

Organizing Domestic Workers

From a global perspective, the domestic work sector is increasingly the target of specific pro-active government regulation.[3] This is also evident in southern European countries. For example, while attempts have been made to limit or impede new entries of foreign migrants to Italy and Spain, these countries have simultaneously introduced policies to permit the continuing entry of foreign domestic workers (Andall 1997; Escrivá 1997). This type of government intervention can significantly affect the structural conditions of migrant women's employment, allowing minimum scope for individual agency. Thus, in 1991 the Italian government provision that permitted new entries to Italy for domestic work enforced a live-in employment contract on migrant women.[4] In countries like Singapore, work permits issued to foreign domestic workers are contingent on their fulfilling a contractual obligation not to get pregnant or marry Singaporeans (Yeoh and Huang 1999). These examples suggest that, as a migratory group, female migrant domestic workers are globally being perceived by governments to be a socially useful group even where the same governments are actively engaged in impeding other 'less desirable' migration. Moreover, in the Italian case, there is evidence to suggest that more flexible entry provisions for domestic work have been exploited by male migrants to gain legal entry and then transfer to alternative economic sectors.[5]

Historically and globally, the domestic work sector has constituted a marginalized sector of employment and has proved notoriously difficult to organize. This is partly a consequence of the highly personal-ized relationship between employer and employee but also because domestic work itself has frequently been categorized as a sector beyond 'the boundaries of the productive working-class' (Wrigley 1991: 323). The ACLI-COLF established itself in the Italian post-war period as the only body to occupy itself specifically with domestic workers. It is therefore an important, if not unique body, in the post-war European context.

The ACLI-COLF, like its parenting structure the ACLI (Italian Christian Workers' Association), based its practice on Catholic social teaching. This meant that it aimed to help workers formulate solutions to their problems based on the conciliation of capital and labour (Bedani 1995). As I have argued elsewhere (Andall 1997)[6] this clerical perspective largely benefited the employers of domestic workers as working-class Italian domestic workers were encouraged to accept their exploitative working conditions. Indeed, they were not even encouraged to view their employment as work, but rather as an extension of their natural maternal roles.[7] This perspective prevailed within the association until the early 1970s, when the effects of the social and political turmoil of the late 1960s began to be felt. This period culminated in the political division of the association, with the conservative, clerical group form-ing a new association, the API-COLF in 1971.[8] The ACLI-COLF, on the other hand, changed its ideological direction and adopted a radical class-based analysis of the sector. None the less, despite the early moderate and clerical position of the ACLI-COLF, its very existence did ultimately contribute to a perception of domestic workers as workers and moreover led to structural improvements in the sector. For example, in 1953, the right to a thirteenth month addition to the annual wage was extended to domestic workers and in 1958, a more substantial legislative Act was introduced that attempted to regulate working conditions at the national level.

The ACLI-COLF's central positioning within the domestic work sphere signified that it had an early awareness of class and ethnic stratification amongst women. Thus, here was an organization that experienced tangible proximity to notions of privilege, subordination and exploitation within the category of gender. This was at a time when the Italian women's movement tended towards a marginaliza-tion of these differences through its validation of the concept of women's commonality (Caldwell 1991) Although in the 1970s, the ACLI-COLF was primarily concerned with positioning itself within the trade-union movement, it did additionally seek to respond to the emergence of the Italian women's movement. To some extent, the visible social profile of the feminist movement, which reached its political peak as a mass movement in the mid/late 1970s, forced the issue of class differences between women onto the ACLI-COLF's agenda. Who would be its natural ally – working class workers (men and women) or (largely) middle class women? The following sub-section will explore the evolution of the association's relationship with the women's movement as a useful frame of reference for assessing shifts in interpretation as the presence of migrant women in the sector became more prominent.

Between Italian Women: The ACLI-COLF and the Women's Movement

The prominence of the women's movement in the 1970s with its early emphasis on the value of domestic work (unpaid) and the ACLI-COLF's engagement with domestic workers (paid) might lead one to anticipate a natural relationship between these two spheres. However, it had been the Catholic (conservative) sector, and not the progressive sphere of women's political activism, which had established and maintained a privileged relationship with domestic workers in the post-war period. Margherita Repetto, a prominent figure within the national women's organization UDI,[9] acknowledged this in her speech to the ninth ACLI-COLF national congress held in 1976:[10] 'The work carried out by the ACLI towards a sector like the domestic work sector is extremely significant . . . because it has bridged a gap left open by other social forces; and this is a reason for self-criticism for all of us, even for an Association like the UDI[11] (ACLI-COLF 1976: 7).[12] Repetto did, however, argue that domestic workers should be incorporated into the wider battle regarding women's situation and envisaged that there could be some co-operation between the two associations. The prospect of transforming domestic workers into 'family assistants' was interpreted as an important sign of female solidarity, necessary for improving women's general situation.

By 1979, when the ACLI-COLF held its tenth national congress in Assisi, the social presence of the feminist movement was much stronger. This could be seen in the address given by the national secretary of the ACLI-COLF, Clorinda Turri. She felt that the association should prioritize committing itself as women and as women workers to connecting the specific problems of domestic work with the women's liberation movement. Despite this objective, the nature of domestic work accentuated a problem implicit within the concept of female solidarity. This was aptly summarized by Turri:

what has become increasingly apparent in these years is that the domestic work relationship and the unjust conditions that it imposes on hundreds of thousands of women is not a sectoral or marginal problem; it can be seen increasingly as a phenomenon which is closely tied to a number of social processes; in particular as a consequence of the refusal, on the part of women, to continue to accept a sexual division of labour which confines the housewife . . . to do domestic work even when this represents a double work burden; however this legitimate instance of women's liberation is causing a new contradiction because domestic work . . . is being off-loaded onto other women who find themselves confined to a role of 'reserve housewife' . . . (ACLI-COLF 1979: 7).[13]

A very basic contradiction between different constituencies of women was thus registered. It is however crucial to note that in recognizing that both the workers' movement and the ACLI-COLF were calling for the development of social services to deal with the issue of reproductive care and domestic labour, Turri warned of the danger of seeing these services as simply beneficial to women. She argued that the tendency to do this was a direct consequence of men's refusal to engage in a transformation of gender roles and maintained that it was imperative for the workers' movement to engage with this issue as an integral component of its general strategy. I emphasize this point here, because, as will be argued below, the 1980s and early 1990s witnessed a gradual shift away from such a position. The notion of greater male participation with regard to domestic work was submerged and female solidarity was increasingly called upon to resolve the difficulties Italian women encountered in reconciling family and work roles. Such a shift in fact entailed a buttressing of the traditional division of labour within the home through the employment of one woman, normally supervised by the female employer, to execute domestic tasks. This situation did not therefore call into question the necessity for a transformation of men's roles but rather reinforced the notion of women's traditional responsibility for reproductive care.[14]

By 1979, although the importance of the women's liberation movement had been acknowledged, ACLI-COLF was nevertheless critical of its neglect of the domestic work sphere:

If we are placing at the centre of our strategy . . . our refusal to be 'reserve housewives' it is partly because we believe that the problem of domestic workers as women and of the contradiction that the domestic work relationship increasingly creates between women has not been properly addressed even by women's movements . . . Addressing this problem means placing at the centre of the debate on the woman question, the structural aspect of domestic work, of a different qualitative and organisational form for it, as a central issue for any process of emancipation or liberation for women (Turri, ACLI-COLF 1979: 8).

Furthermore, there was a forthright rejection of the domestic work sector functioning to facilitate gender privilege: 'our sector [knows] that the price of female emancipation for certain sectors of the middle class cannot be paid by other women who still endure material hardship' (Turri, ACLI-COLF 1979: 8). This perspective would inform the association's strategy in relation to the organization of the sector. Already, the debates of the 1973 and 1976 national congresses indicated that the association was keen to implement a radical transformation of both the working conditions of employees and the status conditions of employers. In particular, the association sought to overcome the private nature of the employer–employee relationship, envisaging a new figure of 'family collaborator' or 'family assistant'.[15] The proposal was for such assistance to be organized as a social service rather than as a private one, with direct links to public bodies. In terms of the service users, the ACLI-COLF anticipated that these family assistants would be employed in response to social exclusion rather than social privilege. Thus 'family collaborators' would provide care in the community for groups such as the elderly, hospitalized and disabled people.[16] The ACLI-COLF, therefore, was, unequivocally focused on improving conditions for working-class female domestic workers (and increasingly ethnic minority women) and in assisting marginalized families rather than privileged families. This was reflected in their new philosophy guiding the association's training courses for domestic workers. Domestic workers would no longer be trained to graciously accept their subservient position in relation to the employer. As the then national secretary, Pina Brustolin, had stated at the 1973 congress:

> Everyone will understand how our approach to training and professionalism is quite different to the past where we prepared workers for bourgeois families, while today we are called to respond to the needs of working-class families.[17]

Nevertheless, support for the underlying ethos of the women's movement led to a belief that the relationship between the female employer and the female employee could be transformed:

> let us here relaunch the proposal to re-establish . . . – amongst domestic workers and female employers open to this message –, that solidarity between women which is at the root of the feminist movement. Not in order to mystify, with a form of left-wing paternalism, the nature of the domestic work relationship, but to understand that it is the source of

common subjection and that together it is possible to take the initiative to change it, to overcome its current characteristics.

It is a proposal which we already put forward at the last congress but which has not had a concrete reply up until now. With the risk that amongst domestic workers ... feminism could be seen as an elite phenomenon, which is only relevant to women belonging to socially privileged classes (Turri, ACLI-COLF 1979: 9).

A number of the delegates however, were, if not explicitly critical of aspects of feminist ideology, certainly particularly sensitive to the issue of gender privilege and exploitation in the struggle for liberation from men. Carla Lazagna, a delegate from La Spezia, was overtly critical of the feminist movement:

the women's movement cannot grow on the backs of domestic workers. Behind every woman who is able to embark on a process of emancipation is a mother or a domestic worker. In other words, there is a woman who carries out the role of housewife. This means that the housewife role in our society is indispensable and this also explains why amongst domestic workers there is clear contempt for that feminism which constructs its liberation on the backs of other women black or white (ACLI-COLF 1979: 16)[18].

Judging from the experiences articulated by women delegates during the national congresses throughout the 1970s it would have been difficult for the concept of sisterhood and female solidarity, as espoused by the Italian feminist movement in the 1970s, to be uncritically accepted by domestic workers. Many of the women who participated in these congresses were likely to be materially experiencing something quite antithetical to the concept of female solidarity in the private context of their employers' homes.

By the time of the 1982 ACLI-COLF congress, specific awareness of gender, as opposed to a reductive focus on class, had begun to affect the ACLI-COLF analyses. Nonetheless, the organization's intrinsic involvement in the domestic work sector meant that the question of exploitation between women remained a central and difficult contra-diction which would constantly resurface. The views of Rosalba Dessì, a provincial delegate for Rome were indicative:

But we professional (or reserve) housewives who experience personally the contradiction of the double day, what should we say? ... When women, through employment, find the means to escape from the ghetto of the family in order to affirm themselves, they force the domestic workers who substitute them to pay for this emancipation. This is then the contradiction: women liberate themselves 'using' other women (ACLI-COLF 1982: 40)[19].

The notion not only of privilege between women but also the exploitation of this privilege was therefore repeatedly articulated by activists within the association throughout the 1970s and early 1980s. A decade later a quite different picture had emerged. The overt recognition of exploitation between women in the 1970s may be attributable to the fact that during this period, it was the workers' movement rather than the feminist movement with whom the ACLI-COLF sought a closer relationship. This implied a vision of their disadvantage as workers rather than as women and indicated that they saw class differentials as the basis of their exploitation. Despite some attention to the issue of gender, class stratification continued to dominate their analyses in the 1970s. Their emphasis on class and their desire to form alignments with the workers' movement was problematic however, and the marginalization of domestic workers by the trade union bodies continued into the 1980s.

Between Italian Women and Migrant Women: the ACLI-COLF and Ethnicity

But what of the ACLI-COLF's relationship to ethnic minority women and hence to the position of subjects that were both racialized and gendered? In the 1970s, the ACLI-COLF evolved into an association with a clear class perspective, enabling it to see through the pious mystifications of its former conservative ideology and to focus on the structural dimensions of exploitation. For this reason, it is perhaps no accident that it was during the 1973 congress that the question of migrant domestic workers was raised for the first time. Consonant with the association's new class perspective, the presence and employment of migrant women was viewed essentially as a weapon of the employers to fracture working class mobilization and strength. As Pina Brustolin stated:

> In terms of recruitment, we cannot help but be worried by the spread of the phenomenon of 'importing' coloured [sic] domestic workers which certainly represents an unscrupulous response from employers to their obligations, which today are a result of legislation and in the future will be guided by contractual duties. In fact many of these workers are employed without a regular work permit . . . and therefore any obligation to pay insurance contributions is avoided. This is an obvious attempt to use these workers, available to work under any conditions, as a 'reserve army of labour', just when there is a more mature combatant mood within the sector to take forward its battle for emancipation.[20]

Ianniello Rosetta, a delegate from Rome, graphically described the nature and extent of the exploitation perpetrated against migrant domestic workers:

> our comrades who come to our country to work are not protected in any way, they work like animals, they are treated like dirt and they earn just enough to survive . . . The problems of foreign female workers is a hot issue which affects all of us, and we must all take on board their difficulties and the obstacles that they encounter to carry out their work.[21]

Generally, it was recognized that the association had little knowledge of the true dimensions of the phenomenon of migrant domestic workers and the ACLI-COLF committed itself to a detailed national survey of the general conditions of domestic workers.[22] On the whole, however, this lack of knowledge and the enormous changes that were occurring both within the ACLI-COLF and the workers' movement meant that migrant women's conditions would, in this period, remain largely peripheral to the practical and theoretical concerns of the association. In 1976, the question of ethnic minority women still appeared to be relatively marginal to the principal concerns of the association. As the theme of the ninth congress in 1976 indicated,[23] the association remained centrally concerned with its relationship to the workers' movement. Thus, at this stage, both gender and ethnicity were subordinated to issues of class. In her address to the 1976 congress, the national secretary Pina Brustolin did not include migrant women in her analysis and the concluding motion to the congress prioritized the renewal of the national contract. This is not, of course, to argue that migrant women were to be excluded from any gains made by the sector but rather to suggest that their specific positioning within the sector had yet to be properly addressed. By 1979 however, and probably as a consequence of the growing numbers of migrant women entering Italy and working as domestics, the ACLI-COLF began to adopt a more inclusive conceptual and practical approach towards migrant women. The new national secretary, Clorinda Turri, suggested that the presence of migrant women and the rejection of domestic work by Italian women constituted two important new processes within the sector. The employment of migrant women continued to be viewed as a means for employers to avoid the contractual gains achieved by Italian women workers. There was also an explicit acknowledgement of migrant women's weaker position in comparison to Italian domestic workers – they were generally paid less, were frequently irregularly employed and worked longer hours. Their employers also appeared to have reverted to an out-moded formulation of the employer/employee relationship. According to Turri (ACLI-COLF 1979: 5):

> [they are forced] into almost total subjection at the hands of private agencies and employers. A type of subjection which recreates real conditions of servitude which we thought we had overcome for ever in our country.

In the face of this, it was argued that a paternalistic attitude was not an appropriate response to migrant women's situation but rather 'a clear and militant solidarity' was called for (ACLI-COLF 1979: 5). Turri suggested that the association should liaise with the organizations of migrant workers. Underpinning her calls for solidarity with migrant women was an understanding of a common exploitation based on class. Turri expressed some concern that the economic crisis of the 1970s had led to more Italian women offering their labour as domestic workers. It was felt that this might lead to a 'war amongst the poor' between Italian and migrant domestic workers.

In some ways, this latter consideration marked the beginning of a flawed interpretation of migrant women's positioning within the domestic work sector. It assumed a similarity of structural conditions dictating Italian women's and migrant women's participation in the sector. Such an interpretation in fact diminished evidence of a racialized structural segmentation within the sector, where migrant women would work only as live-in workers and Italian women were beginning to work principally on an hourly paid basis. This structural differentiation had in fact already been observed by Turri at the 1979 congress.[24]

Reference to a war among the poor implied a similarity of circumstances that did not in fact exist. Certainly, some competition might have existed with the older live-in Italian workers. However, judging by the ease with which migrant women could find alternative employing families (Andall 1999) it seemed that, during the 1970s, the demand for live-in workers began to outstrip the supply. Migrant women, however, appeared to be sensitive to the accusation that they were taking jobs away from Italian women. In her address to the national congress in 1979, Brito Tiago, a representative of the Cape Verdean association in Italy, emphasized both that Cape Verdeans did not want to compete with Italian workers and also presented the Cape Verdean presence as a temporary one.[25]

By the end of the 1970s, the ACLI-COLF had begun to interpret the increased demand for domestic workers as a replacement for the housewife figure. The employment of a domestic worker was seen as a functional solution to the rigidity of working hours in Italy, the lack of free time and the poor quality of social services. Issues of ethnicity, gender and class were all considered relevant to the domestic work situation. This could clearly be seen in the association's identification of groups with which it should establish alliances – female migrant workers, women's movements and marginalized workers. With regard to female migrants it was stated:

> We must get used to considering domestic workers from other countries as an integral part of our sector. Not only, we must also not forget that our choice to be part of the workers' movement obliges us to a fraternal solidarity with workers and exploited peoples all over the world (Turri, ACLI-COLF 1979: 14).

In contrast to migrant women's absence in the concluding motion of the 1976 congress, in 1979, the concluding motion recognized the grievances presented by migrant delegates at the congress and aimed to publicize and respond to them. Throughout the 1980s increasing attention was given to the issue of migrant workers. At the 1982 congress a number of the interventions referred to the general situation of migrant domestic workers[26] and delegations of migrant workers participated in the national congresses.[27] Concern continued to be expressed by Italian activists over whether the recently acquired gains of the sector would be undermined by the presence of migrant workers. As one of the members of the national executive argued:

> employers prefer migrant domestic workers precisely because they can pay them less, speculating on their dramatic situation and on their disinformation with respect to rights which should be guaranteed within the employment relationship.[28]

In her introductory speech to the congress, Clorinda Turri, still acting as national secretary, argued that it was important to formulate legislation that was inclusive of the specific situation of migrant domestic workers to counter their exploitation by employers. This position in fact encouraged the ACLI-COLF to support wider state legislation to regulate the position of migrant workers in general. The association's approach was thus unequivocally inclusive of migrant workers, dictated by the value of class unity: 'We need to break the natural hold of the bosses by uniting the sector and overcoming the temptation for opposition between the two groups' (Turri ACLI-COLF 1982: 7). To this end there was strong support for legislative gains within the domestic work sector to be applicable to migrant domestic workers and the association argued for the inclusion of an explicit reference to migrant women in the collectively bargained national contracts.

By the early 1980s then, the question of ethnicity with regard to the domestic work sector had unquestionably entered the vocabulary of the ACLI-COLF. This attention would increase in intensity as the issue of immigration attracted sustained consideration at the wider national level. This can clearly be seen in the proceedings of the 1985 ACLI-COLF conference, which occurred a year before the promulgation of law 943, the first comprehensive piece of government legislation on immigration. During this congress, a special round-table discussion was held on the question of migrant domestic workers. It should be noted that this did not signify that the issue of migrant domestic workers was subsequently excluded from the rest of the proceedings. In fact, a number of migrant representatives spoke during the main proceedings[29] and Italian delegates continued to make reference to the situation of migrant domestic workers in their speeches. It was the round-table discussion, however, which provided the forum in which the ACLI-COLF could spell out its position regarding female migrant domestic workers.[30] The opening speech by Clorinda Turri (now deputy national secretary) indicated that the condition of migrant domestic workers was seen to be closely intertwined with their general situation as migrants.[31] This seemed to imply that although class location was seen as fundamental, ethnicity and a migrant status were privileged over gender as causes of disadvantage. It was for this reason that the ACLI-COLF called for the implementation of appropriate national legislation governing migrants as a whole. The association reiterated its opposition to special employment norms for migrant domestic workers as it was felt that these would be abused by employers hoping to find docility in their overseas domestic workers. The ACLI-COLF perspective to some extent emulated the Christian solidarity position of its parenting structure, the ACLI. Aldo De Matteo, for example, then vice president of the ACLI, unequivocally stated: 'foreign workers . . . are not stealing jobs, but are pioneers. They have accepted heavy jobs, often rejected by Italians and it is unfair to accuse them of competing when this is not the case' (ACLI-COLF 1985a: 56).

Given that in the 1970s and early 1980s migrant women were employed almost exclusively as live-in domestic workers, it would have been virtually impossible for an association such as the ACLI-COLF to ignore their presence. This proximity meant that the ACLI-COLF pre-empted both national government and the more progressive arena of women's politics in responding to the specific situation of migrant women. It would ultimately adopt an inclusive stance, paying sustained attention to migrant women's specific difficulties at its national congresses. Inclusiveness in itself would not necessarily improve their situation. Rather, the nature of the general strategy of the association into which migrant women were being integrated would be the critical factor in instigating change. Given the ACLI-COLF's development of a radical position during the 1970s and early 1980s, to what degree would it have the potential to transform the position of migrant workers through its wider understanding of and strategy for the domestic work sphere? I want to argue that by the mid 1980s the association had reverted to promoting an ideal of sacrifice for the domestic worker (albeit to a lesser extent than the conservative API-COLF), but this time in the name of female solidarity. In the following sub-section, I shall engage with the ACLI-COLF's contemporary conceptual interpretation of domestic work. I argue that while in the early 1970s the relationship between (largely Italian) female domestic workers and their employers was initially seen to be marked by an exploitative class relationship, by the late 1980s this position had been modified. The ACLI-COLF now emphasized the intrinsic value of the female relationship between employer and employee. This emphasis minimized emerging evidence that indicated that the relationship between women in the domestic work sector could not simply be reduced to a gender relationship as it was being increasingly structured by the interrelationship of gender, class and ethnicity.

The ACLI-COLF and its New Interpretation of Domestic Work

In the early 1990s, a series of articles was commissioned by the ACLI-COLF with the express purpose of contributing to the creation of a new theoretical framework with which to analyse domestic work.[32] It is my contention that the analyses put forward in these articles revealed the association's tendency to obscure class and ethnicity as important factors inscribed within the domestic work relationship. This was evident from the nature of the debate that centred principally on explaining and interpreting *Italian women's* need for domestic workers. This focus functioned to minimize the interests of the domestic worker, thus producing a reductive account of supply and demand factors operating within the sector.

In discussing the relationship between Italian families and the demand for domestic workers, Alemani (1992) maintained that it was the emerging diversity of existing family relationships (one parent families, single people, and so forth) which had not only modified the type of demand for domestic work but had also affected the employer/employee relationship. She argued that the increasing propensity for the female employer to work outside the home had led to a greater willingness on the part of the employer to delegate rather than to supervise, thus permitting the possibility of autonomous management for the domestic worker. She did attempt to interpret the new demand for live-in work but failed to fully engage with the racialized dimension of the new labour supply. In her analysis, demand was attributable to a series of factors. These included the insufficient number of nursery places, the limited number of schools operating an extended day and the increase in the number of pensioners who frequently require company as well as assistance. She maintained that women often had no option but to use private organizations or live-in domestic workers as strategies to facilitate family life. Livraghi's (1992) contribution replicated some of these ideas, as she too focused on how the transformation of Italian families had led to a new plurality of service demands. Marina Piazza (1992) similarly sought to highlight the Italian employers' perspective by stressing the multiple pressures inherent in their 'double presence' (in the home and at work) and the rigidity of city times which caused specific difficulties for women. Di Nicola's[33] article centred on analysing the reasons for Italian women's postponement of maternity. In her view, for Italian women to combine motherhood with both paid employment and a social life, they must have support from parents, in-laws, other relatives or 'be able to afford the luxury of a domestic worker who today represents the last hope not only for bourgeois families, but for all those middle class families who have specific caring needs' (Di Nicola 1994: 176).

As I have demonstrated above, in the 1970s, the ACLI-COLF explicitly recognized the contradiction of women exploiting other women for reproductive work. In the early 1990s, none of the contributors sought to explore this. Alemani (1992) touched on this issue, maintaining that one of the fundamental contradictions that women's movements have consistently been unable to resolve is that of women achieving their liberation/emancipation through the sacrifices of other women. During the 1970s and early 1980s, the ACLI-COLF had acknowledged that ethnicity or a migrant status had caused greater and specific disadvantage for migrant women, but by the 1990s this perspective had quietly faded from view. The series of commissioned articles in the early 1990s focused on the female (Italian) employer and this prohibited the development of any framework that could accommodate the complexity of women's interaction within this relationship. By emphasizing the difficulties that Italian women encountered in reconciling their family and work roles, these articles served only to validate Italian women's increasing propensity to employ domestic workers.

This new ACLI-COLF interpretative model can be situated within Romero's (1992) typology of the relationship between domestic workers and their employers. Her description of employers in the north American context identified several categories but it is the Common Victim proposition that best accommodates the ACLI-COLF perspective. The Common Victim view maintains that the sexist structuring of society signifies that whilst professional women have to compete in a man's world, it is still assumed that they will take responsibility for housework and childcare. The female employer thus views herself as no less a victim than the domestic worker.[34] One problem with this typology is that it replicates the notion that it is other women (often privileged by class and ethnicity) who gain from the work of domestics. This occurs because the work executed by the paid domestic worker is assumed to be the work of the wife/mother, thus it is she, and not other members of the family, who is expected to supervise the fulfilment of household tasks. These patriarchal assumptions do not, however, mean that women can totally distance themselves from their own responsibility within the employment relationship. As Romero (1992: 169) has argued:

> Feminist analysis should consider not only the privilege and benefits that husbands obtain at the expense of their wives but also those that one group of women obtain at the expense of another. Certainly, as employees, professional women are sometimes victims of sexism, but they still make decisions that ultimately result in shifting the burden of sexism. Hiring household workers to take the place of wives or mothers maintains male privilege at home.[35]

The propensity to conceptualize the issue of domestic service in terms of the Common Victim proposition has a repressive function in that it diminishes the weaker position of the (migrant) domestic worker. In other words, the Common Victim perspective somehow fails to encapsulate the extent of the power disparity inscribed within this relationship.

It would seem that the ACLI-COLF gradually began to assimilate and promote this notion in the mid 1980s and this was likely to have consequences for its conceptual and strategical development in the future. A clear example of this can be found in the Charter of Responsibilities and Rights drawn up for domestic workers for the occasion of its twelfth national congress in the mid 1980s. Here, the Common Victim syndrome is explicitly acknowledged:

> We suffer particularly as a result of the contradiction that is created in
> the relationship between women; many of them can improve their own
> quality of life and minimise the discrimination that affects them in the
> current division of roles in society by utilising our work to free them-
> selves from domestic work. We domestic workers, on the other hand,
> cannot use for ourselves or for our families the services which we offer
> to other women (ACLI-COLF 1985b: 2/3).

Nevertheless, and quite significantly I would argue, one finds con-
tained within the section outlining the responsibilities of a domestic
worker, approval for the domestic worker to view her relationship
with her female employer as an act of solidarity between women:

> The domestic worker, as a woman, sees the importance of valorising the
> fact that she is in an employment relationship with other women, whether
> they are traditional employers of domestic workers or women who use
> a home-help service. The domestic worker feels, as a woman and as a
> female worker, that this relationship between women must be solid for
> a journey of personal liberation and to promote a common battle for
> social services which all women can use (ACLI-COLF 1985b: 2/3).

This document does note the contradiction 'between women' in its
preamble, however, the onus of sacrifice and solidarity is placed on
the disadvantaged domestic worker. It is she who must make sacrifices
in order to promote a battle that will ultimately be beneficial for all
women. Notably absent from the section dealing with the domestic
workers' rights is any suggestion that female employers should also
make sacrifices as a contribution to women's struggle, let alone encourage their male partners to make some.

This mode of analysis had begun to prevail by the late 1980s and
was readily applied to the specific situation of migrant women. The
acceptance of Italian women's need for female migrant labour to
perform a live-in function and the concurrent emphasis on the perceived advantages of this for migrant women were used to validate
this perspective (interview, ACLI-COLF).[36] The position adopted by
the association suggests that ascribing a victim label to domestic
workers may have been applicable when employers emanated essentially from the upper classes, but the emergence of employers from
within middle income categories has tended to invalidate this notion,
conferring instead a Common Victim status on both service user and
provider. As Sacconi (1984: 40–1) has written in relation to this structural change in the background of the employers of domestic workers:
'far from being a luxury . . . it is becoming a real necessity in all those
families with young children or elderly members'.

By the early 1990s, the drift towards a narrow gender analysis was consolidated and used to interpret the findings of a major survey of domestic workers undertaken by the ACLI-COLF in the early 1990s:[37]

> the hypothesis which informs our work is that the tensions [and] imbalances . . . which we find in the domestic workers' conditions are to be found in the tensions and imbalances which characterise women's condition . . . the conditions of the domestic worker then as a mirror of women's condition . . . (IREF/ACLI-COLF 1994:9).

Although the ACLI-COLF argued that the presence of migrant women as domestic workers constituted the most important new feature within the sector and acknowledged that their insertion into the live-in sphere had exacerbated their working conditions, its over-riding perspective stressed the useful reconciliation of migrant women's needs and Italian women's needs: 'The type of supply that the migrant domestic worker is prepared to offer reconciles itself well with the needs exhibited by a part of the service users' (IREF/ACLI-COLF 1994: 11). Thus, the perceived advantages of live-in domestic work for migrant women (provision of accommodation, food, greater savings potential and therefore the possibility of larger remittances) have been used by the organization to present migrant women's location within the live-in sphere as a preferred choice. Evidence from different national and historical contexts indicates that domestic workers will abandon live-in work for day work or other employment sectors as soon as this becomes available.[38]

The analysis used to account for the fact that Italian women have largely rejected employment as live-in workers, confirms that a reductive gender focus is not sufficient to understand migrant women's and Italian women's position:

> Italian domestic workers prefer to be employed on an hourly paid basis rather than on a live-in basis as this would mean them having to give up an autonomous life-style or the impossibility of looking after their own nuclear family (IREF/ACLI-COLF 1994: 13).

Remarkably, the pertinence of this statement for migrant women is totally overlooked. The ACLI-COLF additionally asserted that young (Italian) women avoid the domestic work sphere because they view it as anachronistic in view of women's changed circumstances (AAvv 1994: 42). Again, there is no indication that such a view might be equally pertinent to many of the young and professional migrant women who cannot exercise such a choice. This view may be conditioned by what Morokvasic (1991) refers to as pervasive ethnocentric assumptions about migrant women's backwardness. In other words, their conditions in Italy are acceptable given that it is assumed that they are not only an improvement on conditions in their country of origin, but also provide escape from oppressive cultural traditions. To this end, the ACLI-COLF failed to engage with the reasons why migrant women work as live-in domestics, and in so doing evaded the issue of ethnicity within the sector. This omission was determined by a paternalistic approach to migrant women which focused on the advantages of live-in work for migrant workers and perceived the disadvantages as being largely related to problems of the sector as opposed to their structural location as female migrants confined to a specific area of the economy. In this way, the severe social consequences of live-in work for migrant women could be marginalized. This perspective is also being used to privilege the gendered ethnicity of Italian women against that of migrant women. The importance of Italian women's family role was explicitly acknowledged as a valid reason for their repudiation of live-in work. The family role of migrant women, on the other hand, was entirely overlooked. This conceptual omission suggested that although the association had ostensibly adopted an inclusive approach to migrant women, in reality it continued to be principally concerned with representing the interests of Italian women, not only as domestic workers but increasingly as employers of domestic workers.

The foregrounding of gender for the analysis of the IREF/ACLI-COLF study can thus be said to have led to some debatable conclusions. One of the questions included in the survey regarded the relationship between female employers and their employees. This was used to assess the extent to which gender could constitute an element of cohesion between women. The results indicated that a greater degree of familiarity was apparent between women within the employer/employee relationship.[39] This led to a very positive assessment of the potential for increased collaboration between women. By the 1990s then, the belief that the relationship between female employer and female employee was no longer conflictual led to an apparent resolution of the old and familiar dilemma regarding privileged women's exploitation of disadvantaged women. The new position was decidedly different from that described above with reference to the 1970s:

> Is the affirmation still valid that the emancipation of women necessarily negates the same emancipation of other women forced into a domestic role? The responses relating to this seem to indicate that this antagonistic vision has been overcome and is allowing space for comparison and dialogue from which a new relationship between women can develop (IREF/ACLI-COLF 1994: 14).

Indeed, even the presence of migrant men in the sector was promoted as a positive :

> It is indicative . . . that male [migrants] . . . are willing to carry out tasks which have typically been assigned to women and that families are accepting men to fulfil certain tasks. A step forward perhaps for a different and more equal re-distribution of reproductive care work within the family . . . ? (IREF/ACLI-COLF 1994: 13)

It is I think extremely pertinent that migrant men, are here lauded for standing at the vanguard of a transformation of gender role stratification within Italy.[40] At the same time, an unspoken compliance with Italian men's reluctance to participate in this transformation is evident in the apparent acceptability of hiring other women to do domestic labour.

The unmistakable prominence of gender and the value attributed to the domestic work relationship between women has had important implications for the nature of migrant women's inclusion into the ACLI-COLF's analysis. Privileging migrant women's gender over their ethnicity has functioned to obscure the ongoing racialization process within the sector, leading to false assumptions regarding women's solidarity. Indeed, this focus on solidarity, while not totally negating the existence of exploitative relationships, has effectively marginalized themes of exploitation. A number of hypotheses could be put forward to explain the ACLI-COLF's gradual change of emphasis. Firstly, there had been changes in the political climate. The progressive collective action of the 1970s had led to a retreat into private life in the 1980s, culminating in more moderate forms of activism and analysis. Secondly, there had been some improvement in domestic workers' situation via the collectively bargained national contracts. Thirdly, the ALCI-COLF's most recent survey had indicated an improved relationship between employer and employee. Finally, and perhaps most significantly, is the relevance of the structural change in the status of employers. The blatant class exploitation between upper-class leisured female employers and working-class women had become much less apparent in Italy. Now middle-class women, with new aspirations and roles, were seen to have a functional need rather than a superfluous desire for domestic workers. This undoubtedly contributed to the new focus on gender. Nevertheless, the marginalization of ethnicity by the ACLI-COLF meant that Italian women's needs, both as employers and domestic workers were implicitly seen as more important than those of migrant women.

Conclusion

The continued demand for live-in workers by Italian families has accentuated the unresolved tension between productive and reproductive care in Italy. This has led to the co-existence of a flexible hourly paid domestic work sphere (dominated by Italian women) and the persistent rigidity of the live-in sphere (dominated by migrant women). This duality within the sector suggests that migrant women's situation cannot simply be explained by reference to gender stratification alone. Rather, attention must also be paid to their migrant status and the rigid structural constraints of live-in work. Recent trends within the ACLI-COLF indicate a privileging of Italian women's gendered ethnicity as middle-class employers and as (largely) hourly paid working-class domestic employees. In relation to migrant women, this has contributed to what Frankenberg, in her study into the social construction of whiteness, describes as power evasion:

> power evasion involves a selective attention to difference, allowing into conscious scrutiny . . . those differences that make the speaker feel good but continuing to evade by means of partial description, euphemism, and self-contradiction those that make the speaker feel bad (Frankenberg 1993: 156–7).

Once the ACLI-COLF had left behind its clerical response to the domestic work sector and moved on to a class and gendered interpretation, it was able to explicitly articulate those factors responsible for domestic workers' subordination. More recently, however, it has been loath to explicitly verbalize the manner in which a migrant status functions to subordinate ethnic minority women within the domestic work sphere. At its fourteenth congress in 1994, it did recognize migrant women's need for more political space and autonomous representation within the association and also pledged to support them in their need for housing (ACLI-COLF 1994). Generally, however, the 1990s saw a shift towards the acceptance of the *utility* for Italian female employers to have access to live-in domestic workers, seeming to typify Frankenberg's concept of power evasion. This could equally be observed when the ACLI-COLF asserted Italian domestic workers' preference for hourly paid work to facilitate their family roles but failed to fully investigate the implications of live-in work for the family life of migrant women. The ACLI-COLF's focus on women as a disadvantaged group not only avoids acknowledging the weaker position of migrant domestic workers but it equally masks class differences between Italian women by validating the choices of those middle-class families who are financially able to employ live-in domestic workers, without engaging in a corresponding discussion of working-class women's inability to do so. Interestingly, then, it would seem that the potential for an inclusivity that acknowledged the specific structural location of migrant women was more prevalent in the 1970s than in the 1990s. In the 1970s, there was no attempt to fuse the interests of middle/upper class women with those of working class women. Rather the exploitation seen to be inherent within the domestic work relationship was something to be challenged and, indeed, radically altered. By the 1990s such a fusion of interests had become an integral component of the ACLI-COLF's strategy and it is precisely the attractiveness of interpreting migrant women's presence in the live-in sphere as a straightforward and useful reconciliation of supply and demand that in fact suggests that the contradiction at the basis of the domestic work relationship remains unresolved.

Notes

1. It was initially known as the Domestic Workers group (GAD) within the ACLI (Italian Christian Workers' Association). The ACLI was established in 1944 as an association for workers aiming to promote Christian values. COLF is an abbreviated form of *collaboratrice familiare*, 'family collaborator'.

2. For more discussion on this period see Duggan and Wagstaff (1995)

3. See Yeoh and Huang (1999) for an example of this.

4. Circular n.156/91 of *Lavoratori extracomuntari da adibire ai servizi domestici – nuovi ingressi*, dated 29 Noember 1991.

5. In 1992 for example, male migrants constituted 61 per cent of domestic workers in Sicily (see ISMU 1996).

6. For a more detailed analysis of the ACLI-COLF's pre-1971 position, see Andall (1997).

7. See Crippa (1961).

8. Professional Association of Italian Family Collaborators.

9. Union of Italian Women. This organization was composed principally of communist and socialist women activists and was originally closely tied to the Italian Communist Party.

10. The UDI's participation in this congress was indicative of the new left-leaning direction of the ACLI-COLF.

11. All translations from original Italian sources are my own.

12. This is an abbreviated reference as the congress proceedings were published in a special addition of *Acli-Oggi*, the ACLI's periodical.

13. This is an abbreviated reference as congress proceedings were reproduced in a special issue of *Acli-Oggi*.

14. Vaiou (1995: 43), in her study of southern European women has confirmed that 'male identities in the south do not include in their definition caring and domestic labour'.

15. The new appellation to refer to domestic workers had been introduced by the ACLI-COLF during its fifth national congress held in 1961. It was used to reflect the professionalism of the sector and also as a means of acknowledging domestic workers' contribution to family life..

16. The national secretary of the UDI, Costanza Fanelli, saw cooperatives as the way forward in overcoming the individual work relationship of the domestic worker. See her intervention at the 1979 national congress (ACLI-COLF 1979)

17. See 'Relazione Organizzativa dell'incaricata nazionale: Pina Brustolin', Assemblea Nazionale Congressuale, Siena 1973, p. 7.

18. See also the interventions of Bianca Buri from Milan and the trade-union representative Gianna Bitto on this point at the 1979 congress.

19. This delegate would become the national secretary by the time of the 1985 congress, at which time she called for greater links with the women's movement. See ACLI-COLF 1985a: 19).

20. Relazione Organizzativa dell'incaricata nazionale: Pina Brustolin', Assemblea Nazionale Congressuale, Siena 1973, p. 10.

21. Intervention published in *La Casa e La Vita*, maggio-giugno-luglio 1973, p. 4.

22. In the event, they were excluded from the survey carried out in 1974. It was in fact the conservative API-COLF that first investigated the conditions of migrant domestic workers in a 1976 survey. These findings were eventually published in book form in 1979 by Father Erminio Crippa, an influential figure within the pre-1971 ACLI-COLF. See Crippa (1979).

23. The theme was 'Domestic Workers in the workers movement for the development of social services for a new life-style model'.

24. This structural differentiation had in fact already been observed by Turri at the 1979 congress. See (ACLI-COLF 1979: 5).

25. See her intervention in (ACLI-COLF 1979: 16).

26. Even the contributions by the representatives of the main political parties referred to the question of migrant workers. See interventions by the Christian Democrat member of parliament Giuseppe Costamagna and that of Mariangela Rosolen, a member of the Italian Communist Party's national women's committee (ACLI-COLF 1982).

27. This in itself was significant as it suggested that the ACLI-COLF did attempt to integrate migrant women into its organizational structures at an early stage. See intervention by Rita di Maio (ACLI-COLF 1982: 33).

28. See intervention by Rita di Maio (ACLI-COLF 1982: 33).

29. See interventions by Yeshi Habits, the Filipino representative Corazon Sim, and an Eritrean representative Alì Moussa.

30. The discussion was entitled 'Le Colf immigrate in Italia: linee d'impegno dell'associazionismo'.

31. In fact the congress sent a telegram to the Home Secretary regarding the urgency of an immigration law and asked to hold a meeting with him to present the specific case of domestic workers. The original telegram is reproduced in the proceedings of the 1985 ACLI-COLF congress.

32. These were published in 1992 and 1993 in a journal, *Quaderni di Azione Sociale*, a debating forum for Italian associationism. Claudia Alemani, an ACLI-COLF representative, opened and closed the debate with two articles entitled: 'Le colf: un'identità molteplice tra persistenza e mutamento' and 'Le Colf: emblema del femminile'. The intervening articles consisted of Marina Piazza: 'Le implicazioni attuali del concetto di doppia presenza'; Renata Livraghi: 'Le famiglie e la produzione di servizi'; Giulia Paola Di Nicola: 'Le sfide sociali della maternità'. Some of these articles were reproduced in the ACLI series 'Transizioni' in 1994 in a publication reporting the results of a survey into the conditions of domestic workers. See AAvv (1994).

33. This article was also originally published in *Quaderni di Azione Sociale* but references here are to the reproduction of this article in AAvv (1994).

34. Jacklyn Cock (1980) presented a similar thesis regarding the situation of Black domestic workers and their employers in South Africa, which she describes as a politics of mutual dependence.

35. See also Ramazanoglu (1989) on this point.

36. The interview was carried out with an ACLI-COLF representative in 1993.

37. The interpretative framework adopted for the survey was established during the course of a seminar organized by the ACLI-COLF and IREF in Rome in February 1991. The research took place between 1991 and 1993. This survey currently constitutes the largest and most up-to-date national survey of the domestic work sector. It was based on interviews with 717 domestic workers, 92.7 per cent of whom were women and 34 per cent of whom were migrants.

38. See De Grazia (1992) on Italian women in the inter-war period.

39. 36.5 per cent of workers considered their relationship with their employers to be 'friendly', with a slightly lower figure for migrant women (32.8 per cent) and a higher figure for Italian women (38.5 per cent).

40. This view was reiterated by the national secretary Maria Solinas in her speech to the 1994 congress. See ACLI-COLF, Le Colf tra nuovi modelli familiari e crisi dello stato sociale, XIV Assemblea Nazionale ACLI-COLF, Roma, 24–26 febbraio 1994.

References

AAvv (1994), *Donne in Frontiera. Le colf nella transizione.* ACLI series Transizioni n. 17. Milan: Editrice CENS.

ACLI-COLF (1976), Le Colf nel movimento operaio per lo sviluppo dei servizi sociali per un nuovo modello di vita. IX Assemblea congressuale ACLI-COLF, 3–4 April 1976 in *Acli-Oggi*, Edizione speciale, anno XIV, No.103–4, 12–13 April.

ACLI-COLF (1979), Le Colf: Da casalinghe di riserva a protagoniste di una nuova qualità del lavoro. X assemblea nazionale ACLI-COLF, 12–13 May 1979 in *Acli-Oggi*, anno XVII, No.164–5, 13–14 June.

ACLI-COLF (1982), Cooperare per la solidarietà, l'autotutela, la partecipazione. Atti dell'XI Assemblea Nazionale. 20–21 November.

ACLI-COLF (1985a), Le Acli Colf per il lavoro associato per nuove forme di solidarietà. Atti della XII Assemblea Nazionale ACLI-COLF. 7–8 December.

ACLI-COLF (1985b), Carta delle responsabilità e dei diritti delle Colf.

ACLI-COLF (1989), Professionalità e diritti per una nuova cittadinanza sociale. Atti della XIII Assemblea Nazionale ACLI-COLF, 10–12 March.

ACLI-COLF (1994), Le Colf tra nuovi modelli familiari e crisi dello stato sociale. Atti della XIV Assemblea Nazionale ACLI-COLF. Roma, 24–26 February.

Alemani, C. (1992) 'Le Colf: un'identità molteplice tra persistenza e mutamento', *Quaderni di Azione Sociale*, May–June, No. 87, pp. 59–69.

Andall, J. (1997), 'Catholic and State Constructions of Domestic Workers: The Case of Cape Verdean women in Rome in the 1970s', in K. Koser and H. Lutz (eds), *New Migration in Europe: Social Constructions and Social Realities.* Basingstoke: Macmillan, pp. 124–42.

Andall, J. (1999 forthcoming), 'Cape Verdean Women on the Move: "Immigration Shopping" in Italy and Europe', *Modern Italy*, Vol. 4, No. 2.

Bakan, A. and Stasiulis, D.K. (1995), 'Making the Match: Domestic Placement Agencies and the Racialization of Women's Household Work', *Signs*, Vol. 20, No. 21, pp. 303–5.

Bedani, G. (1995), *Politics and Ideology in the Italian Workers' Movement.* Oxford: Berg.

Caldwell, L. (1991), 'Italian Feminism: Some Considerations, in Z. Baranski and S. Vinall (eds), *Women and Italy*, Basingstoke: Macmillan.

Caritas di Roma (1997), *Immigrazione dossier statisico '97*. Rome: Anterem, pp. 95–116.

Chell, V. (1997), 'Gender-Selective Migration: Somalian and Filipino Women in Rome', in R. King and R. Black (eds), *Southern Europe and the New Immigrations*, Brighton: Sussex, pp. 75–92.

Cochrane, A. (1993), 'Looking for a European Welfare State', in A. Cochrane and J. Clarke (eds), *Comparing Welfare States. Britain in International Context*, London: Sage, pp. 239–68.

Cock, J. (1980), *Maids and Madams: A Study in the Politics of Exploitation*. Johannesburg: Raven Press.

Crippa, E. (1961), *Le sante del nostro lavoro*. Torino: Casa Serena.

Crippa, E. (1979), *Lavoro amaro: le estere in Italia*. Rome: API-COLF.

De Grazia, V. (1992), *How Fascism Ruled Women*. Italy, 1922–1945. California: University of California Press.

Di Nicola, G.P. (1994), 'Le sfide sociali della maternità', in AAvv (1994) *Donne in Frontiera. Le colf nella transizione*, ACLI series Transizioni n. 17. Milan: Editrice CENS, pp. 165–200.

Duggan, C. and Wagstaff, C. (1995), *Italy in the Cold War*. Oxford: Berg.

Enloe, C. (1989), *Bananas, Beaches and Bases: Making Feminist Sense of International Politics*. London: Pandora.

Escrivá, A. (1997), 'Control, Composition and Character of New Migrations to South-West Europe: The case of Peruvian women in Barcelona, *New Community*, Vol. 23, No. 1, pp. 43–58.

Frankenberg, R. (1993), *The Social Construction of Whiteness*. Minnesota: University of Minnesota Press.

IREF/ACLI-COLF (1994), La condizione delle collaboratrici familiari in Italia.

ISMU (1996), *Migrations in Italy. The First Report 1995*. Milan: Franco Angeli.

Korsieporn, A. (1991), 'International labor migration of Southeast Asian Women: Filipina and Thai domestic workers in Italy', Ph.D. Dissertation. Cornell University.

Leibfried, S. (1993), 'Towards a European Welfare State?', in C. Jones (ed), *New Perspectives on the Welfare State in Europe*. London: Routledge, pp. 133–56.

Livraghi, R. (1992), 'Le famiglie e la produzione di servizi', *Quaderni di Azione Sociale*, July–August September–October, No. 88–89, pp. 115–127.

Morokvasic, M. (1991), 'Fortress Europe and Migrant Women', *Feminist Review*, No. 39, pp. 69–84.

Nakano Glenn, E. (1992), 'From Servitude to Service Work: Historical Continuities in the Racial Division of Paid Reproductive Labor', *Signs*, Vol. 18, No. 1, pp. 1–43.

Pereira De Melo, H. (1989), 'Feminists and Domestic Workers in Rio de Janeiro', in E. Chaney and M. Castro (eds), *Muchachas No More. Household workers in Latin America and the Caribbean*. Philadelphia: Temple University Press, pp. 245–67.

Piazza, M. (1992), 'Le implicazioni attuali del concetto di doppia presenza', *Quaderni di Azione Sociale*, November–December, No. 90, pp. 105–111.

Ramazanoglu, C. (1989), *Feminism and the contradictions of oppression*. London: Routledge.

Rollins, J. (1985), *Between Women: Domestics and Their Employers*. Philadelphia: Temple University Press.

Romero, M. (1992), *Maid in the USA*. London: Routledge.

Sacconi, R. (1984), 'Le colf, queste sconosciute', *Politica ed economia*, January, No. 1, pp. 39–46.

Tan, T. and Devasahayam, T. (1987), 'Opposition and Interdependence: The Dialectics of Maid and Employer Relationships in Singapore', *Philippine Sociological Review*, Vol. 35, Nos. 3–4, pp. 34–41.

Vaiou, D. (1995), Women of the South after, like before, Maastricht?', in C. Hadjimichalis and P. Sadler (eds), *Europe at the Margins*. Chicester: Wiley, pp. 35–50.

Wrigley, J. (1991), 'Feminists and Domestic Workers', *Feminist Studies*, Vol. 17, No. 2, pp. 317–29.

Yeoh, B. and Huang, S. (1999) 'Migrant Female Domestic Workers: Debating the Economic, Social and Political Impacts in Singapore', *International Migration Review*, pp. 114–36.

Female Birds of Passage: Leaving and Settling in Spain

NATALIA RIBAS-MATEOS

Introduction

This chapter examines new female migration into Spain, specifically to Catalonia, through the study of three groups of migrants (Filipino, Gambian and Moroccan). Fieldwork in Catalonia and in the countries of origin has been organized in terms of three migratory models in respect to gender: highly feminized (Filipino), a masculine type in transition (Moroccan) and a highly masculine one (Gambian). Important information on the context of migration is provided in terms of labour markets, social organization (ethnic, family and religion) as well as cultural and symbolic identity. This chapter describes the meeting of various spaces, which configure the stages before and after within the migratory cycle. Represented by a 'woven carpet' of places, the reader is able to consider a complex network where the material and the cultural structure are woven together.

In Spain, as in other southern European countries one of the most important recent changes in the sociology of migration is attention given to the growing feminization of flows, and its significance in the context of migration patterns of the so-called 'new immigration countries' of the European Union. This phenomenon will be analysed not only in relation to gender dynamics, but also in relation to other factors such as the diversity of origins of the migrants.

With the break-up of the 'gastarbeiter regime' (1973 and 1974),[1] more-or-less present in all the old immigration countries of northern Europe, a new phase has emerged in massive labour migrations (Castles 1984). This period is important because it situates a time on one side when family reunification processes were starting to take place in northern Europe and on the other, the very beginning of the emergence of the new immigration in southern Europe. Countries like Italy, Spain, Greece and Portugal have now become destinations for potential migrants. Therefore, in contrast with past decades, the 1980s showed a migration turnaround (King and Black 1997) in southern Europe. Flows became immigratory instead of emigratory and internal migration processes have decreased. The feminization of migration in the whole of Europe may be playing an important role in this migratory turnaround. The international migration of women into the new countries of immigration stretches the capacity of the classical theoretical models for explaining this set of phenomena. In order to give an understanding of the feminization of flows it is important to look at a number of factors.

First of all, international migration policies contribute to the composition of flows as well as to the social vulnerability of women in migration processes. On the Spanish side, the role of the state has contributed to a specific migratory dynamic since 1993 through a quota policy system predominantly covering domestic service, which is mainly functioning as a way of 'covered regularization'. This has been the official answer to the gendered demand in the labour market for foreign women as domestic workers. On the country of origin side, women can contribute towards the living standards of the family through women's migration process. By looking at female migration we are stressing a neglected area of economics that deals with household strategies. Therefore, this analysis goes beyond the classical model, which understands migration as shaped according to market and policy processes and in terms of individual strategies.

Secondly, female migrant labour has to be seen in terms of the demand for jobs relating to health care, domestic service and leisure. Furthermore, these demands are dependent on changes in employment for local women, changing conceptions of the family and the existence of weak welfare state regimes. In the case of Spain, migrant women usually find jobs rejected by local/Spanish women, as in the case of the extended system of live-in domestic service in southern European countries. Notwithstanding, female domestic service demand occurs mainly (but not exclusively) in big urban spaces (in the Spanish case, Madrid and Barcelona, in Italy, Rome and in Greece, Athens) and is related to gender changes within the urban middle classes.

In the case of Spain, many migrant women find jobs as live-in domestic servants, which in southern European countries are based on diverse employer–employee arrangements. Izquierdo (1997)[2] suggests that migration flows could be a response to labour demand but they could also be a response to political decisions or quota system patterns (which are often a disguised regularization process). According to his argument, two characteristics are important in the Spanish model, which are: the irregular and multiple regularization processes and the growth of female flows (probably attracted by the quota system, which is very dependent on domestic service). Apart from the economic and political implications, this type of migration reproduces the Spanish lifestyle, and involves an organization of the household (food, cleaning, caring for children) which perpetuates tradition.

Thirdly, there are also factors relating to changes in the countries of origin; this will be the central core of this chapter. In this case the changes are related to labour market disintegration, suggesting that the feminization of flows could be the result of a female proletarianization process within international labour migration. Different aspects related to this issue will be analysed through Filipino, Gambian and Moroccan flows to Catalonia, Spain. The context of the work will be to give evidence of the heterogeneity among foreign immigrants through these three different national groups. This underlines how different groups interact with different locals markets and immigration policies and the extent to which this results in diverse outcomes. My main focus here will be to emphasize heterogeneities between different national groups. However, I also have to stress that there are significant limitations in using the 'national group' as a category, because groups are not homogenous internally. I will be using basically qualitative data from research carried out in 1992, 1993 and 1994, in three countries or origin: The Philippines, Morocco, and the Gambia, respectively.

The Case of Spain: Gender as a Barometer

Firstly, I want to briefly examine the conversion of Spain into a country of immigration. The development of Spain as one of the 'new immigration countries' together with the rest of the southern European nations goes hand-in-hand with the 'Europeanization'[3] of Spain. I will look in particular at the case of Catalonia.

Apart from the growing number of nationals from less-developed countries, a series of other events have set the new agenda relating to the Common European Market. In 1985 Spain entered the Common European Market and in the same year a new 'Alien's Law' was passed. After this date the country experienced repeated small regularization processes of migrant workers.[4] During this period Spain changed from an emigration country to an immigration country. Catalonia (an 'autonomous community' of Spain) was experiencing flows from outside Spain, leading to different migration patterns (marked by different economic and socio-cultural features). This manifests many of the ingredients of the new European migration areas: the increase of female immigration flows, the old settlement of certain communities (for example, Moroccans since the 1970s, López 1993) in relation to the rest of Spain and the replacement of internal migration by external migration (with variations among different economic sectors). In contrast to other Spanish situations there is the significance of regional or local politics in social integration and the role of language in the construction of a Catalan identity.

If we look at the data for Catalonia we can see that the sex distribution for foreign regular workers for 1990 can be distinguished by a male predominance (72 per cent, compared with 65 per cent for the rest of the Spain). The results of the 1991 regularization reflect continuity in the 'masculinization' of the flows, but this is weaker in comparison with previous years: 32 per cent of the regularization requests of the whole country come from women (mostly from 'Third World' countries), whereas beforehand the total percentage of foreign women was 28 per cent (and 21 per cent when considering only 'Third World' countries). As mentioned above, the feminization process has been promoted by 'quota system policies', which specify sectors of activity less covered by Spanish nationals, specially the domestic service sector. This sector is the highest in terms of quota coverage (in 1993 it was 72 per cent against 2 per cent in agriculture, 20 per cent in personal services and 0 per cent in the building sector (Izquierdo 1996: 123)).

Aragón and Chozas (1993: 104) show how the proportion of women migrants in Spain is similar to other EU countries (France, Denmark and Belgium) and a high concentration of migrant women in the domestic sector (89 per cent of Philippine women, 90 per cent from the Dominican Republic, and 83 per cent from Cape Verde). In contrast, in agriculture and the construction services there is a higher

Table 8.1: Work permits for foreigners in Spain (1988–1993)

	1988	1989	1990	1991	1992	1993
Men	27,978	30,453	33,389	94,661	68,207	66,778
Women	17,561	17,490	17,821	31,439	26,748	25,958

Source: Dirección General de Migraciones 1994: 111.

representation of men: Algeria (99 per cent), the Gambia (98 per cent), Morocco (83 per cent), and Senegal (86 per cent). The 1991 regularization process uncovered the strong presence of women coming from 'Third World' countries, contrary to the common view among researchers that 'foreign women' meant only 'First World women'. The growth of the domestic service sector (60 per cent of the regularized women, Izquierdo 1996) is related to the increasing incorporation of Spanish women in the labour force, as already mentioned. The majority of permits given to women on 31 December 1993 were to those from central and south America (Dominican, Peruvian, Colombian and Chilean) with a smaller representation to those from Asia (Filipinos and Chinese). However, many of the permit renewals were not successful, which meant that many would become irregular again.

In the Spanish data on immigration for 1997 (31 December 1997), women represented 44 per cent of migrants in the country and 35 per cent of workers with work permit. Meanwhile 69 per cent of African people are men (the majority from Cape Verde and Equatorial Guinea are women) and 64 per cent of those from Latin America are women. The important presence of Moroccans, Chinese and Peruvians can be seen for both sexes. Meanwhile Dominican women and Filipinas have a more important presence than men do: 63 percent of Latin-American work permits belong to women. It is necessary to underline the high activity rate of women from the Dominican Republic (11,142 residents with 10,345 work permits), Peru (11,342 residence permits and 9,639 work permits) and the Philippines (6,126 residents and 5,402 work permits). However, although the presence of Moroccan women in the total migrant population is high, their activity rate is lower (30,564 resident women, of which 11,414 have work permits – see also Table 8.1) (Figures on regular migrants, August 1998, Observatorio Permanente de la Inmigración, Ministerio de Trabajo y Asuntos Sociales).

Any explanation of the feminization of migrant labour needs to consider the situation of women in the sending countries (female proletarization), the situation of women in Spanish society (who are now less represented in agriculture and in the domestic service) and the different situation of migrant women according to social variables such as class and ethnic origin. Regarding the role of changes in the countries of origin, we can talk about three different important contributions:[5] Ramírez examines the case of Moroccan women in Spain. She points out that female Moroccan migration to Spain is different from previous migrations to other European destinations. Gregorio examines female migration from the Dominican Republic to Spain, discussing the factors that structure female migration as a consequence of the strategies of 'domestic transnational groups', changes in the sexual division of work, and changes in power and authority relations between men and women. Kaplan gives a central role to changes within communities from western Africa (Gambia, Guinea-Bissau and Senegal) in terms of cultural and social transformation or reproductive organization; establishing new gender relations not only in the receiving countries but also in the sending countries.

My own research attempts to look at the context of female migration in sending countries. According to the 1991 regularization results, the groups from the 'Third World' selected in my research represent the group of the 'new migrations' (with the exception of some Latin-American countries) in Catalonia.[6] I have distinguished the following types: Filipino (highly feminized), Moroccan (mainly male, but 'in transition'), and Gambian (mainly male).

A Sketch of the Past of the Migratory Cycle: the Countries of Origin

As mentioned earlier on, I will consider three countries of origin: the Philippines, the Gambia and Morocco. Important aspects of the country of origin for the sociology of migration are social class and gender divisions. Heterogeneity can be understood in terms of three elements of discontinuity or dissimilarity of the target population: relating to the country of origin (through a study of origin and destination), the social class to which one belongs (different socio-economic reality and a different positioning in the labour market) and gender. The analysis of social heterogeneity in the social integration of migrants results from a qualitative study within the countries of origin (the Philippines 1992, the Gambia 1993 and Morocco 1994), and of destination (Catalonia, in Spain).

Qualitative analysis in the countries of origin was chosen in order to discover structures and processes that can help us to understand migratory trajectories. My interest in the countries of origin emerged from a general investigation on migrant women in Catalonia (see Solé 1994) which stressed the peculiarities of the new migration profile in the 1990s. It was hoped that through in-depth interviews new knowledge concerning various female strategies from different countries of origin would emerge, as well as indicating the growing significance of urban women involved in an 'autonomous project' (in opposition to the family reunion one). Other facets of investigation were the linguistic and ethnic differences between groups, the disparity in education levels (especially among Moroccans) and the attraction of a segmented labour market (concentrated in domestic work).

The Significance of the Country of Origin

There are a number of reasons why studying the sending countries is important. Firstly looking at the emigration policy of these countries is crucial for understanding the international migration scenario. The nation state has established itself as a mediator in the relations between capital and the migrant labour force. What started as a temporary measure in the Philippines and Morocco in the 1970s has become a specific feature of the socio-economic system. In the case of the Philippines international migration through recruitment agencies was an attempt to stabilize the balance of payments, in this sense, we are encountered with criticisms related to the government's use of short-term measures. These measures arise from old colonial relationships; the colonial role of the recruitment of cheap labour through the 'hacendero system' is especially reproduced in the countryside (see Ribas 1994).

In addition there is a connection between development and migration in the Gambian case study. Various social disadvantages are intertwined: poverty, unemployment and social inequality. Understanding development involves analysing remittances from the receiving countries as well as the examination of the socio-economic achievements of returnees. The following aspects of the relation of development and migration have been seen:

(1) A review of the colonial past illuminates the process of development and modernization in countries of origin and destination. Furthermore, colonial history structures the patronizing attitudes towards the African continent and towards Africans.

(2) Gambia is an example of a society where there is cohabitation among members of different cultures. It is a small country in western Africa, with a unique jumble of cultures and history, which means working in a very diverse society comprised by many ethnic groups. Therefore, this context of diversity is significant when considering the limits of using the country of origin as a category for understanding social integration in the settlement countries.

(3) Development aims to improve women's status through education – formal, Koranic or informal. The role of peasant women is often emphasized, as 80 per cent of African women live in rural areas (Adepoju 1994: 17). In this context, it is important to note the

role of Serahule women, who are very active in the area of production, contrary to general belief in the receiving society. This helps to challenge stereotypes of migrant women.

The colonial inheritance of the nineteenth century explains part of the present migratory phenomenon. There are economic, political and cultural facets of this inheritance such as the impoverishment of the south, ecological degradation, political colonialism (in the case of the Gambia, based on the English model of democracy), and cultural colonialism (in the Gambia, English language and culture are an educational vehicle). These are all indirect causes of rural exodus from the inner lands and of emigration to other African countries and to Europe.

In the case of Morocco, colonial policies explain in part why migration changed from a provisional and short-term phenomenon to a durable and structural one, because it had been framed, from the very beginning, by the economic relations of colony and metropolis. However, migration cannot be conceived only as a phenomenon related to economic processes; a multidimensional perspective on migration is needed. For instance, household strategies have rarely been considered in understanding migration. As suggested above, to grasp the historical origin of Moroccan migration to Europe requires a review of colonial politics. In Morocco, one of the basic consequences of colonial politics, both French and Spanish (through the *Proctectorado*) was the settlement of a nomadic population, which affected traditional life and accelerated urbanization. One of the effects of this was the rise of Moroccan migration flows, in this first period, to Algeria.

Migration to international labour markets means a contribution to the income of families in the country of origin. Thanks to this income, the maintenance of traditional social and economic structures is possible. The spatial distribution of the city can be considered as a direct and indirect subproduct of migration to foreign countries (Fadloullah and Berrada 1990; Popp 1992; Berriane 1992; Hopfinger 1992). Furthermore, rural exodus is also a consequence of international migration. Migrants encourage their families to move to urban centres so as to be able to take advantage of a number of services offered by banks, schools and so forth.

To sum up, the significance of the country of origin uncovers two important issues: the importance of connecting migration issues with development issues and the legacy of the colonial context.

Filipino, Gambian and Moroccan Migration:[7] Beyond the Push-pull Scheme

In this section I will look in turn at Filipino, Gambian and Moroccan migration. Migration from the Philippines to Europe is characterized by female migration and family reunion encouraged by women. At the time of the research, Philippine immigration was the most feminized non-European flow in Spain, followed by immigration from the Dominican Republic. When a female migrant is able to save sufficient money and has enough information about the administrative procedures relating to family reunion, she attracts the rest of her family, establishing a Philippine settlement on the basis of extended family groupings. Most of my interviewees wanted to migrate so as to be together with their family and so used family reunion mechanisms in Spain. The period of the field study (1992) in the Philippines coincided with a period in Spain, which was open to family reunion.

The family chain offers the context of support for the individual in an unknown place, and the house of the employer comes to symbolize the security offered by its living quarters. It should be stressed that family reunion is not limited to one country. The family may be dispersed in different countries, in small divided family groups. Apart from Catalonia and other zones of Spain, most of the interviewees had family in other countries: the US, Canada, Hong Kong, Saudi Arabia and some European countries. However, it is interesting to see how men are over-represented in Filipino migration to other countries in contrast to Italy and Spain. It is the demand for live-in maids, as well as the quota system from the Spanish government, which determine this feminized flow from Asian and Latin-American countries. Filipinas together with Latin-American women represent the highest feminized flows. The most feminized flows in Spain are from the Dominican Republic (80 per cent), Colombia (72 per cent), Ecuador and Brazil (69 per cent), Equatorial Guinea (66 per cent), Philippines and Peru (65 per cent) and Cape Verde (60 per cent) (Colectivo Ioé 1998, using 1997 data of regular residents from the Comisaría General de Extranjería 1998).

With respect to the Gambia we can speak about a male 'cyclic' migratory model, typical of Gambian emigration of the 1980s. However, another type of woman, who comes on her own, with knowledge of English and with formal education is also recently found. This type of migration is similar to Moroccan migration during the 1960s and 1970s and is characterized by a cyclic model of new return migrations of the 'young and strong' man of the family. The cycle is shared by different men of the family, depending on the needs of the *compound* (units of shared living quarters). In the rural zones of the Gambia the *state bengo* is the main decision-making space of the village, whereas migration decision-making takes place in the compound and in the extended family. Consequently, the elderly person of the compound is an important political decision maker where international migration is concerned. In Gambian society, welfare needs are met through the extended family structure. Family, and especially women, are the caretakers of society.

According to Webb (1989), economic factors are the principal motivation for migration for all social groups of the Gambia. This motivation is channelled in two ways: temporary internal migration (in which young people have a decisive influence) and migration abroad. Since this second choice is an important project, the heads of the compound need to support it. It is up to them to hold the decision-making power and it is also them who stress the need for economic improvement.

For the average Gambian family, cash is not the major indicator of wealth or poverty. Nutritional security, land and livestock, credit, technology, education and integration into the family system, are perceived as more important than income and consumption levels (Government of the Gambia 1994: 9). Women and children are the most vulnerable social actors in terms of access to resources and services. In the Gambia, the risk groups include women from rural areas and unemployed women of urban zones. These women have less chance of being candidates for international emigration, as opposed to the 'educated' migrant man.[8]

The Moroccan type of migration, on the other hand, may be defined as a transitional type and is no longer exclusively male. The present profile of the Moroccan emigrant abroad is young (the majority between 20 to 29 years of age), single (66.5 per cent), economically active (66.3 per cent are economically active, 11.9 per cent are unemployed), and relatively educated (45.3 per cent equal or superior level of second cycle of secondary education, 17.7 per cent are without schooling) (GERA 1992). Individual reasons for migration are complex and not only economic (GERA 1992: 5–6). Nevertheless, Moroccan migration to Spain was initiated much later and under different circumstances (such as socio-economic conditions of departure, and a higher presence of female migration) from the rest of northern Europe. However Morocco now tends to share trends with the traditional immigration countries: family reunion, feminization of flows and unemployment.

There is a feminization of Moroccan migration in Spain: 10.7 per cent of women coming from the Rif, 45.3 per cent from Jebala and 24 per cent from the Garb/Atlantic area (López 1992). With the increase in Moroccan migration to Spain, behaviour patterns tend to become increasingly similar among the different regions; including the feminization of flows. With regard to female migration, there are important differences according to social class. In Catalonia, most migrants are low-skilled workers, who are more culturally rooted in a 'traditional' model of femininity.

Female Moroccan migration differs in terms of the nature of the decision making: depending on whether decisions were 'autonomous' or 'dependent'. I have found five different types of female migration: (1) voluntary autonomous migration (for education/better work); (2) forced autonomous migration related to poverty; (3) forced autonomous migration (resulting from changes in agriculture, and lack of male descendants to migrate); (4) female migration due to male migration (as a function of the migratory chain headed by the husband): 'Because in the country women dream of living in a city, but especially in Europe, with their husbands' (interview in the Rif, Morocco), and (5) migration due to the abandonment of the rural zones: 'The Rif is extremely abandoned. We are isolated in all aspects' (Moroccan women in Alhucemas, Morocco).

On the other hand, the Moroccan women interviewed in Catalonia (see Solé 1994) were from the following backgrounds: (1) from a rural background or from a group of 'neo-urbans', who had migrated through a family reunion process; (2) a low-skilled working class background who migrated because of divorce/repudiation and low economic status; (3) women with secondary or university education involved in autonomous emigration, because they could not obtain a job in accordance with their qualifications. It is possible to suggest that women from rural contexts are generally illiterate and gain access to migration through a family reunion process. On the other hand, in the urban contexts two poles of migrants can be distinguished: university educated women (completed or uncompleted) who were outside the labour market, and illiterate or poorly educated women belonging to the urban working class. The criterion of education is significant for both rural and urban groups when opting for an autonomous migration project. It is important to elicit whether female migration is dependent or autonomous as this is significant in the migratory process and in social integration in the destination countries. Autonomous migration is a relatively new phenomenon and it challenges the stereotype of the Moroccan woman in the receiving society.

Returning to the first research on migrant women in Catalonia (Solé 1994), and analysing the interviews of Moroccan women, a number of points can be made in order to understand research done in Morocco and in Catalonia:

(1) Women born before 1950, who work in Morocco, migrate almost exclusively because of lack of resources, in general terms, a synonym for the absence of husband. Among the migrant working class there is a constant correspondence between two occupations: the husband occupied in the construction sector and the woman as a domestic worker (whether by part-time or full time frequently depends on the number and ages of their children).

(2) Women within the family contribute towards the education of younger brothers and sisters. One of my interviewees tells how sisters who have migrated contribute towards the interviewee's university studies with their financial support. In practical terms, whether or not this sacrifice for education will be of benefit is uncertain if one takes into account the devaluation of studies during migration (for example difficulties with the recognition of qualifications).

(3) Where there is a mix of social classes within one extended family, those from the lower-middle class stay in the country and those from the working class migrate.

(4) A more acute reduction in social status will be experienced by women migrants than by men. As far as students and 'housewives' are concerned, both tend to become domestic helpers. One of the hurdles faced in Spain, is the difficulty women have in getting jobs according to their qualifications. In general the only way to escape from this fate is to work as mediators within their own migrant community.

More and more importance is given in migration studies to the construction of migratory networks, previously ignored because of a dominant macro-social focus. Networks allow an alternative migratory structure to those created by governments, and are a source of information, lodging, and money transfers and ethnic enclave formation. They are also the origin of spatial concentration according to ethnic difference as in the case of the people from Nador in Catalonia. Apart from migratory networks in choosing the country of destination, some of the interviewees also mentioned the weight of the colonial legacy and their connections with Spaniards. However, economic factors are usually the main reason given.

Socio-economic Situation, Social Class and Country of Origin

The socio-economic situation of the various countries of origin has been a fundamental spur to migration. However, socio-economic factors do not influence all women in the same way. Socio-economic pressures range from extreme cases of poverty to the search for a general improvement in working conditions. In the interviews carried out in Morocco, for example, multiple reasons were given for migration including the search for a new job, the bad situation of women in the labour market, feeding and education of children, improved lifestyle, consumption as a form of prestige, escaping from a rural environment, eluding social control, and a wish for freedom.

The Filipino case

Migration from the Philippines shows the importance of the *balahan* attitude (there is always hope) even in the worst situations, 'in the foreign country God will take care of my situation'. The migratory tradition of the country and the penetration of migration into all aspects of society (from government to all types of employment agencies, travel agencies, banks, business administrators, and so forth) has produced the so-called 'migration mentality' in the population. Despite the fact that the majority of female migrants are single, I have chosen to examine the migratory strategies of the married Filipina with children because it is in this context that family migration issue can be better understood.

Migratory strategies are usually similar for all women, as far as they involve a family-related goal: from the role of the eldest daughter as a family support as well as other forms of support within the extended family. The 'immediate' economic reasons for the interviewees in the Philippines were the following: nutrition and education of the children in the family and survival. Secondary reasons include possibility of a higher standard of living and the eagerness to travel. In a society without a welfare state, the woman is frequently the person responsible for carrying out the migratory project. She has to support the family, make economic pressures more bearable and shape a better economic future, either in or away from the Philippines. However, children are the most important consideration for the women. The role of the mother and maternal sacrifice is the motor of migration. Nevertheless, other objectives are also present, such as helping other members of the family, or migration as an 'autonomous act'. In general, the migratory project has three aspects. On a short term basis, survival – the feeding of the family – is important, 'We are supposed, Filipino women, to stay at home, but we have to go abroad because of good income, because of no employment, because of the children' (a Filipina in Manila). On a medium-term basis, children's education and on a long-term basis, improving social status and social position are important. The long term objective is understood through a conception of the future, a future of family stability, achievable through sacrifice as a mother and through a work ethic based on savings for a future life (that of her children, her own life, and even including the rest of the extended family). There is a strong hope to return to the homeland. Generally speaking, the idea of return depends on the economic circumstances of the Philippines and on the obstacles for occupational mobility in the receiving labour markets.

For the Filipino 'blue collar' worker, the aspiration is to become a 'white collar' worker and to be able to allow himself/herself a 'Western white collar' lifestyle. As in many other 'Third World' countries the distance between the rich and the poor is translated into the different opportunities for being able to enjoy a Western lifestyle. For the poor, the dream can come true by migrating to a 'Western' country, where they know that wealth is distributed in a more homogeneous form. At the same time, an abysmal disparity is evident between Spain and the Philippines in terms of per capita income (see Ribas 1994). There is also a great disparity between consumption costs (for example, for fuel).

Depending on the socio-economic situation of the person who wishes to migrate, a number of possible destinations is open to him/her. From the perspective of a person who lives in the countryside, the cheapest would be to migrate to Manila (although it might not be as fruitful). The second place would be Hong Kong and Singapore, the third Saudi Arabia, the fourth place Europe, and the fifth north America. On many occasions selection of the country is made on the basis of the highest salaries. According to official data, Spain offers medium-range salaries, Canada very high ones and Singapore and Kuwait low ones, (POEA 1989). This will often neglect working conditions. This shows a low degree of consciousness regarding the crucial aspects of the migrant worker's life in the destination country (such as working hours and contact with the employers). According to the women interviewed, wages for domestic helpers in Catalonia would multiply the salary of a domestic helper in the Philippines by 23. This type of work is considered neither unworthy nor shameful. What is more, to work and live in the same place – the home of the employer – is seen as the safest type of work for a Filipino.

The woman, considered in the receiving society as a social integration agent, is seen in the country of origin as an agent of modernization and development. Labour market conditions and social and family organizations are important when analysing gender in these contexts. The low-income that women obtain from their businesses (*carinderia, sari-sari* – small shops, crafts, peddlers, and shops in local markets), together with the low wages and bad working conditions and the discrimination against Filipinas in the labour market, are some of the main obstacles to economic integration. In the city a climate of work dissatisfaction is an added pressure pushing people to migrate. 'Socio-economic frustration-emigration', in terms of high cost of goods and very low salaries, bad working conditions and the discrimination of women in the labour market is very common. The interviews show how it is usually women with more education and more social consciousness who refer to discrimination: 'in the bank they don't want you, if you are married, they want you single' (Interview in Pangasinan, the Philippines).

Female literacy rates are very high, as well as the number of women with university degrees. The Philippines counts for the highest educational levels in south-east Asia and shows even less contrast than Spain in the sex distribution of literacy rates (Ribas 1996).

Furthermore, the presence of women in both productive and reproductive tasks intensifies the pressures on women. Their answer to the crisis is expressed in the feminization of the rural exodus (as occurs with emigration flows to Catalonia) and in the feminization of labour migration to foreign countries.

During my fieldwork in the Philippines I was aware of a general view which perceived migration to be easier for women than for men. Reasons include the fact that the jobs on offer in foreign countries are mainly domestic help, which is typical women's work as well as suited to the qualities attributed to the Filipino woman. These included perseverance, courage, a work ethic (at the same time as they are also tagged as 'the ones who sacrifice themselves for the family'). Level of education is an important criterion for migrant selection by recruitment agencies. In my qualitative study Philippine women had a higher level of education than men did. The number of children may also have a positive effect; the more children, the bigger the needs, and this becomes 'another variable pressuring women to emigrate'.

The reason for migration is the difference in salaries and the fact that this sort of job in the immigration country is not perceived negatively. Moreover, domestic work does not imply a loss of status in the eyes of the women's own community for it is well looked upon (even when the women are overqualified for the job). However, it is not well considered if done in the Philippines. This is because the women who do domestic work in the Philippines, besides being poor, are not educated. Curiously enough, many of the women who migrate employ domestic workers in their Filipino homes, but not under the same work conditions as in foreign countries. As in the case of Morocco, most frequently these workers are family members; young girls who have to leave home due to poverty or else in order to be able to study in the town; most come from remote places.

One of the most alarming results of the fieldwork conducted in the Philippines has been that it verifies the sacrifice involved in long-term separation in order to achieve migration objectives: the migration of married women with young children and the separation of the couple, even for such long periods as ten or twelve years. The children who remain in the Philippines are often left in the care of the father, the grandparents or other members of the family while the woman works in Catalonia. It is understood that the separation of the couple due to migration is part of a couple's commitment to a family project. On the other hand, there are cases that suggest a non-official separation of the couple, taking into account that in the Philippines there is no divorce. In many cases, the married woman lives in Catalonia and has small children in the Philippines.

The Gambian Case

The causes for Gambian migration coincide with the main objectives of social integration in the receiving country, generally referred to as socio-economic factors (for example the agricultural crisis and its impact on women, fast urbanization processes) and socio-cultural ones (women's education and their representativeness in the informal sector of the economy). The causes of migration (socio-economic) are also the reasons why a return is not opted for: the low salaries in Europe (which do not encourage savings), the difficulty of returning money that was lent to them and the level of satisfaction with social services in Catalonia (especially education and health) in contrast with the Gambia. A few distinctions have to be made in order to take into account conditions of departure for Gambian women (rural-urban context, ethnic group etc.) First of all, in the Gambia the gender system is particularly shown through changes in the extended family, which vary according to the diverse ethnic groups. Secondly, women in agriculture have to put up with the persistence of family values and with the severe economic crisis which heavily affects their everyday life, making them much more invisible in international migration, because they seem to opt for family reunion models. Thirdly, in the city, even though women live with grave difficult conditions in the informal labour market are more prone to autonomous migration projects.

The Case of Morocco

Regional inequalities and urban and rural contrasts shape a complex socio-economic picture. In Morocco, the socio-economic context includes a politically and socially oppressive life (lack of freedom and human rights, political discontent). The interviews also point out to other factors, such as escaping from social control, the need for change and the lack of opportunities in northern Morocco. There is however, also an entirely imaginary perception of the receiving place, Catalonia, as an industrial zone, a good climate and a Mediterranean environment.

In northern Morocco in the public sphere the rural souk, through migration, has seen a deruralization of goods as urban products increase and the exchange of traditional commerce decrease. The increasing value given to consumer products also justifies incorporating women in the labour market as they can contribute to the family income. In the rural Rif in particular, migration can be understood as a result of: Firstly, the devaluation of life in the countryside. Secondly, the over-valuation of urban life (Europe being the maximum exponent). Thirdly, expectations for family reunion in Spain.

In Morocco, schooling, fast urbanization, the women's increasing involvement in industry and the third sector – the decline in age of marriage, and the development programmes aimed at women, are all factors that have propelled demographic change. Development during the 1980s was focused on the rural zones. According to the 1982 Census data: 78 per cent of women were illiterate, 95 per cent in the rural areas. There was also a weakening of family solidarity: an increase in the number of unmarried mothers, of mothers who were heads of the household, of women who work in the informal economy as domestic helpers and in the carpets handicraft. The breakup of tradi-tional forms of production structures and the change in the agricultural sector opened doors to the female labour force. As in many other countries, girls and women abandon the countryside in order to work in the homes of urban families. They would principally opt for a job in a factory or an office, but unfortunately they often have no experience on the one hand, or preparation, on the other. For this reason, becoming a domestic helper was the only choice for this type of woman. In Morocco, we have a tendency towards female proletarianization. Nevertheless, given the limited access to higher education for girls there is an overwhelming high male presence in most qualified jobs.

Marriage instability is more acute amongst the proletariat and the sub-proletariat. The woman with poor economic means is the one who is obliged to work. The absence of the man is precisely the cause of her poverty (the more we descend socially, the more we find that the head of the household is a woman). Proletarian and divorced women (and also widows) are important actresses in autonomous migration.

During the interviews carried out in the zones of Temsaman (Rif) and in the zone of Driuch (also in the Rif), various push factors related to illiteracy were observed as well as the lack of social services and the use of traditional structures of solidarity. Women, who desire to leave the country, do it as a search for social rights and services, pursuing the benefits of the welfare state. This idea is mediated by an idealized perception of social benefits in Europe: 'Over there everything is easy'. 'Now everybody goes to school and people now have the right to live as Europeans'. All interviewees compared salaries in different countries (Germany, the Netherlands, Spain).

Social class is the principal determinant in the decision making of the migratory process. A good example of this is the role played by internal migration in the construction of social structure. The city, a space of power, represents a dichotomy in Moroccan society, the differences between Arabs and Berbers, between urban and peasant people. These differences result from unequal development in the different zones and regions. Inequalities have moulded urban, rural and tribal stereotypes. The potential working class migrant comes from the sector of the population that has experienced internal migration processes most intensely. The study of this sector of the population is crucial, because it forms part (using Martin's 1994 terminology) of the sector excluded from modernization, in opposition to the elite and middle classes as sectors that were beneficiaries of modernization. The gains or losses of modernization are inseparable from the social processes relating to gender, in relation to Islamism (as a contesting force to confront exclusion), and in relation to international migration. In this context, the beneficiaries of civil society are the modern sector generated by the city and the sectors that have been able to benefit from state feminism (Martin 1994). Participation in social movements is also linked to the benefits of modernization: human rights associations, women's groups, etc.

Settling in Spain

One of the main changes related to the settlement of migrant women is the form of labour and class insertion. According to Colectivo Ioé (1998) we can distinguish five different changes in Spain related to female migration:

(1) The perpetuation of the live-in domestic helper. This relates to migrants who have a stable legal position (work permit for five years), have been living in Spain for a few years but they have always kept the same jobs even if they change employer. Family remittances and the difficulties of the Spanish labour market explain this stagnation. Generally speaking, married women are the ones who change most from live-in to live-out domestic help, but sometimes the only opportunities available for the husband involve being employed as a domestic helper (combining the tasks as chauffeur or as gardener).

(2) The change from live-in to live-out domestic helper. In the case of married women, remittances diminish and they usually look for more flexible work times when they have children.

(3) Openings to other activities. There are usually many obstacles to this; on the one hand due to the stereotype of migrant women in the receiving society, and on the other hand due to the restricted labour demand to domestic work. However, other typically feminized activities can be found, like hairdressing in the case of Dominican women or family businesses in the case of Moroccans.

(4) The second most typical activity apart from domestic help (but much less represented) is work in the hotel and catering industry. Most of the activities in this sector are related to cleaning and cooking rather than waitressing. Even though in principle this is a job with more in common with those jobs done by the indigenous population and gives more autonomy, working conditions here are also very precarious.

(5) From inactivity to 'help' in family businesses. This indicates the trajectory of the 'housewife' who enters in the labour market because of a rupture with the initial project of the patriarchal family. It results normally from the unemployment of the husband

or because of the need to increase family income. Women start working outside the home after they have had their children. In this case they follow a trajectory very similar too many Spanish women from the working class, who start live-out domestic help or who 'collaborate' in the family business.

Many women experience downward mobility, especially in the case of Filipinas and in the case of Moroccan women with university diplomas. For others who had similar jobs in their countries of origin their income is now much higher. There are some who have never worked outside the house (for example among Moroccan working class women from urban areas). For others who do not follow an 'autonomous project' the husband was always the first to migrate. This was typically the case until very recently with Moroccan migration to Spain, and it is still the dominant pattern of Gambian migration.

Conclusion

A broad analysis of the conditions of female migration from the Philippines, Gambia and Morocco to Spain has been given. Without doubt, a radical change has emerged in the 1990s related to globalization and to the 'flexibilization' of work in receiving and sending countries. In Spain, rapid deruralization and deindustralization processes as well as the revolution in family structures need to be mentioned as part of the background changes. Migrant women, as a form of labour supply, need to be seen in this context. At a regional level, the most notable conclusion is that gender changes in southern Europe and in south-east Asia (the Philippines), the Maghreb (Morocco) and western Africa (the Gambia) provide a framework for understanding the feminization of migration to Spain. In the last three regions, migration flows are the result of the impact of social change on women, as their entrance to Catalonia is the answer to the impact of social changes on Catalan middle-class women produced after Franco's dictatorship. In the introduction to this chapter some of the reasons for the feminization of flows from 'Third World' countries were raised. We can firstly point out international migration policies and their gender impact; secondly there is the labour supply in the receiving labour market and, thirdly, diverse factors related to the status of women in the countries of origin.

Much has already been said about the role of conditions in the receiving country in relation to migration policies. In the case of Spain, the feminization process is a clear result of the interaction of two factors: the job vacancies established and the quota system established. Gender discriminatory immigration policies correspond to emigration policies in the countries of origin, as in the case of the Philippines, where the government is a mediator for Filipino recruitment in migration.

This chapter has looked in detail at one side of the feminization process, that is to say at the conditions in the countries of origin for the understanding of international migration. A tentative conclusion arises from the changes in those countries related to the labour market and to the consequent changes in the family system. In the family sphere complex changes have to be taken into account, especially changes in generational and gender relations related to the nuclear and extended family structures.

Country patterns and women's migratory strategies have shown a great degree of diversity. For more qualified women, career reasons make them choose the step to the international labour market as a complex social mobility strategy. For poorly qualified women, reasons are mainly related to family position and poverty. In the Philippines, the historical links with Spain have to be connected with the socio-economic transformation of south-east Asia and its impact on gender relations. In Morocco, a transitional society is reflected in women's migration patterns. In the Gambia the traditional household strategies still relegate migration to a male and family-oriented strategy. However, diverse countries of origin, social classes and gender relations (in and out of families) shape multiple strategies, which are often very complex. One thing has become clear, and that is the 'multiple presence' of migrant women. They are asked to be present at the same time in different families and different markets, along with the cultural implications of this multiplicity of locations.

What exactly is the link between the issues related to the country of origin and the changes in the receiving country? In Spain, both the state (through immigration policies) and the market (through the women who employ domestic workers) look at international female migration as the solution to the demands in the reproduction sphere. They look for a way of coping with indigenous women's double presence: in the market and in the home. But, this double presence is also evident for migrant women who have to manage their lives between an internationalized market and a transnational household (in many cases female-headed). Therefore, gender analysis in migration becomes an important element for understanding the globalization process, where not only goods but also human labour are involved.

Within this process, there is an interaction between culture and gender differences. Examining women's strategies from the countries of origin can give us a better understanding of how to overcome cultural ethnocentrism, which defines them as passive. Nevertheless, future research will have to focus on other emerging issues such us the dynamics of new female flows from Cuba (which also shows the consolidation of the Latin-American presence in Spain) and the demand for care services within the family strategies of indigenous women. In particular, private services for the care of the elderly will have to be examined in order to see the potential resource represented by migrant women.

Acknowledgement

I would like to thank Floya Anthias and Gabriella Lazaridis for comments and for helping prepare the final draft of the paper.

Notes

1. However, not all workers were included under this 'gastarbeiter regime'. Many migrants who came from the former colonies of Great Britain, France and the Netherlands had the right to stay.

2. The ideas presented by Antonio Izquierdo and Laura Oso have been extracted from the following conference: Congreso sobre la Inmigración en España. Madrid 16–18 October 1997. Fundación Ortega y Gasset.

3. For practical reasons, I will focus especially on Catalonia. One of the characteristics of the Catalan immigration model in contrast with the rest of Spain is the higher presence of sub-Saharans and Maghrebians. Following the division of the four immigration types in Catalonia, established by GES (1995), we can distinguish the following immigration flows: Central Maghreb (Morocco, Algeria and Tunisia), Western Africa (Cameroon, Nigeria, the Gambia), the Philippines, and South America (Venezuela, Chile and Argentina). If we take the percentage of foreign residents in Catalonia between 1979 and 1990 from the data elaborated by the Colectivo Ioé (1992: 47–49), we can identify the three nationalities with a higher increase as: Moroccan, The Philippines, Uruguay, and in the case of the Gambia – which did not have data for the first year, represented in 1990 2.5 per cent of the total foreign residents in Catalonia. Analysing the 1991 regularization data two peculiarities can be underlined for our research: a very important growth in the number of Moroccans (multiplied by five, representing a quarter of the total foreign population in Catalonia)

and a doubling of the total number of people from the Gambia, the Philippines, Peru and Argentina.

4. In 1986, 1991, and 1996, plus small regularizations through the quota system in 1994, 1995 and 1997. In the quota system for 1993, foreigner residents in Spain could not apply.

5. The ideas presented are a result of a Summer School. (Curso Intensivo Erasmus, 22–25 September 1997. Facultad de Ciencias de la Educación, Universidad de Granada). Here I have used some of the ideas discussed by Yolanda Herranz, Colectivo Ioé, Dolores Juliano, Carmen Gregorio, Adriana Kaplan and Ángeles Ramírez.

6. Analysing data given by Colectivo Ioé (1992, 1995) and GES (1995).

7. The results presented here relate to the following research: The Philippines 1992 with 32 interviews, Morocco in 1993 with 22 interviews, The Gambia in 1994 with participant observation. The interviews were selected through contacts with migrant families in Catalonia, considering the main areas of origin. Interviews took about one-and-a-half hours each and were conducted in different languages, sometimes using local translators. In the Gambia, the research was not carried out through interviews, as I had no access to interviewees. Instead I used participant observation with different families in an urban and rural setting. The fieldwork was mainly centred in three zones as follows. In the Philippines: the island of Luzon; in Morocco: the North, and the Spanish ex-protectorate; and in the Gambia: mainly the Upper River Division. As we will see, the interviews illustrate different realities, different habitats, different social classes and different migratory strategies (within a family, outside the family, alone but for the family, alone but for a career, and so forth).

8. The vulnerability of women, is subject to:

(1) the economic and social crisis (here I also include ecological effects, rapid population increase, high child mortality rate, and so forth)

(2) negative changes provoked by the modernization process such as tourism, migration and urbanization generally reverberate negatively on the woman's status. Within these negative changes, we should list: women's limitations in the formal sector and (contrasted with women's representativeness in the informal sector) the effects on women of the shift to commercialized agriculture products. Having less access to consumption than men, and having less purchasing power implies a weaker position in carrying out the migratory project. Some of the causes for this inequality are lower educational levels than men, lack of property, lack of access to credit and traditional perceptions about the role of women.

References

Adepoju, A. (1994), 'The demographic profile: Sustained high mortality, fertility and migration for employment' in A. Adepoju (ed.) *Gender, Work and Population in Sub-Saharan Africa*, London: ILO.

Aragón Bombín, R. and Chozas, J. (1993), *La regulación de los inmigrantes durante 1991–1992*. Madrid: Ministerio de Trabajo y Seguridad Social.

Berriane, M. (1992), 'Projet de recherche sur la migration internationale du travail et la croissance urbaine (Gran Nador)', in *Cahiers du C.E.M.M.M.* No. 1.

Castles, S. (1984), *Here for Good. Western Europe's New Ethnic Minorities*. London: Pluto Press.

Colectivo, Ioé (1992), *La immigració estrangera a Catalunya*. Barcelona: ICEM.

Colectivo, Ioé (1995), *Marroquíes en Cataluña*. Madrid: Fundamentos.

Colectivo, Ioé (1998), 'Mujeres migrantes en España. Proyectos migratorios y trayectorías de género', in *Ofrim* December, pp. 12–34.

Dirección General de Migraciones (1994), *Anuario de Migraciones 1994*. Madrid: Ministerio de Asuntos Sociales.

Fadloullah, A. and Berrada, A. (1990), 'L´émigration internationale et l'utilisation de l'espace a Nador'. Ford Foundation. July, (mimeo).

G.E.R.A (Groupe d´Etudes et de Recherches Appliquées. Faculté des Lettres et des Sciences Humaines) (1992), *Etude des mouvements migratoires du Maroc vers la Communauté Européene*. Commission des Communautés Européenes, (January).

GES (Gabinet d´Estudis Socials (Aiguabella, Beney, Estivill and Martínez)) (1995), *Els treballadors immigrants estrangers a Catalunya. Perspectives Laborals*. Barcelona: Generalitat de Catalunya. Departament de Política Territorial i Obres Públiques. Acció General de Planificació i Acció territorial.

Government of the Gambia (1994), 'Strategy for Poverty Alleviation'. *The Gambia. Round Table Conference*. Banjul: Government of the Gambia, Banjul.

Hopfinger, H. (1992), 'The impact on migration on urban development. First results of an exploratory project in Nador Province', *Cahiers du C.E.M.M.M.* No. 1.

Izquierdo Escribano, A. (1996), *La inmigración inesperada*. Madrid: Trotta.

Izquierdo Escribano, A. (1997), Congreso sobre la inmigración en España. Madrid 16–18 October 1997. Fundación Ortega y Gasset.

Kaplan, A. (1997), Comments made during the Curso Intensivo Eramus, 22–25 September Facultad de Ciencias de la Educatión, Universidad de Granada.

King, R. and Black, R. (eds) (1997), *Southern Europe and the New Immigrations*. Brighton: Sussex Academic Press.

López García, B. (1992), 'Las migraciones magrebíes y España', in *Alfoz* 91/92.

López García, B. (1993), 'La inmigración marroquí en España: la relación entre las geografias de origen y destino', in *Política y Sociedad* 12.

Martín Muñoz, Gema (1994), 'L´estat de dret i el paper dels ciutadans al Magreb' in *Europa davant la problemàtica jurídica del món islàmic* (course). Barcelona 21–24 November, UIMP. Institut Català d´Estudis Mediterranis.

POEA (Philippine Overseas Employment Administration) (1989), 'Matrix on entry regulations and market barrier in emerging labor markets', in *Overseas Employment Info Series* Vol. 2, No. 3, (December).

Popp, H. (1992) 'Les anciens émigrés marocains après leur retour dans la province de Nador: Présentation du programme de reccherche du groupe maroco-allemand sur la rémigraction'. Cahiers du C.E.M.M.M. 1.

Ramírez, Á. (1994), 'Conferencia sobre la mujer marroquí en España', in *La dona en el context de l´islam*. Girona: Universitat de Girona. Grup d´Estudis Euro-àrabs.

Ribas Mateos, N. (1994) 'Origen del proceso emigratorio de la mujer filipina a Cataluña', in *Revista Papers*, Vol. 43, pp. 101–14.

Ribas Mateos, N. (1996), 'La heterogeneidad de la integración social. Una aplicación a la inmigración extracomunitaria (Filipinas, Gambia, Marruecos) en Cataluña (1986–1996)'. Doctoral Thesis. Universitat Autònoma de Barcelona, Facultat de Ciències Polítiques i Sociologia.

Solé, C. (1994), *La Mujer Inmigrante*. Madrid: Publicaciones del Instituto de la Mujer No. 40. Ministerio de Asuntos Sociales.

Webb, P. (1989), 'Intrahousehold decision making and resources control: the effects of rice commercialisation in West Africa'. *Working Papers on Commercialization of Agriculture and Nutrition n. 3*. Washington DC: International Food Policy Research Institute.

The Position and Status of Migrant Women in Spain

ANGELES ESCRIVÁ

Introduction

Almost all existing literature on immigrants and migration flows from developing countries to Spain has been written during the 1990s. The unexpected and rapid increase in the numbers of newcomers during the late 1980s and early 1990s surprised social researchers as much as the general public. But while migrant men – especially of African origin – were visible within the Spanish landscape, women have remained invisible to the public and in the eyes of some social scientists dealing with migration issues. As usual, it has been women researchers who have been interested in revealing the female realities that remained hidden. The second half of the 1990s has been specially fruitful in producing contributions to the issue of gender and migration. Apart from my own research on Peruvian women in Barcelona, other research has or is currently being conducted on Moroccan, Dominican, Filipino women in Madrid and Barcelona, which are the main locations where migrant women are concentrated (Gregorio 1996; Herranz 1996; Ramirez 1997; Ribas 1996).[1]

These early contributions offer a very general view of the migrants' situation. The focus is placed on numbers and figures rather than on qualitative aspects. Some of the work mentioned above has analysed the experience of a specific migrant group, or compares it with other groups. Others have concentrated on the incorporation of women in the labour market of the receiving society. Very few scholars have looked at the sphere of social and family relations in the country of origin and destination. They stress the socio-economic discrimination migrants suffer due to being both women and migrants. In these studies, in parallel to men's work, the economic aspect of migration becomes a central issue. The difference between those writings focusing on men (the term 'migrant' usually implies men) and those focusing strictly on women, is that the latter focus on women's status. Indeed, the question of women migrants' status has preoccupied international researchers for a long time. In Spain this is a recent issue – as new as the immigration phenomenon of the last decade.

In what follows I will firstly describe policy and administrative measures adopted by the Spanish government to control non-EU immigration since 1986. These measures shape the composition and character of flows in terms of their feminization, country of origin, and labour orientation. Secondly, by concentrating on the position of migrant women we address one of the major questions about female mobility: do women benefit from it in terms of a rise or a maintenance of their social position? Examples will be given from research on migrant women in Spain, focusing on the experiences of Dominican, Moroccan, Peruvian, and Filipino women – which are the most important groups numerically.

Control, Composition, and Character of Flows

Immigration History

Southern Europe can now be recognized as an area that receives migrants after several decades of being a source of emigration to central and northern Europe. In fact, from the 1950s to the mid-1970s there was a negative migration balance in Spain, which became positive in the late 1970s. However, Spanish emigration to Europe and America was still, in the 1990s, numerically superior to the foreign population in Spain, as can be seen from Table 9.1.

Table 9.1: Emigration and immigration in Spain (1970, 1980, 1994)

Year	1970	1980	1994
Spanish population in Spain	33,823,000	37,616,000	39,200,000
Spanish population in Europe and America	2,232,570	1,769,483	1,167,461
Foreign population in Spain	147,700	181,000	484,342
	(0.4% total population)	(0.4% total population)	(1.2% total population)

Source: Manjón (1994).

This change in migration patterns is the result of, on the one hand, significant numbers of returnees, and on the other hand, international migrants, from other European countries and from Asia, Africa and Latin America. Factors influencing the shift from a country of emigration to a country of immigration include the following:

(a) Political and socio-economic changes such as democratization and the economic growth of Spain, making certain work activities and conditions less attractive to nationals.

(b) Free entrance of foreigners as tourists until the early 1990s[2] – poor implementation of the 'foreigner's law' of 1985.[3]

(c) Closure of neighbouring European countries' borders to third country migrants.

(d) Since 1993 the introduction of a quota system for domestic and agricultural services.[4]

(e) Opening and promotion of Spain internationally in the fields of culture, information and economy: for example the Barcelona Olympic games and the Universal Exposition of Seville in 1992; the purchase of telephone and electrical companies amongst others in countries like Peru, Argentina and so on; and the building of many hotels and tourist sites in the Dominican Republic.

(f) Geographic proximity, especially with Morocco acting as a door to Europe for migrants from the rest of Africa.

(g) Colonial common history, cultural-linguistic links, especially with Latin America.

(h) Rise in emigration from sending areas, especially because of the acute political and economic crisis in parts of Latin America and Africa.[5]

Migration Policy

The economic and political integration of Spain into the European Community in 1986 played a major role in the process of regulation of foreign migration. On the one hand, it opened the doors to European goods, capital and people, while on the other hand, it closed them to non-European Union citizens. A 'foreigner's law' was adopted some months before integration. It gave the guideline for border control. The terms of this law were determined by what Borrás (1995) calls the cross-roads of Spanish policy on foreigners, namely: (1) its membership of the European Union; (2) its strong links with Latin America; (3) its geographical proximity to the African coast. Two further influences might be added: firstly, the low birth rate (in 1995 the lowest in the world at 1.2), and the high life expectancy (of about 78 years) that prevail in Spain (Hernández 1995),[6] and secondly the segmented and precarious labour market.

The granting of EC membership to Spain and to Portugal in 1986, represented the end of a long quest for recognition within the economic and political structure of a united Europe. Spain had made tenacious efforts to join the First World Western bloc, but previous efforts during Franco's regime had been unsuccessful, mainly due to the lack of democracy and protection of human rights. Yet many researchers comment that Spain's integration into the EC in fact coincided with increasing tendencies towards violation of the human rights of Spain's many foreign residents and of prospective migrants (Borrás 1995; Contreras 1994; Varios Autores 1994a). Since the 'foreigner's law' of 1985 was enacted a year later, foreign migrants have been required to obtain a residence and work permit in order to become legal citizens. To obtain these permits a formal work contract is necessary, and this is often impossible in a dual labour market society, in which migrants perform marginalized activities. Such regulations mean that migrants are forced to violate the law by using fraudulent contracts and other nominal papers. Other restrictive measures regarding immigration from non-EU countries include limiting one-year permits (types A and B)[7] to a particular activity and geographical area, and discretionary measures such as making the granting of a permit contingent upon the state of national labour demand, and family reunion dependent on the economic and social conditions of the petitioners.

Historical links with Latin America are reflected in the same 'foreigner's law'. Latin American as well as Filipino and Equatorial Guinean migrants receive: (1) preferential residence and work permits; (2) easier renewal of permits and the issuing of longer and more flexible permits; (3) no visa requirement to enter the country (with the exception of nationals of Cuba, the Dominican Republic and Peru); (4) a faster application procedure for the granting of Spanish nationality (Varios Autores 1994b) (see Table 9.2). Proximity to the African coast prevented Spain from making its immigration policy too open. Economic and demographic contrasts within the Mediterranean region, together with the conflict of ideologies of religion and culture, have given some researchers and many other European citizens the impression that migration from this area to its immediate northern neighbours will continue and even increase (Bodega 1995). Whether a myth or a reality, this helps explain why Moroccans do not enjoy the same preferential treatment as Latin Americans, despite sharing historical and colonial links with Spain.

Table 9.2: Listing of administrative preferential treatment measures till February 1996*

Non preferential treatment (all other non-EU foreigners)	Preferential treatment (Latin Americans, Filipinos and Equatorial Guineans)
• Visa requirement • No easier restrictions on work and residence permit • No easier restrictions on renewal of permit • A five-year permit after five renewals of one year • Request for Spanish nationality after 10 years of legal residence • Obligation to renounce previous nationality in favour of Spanish nationality when naturalizing	• No visa requirement (except for Dominicans, Cubans and Peruvians) • Easier work and residence permit • Easier renewal of permit • A five-year permit after two renewals of one year • Request for Spanish nationality after two years of legal residence • No obligation to renounce previous nationality in favour of Spanish nationality when naturalizing (with the exception of Mexicans and Brazilians)

Source: Based on Varios Autores (1994b).
*Since then there has been a slight change in immigration law although preferential treatment for these countries is still maintained.

The formulation of immigration policy in Spain has been influenced by national and European interests in terms of restriction rather than social integration. The fear of political leaders and the general populations of an 'avalanche from the Third World' has promoted defensive positions.[8] In this climate, social workers and other organizations attempt to influence and guide governmental procedures towards some positive initiatives. The extraordinary regularization process of 1991 was the result of such action. It was carried out after the publication of several reports by social scientists and Caritas on undocumented migrants and was an urgent administrative measure, introduced some years after the Spanish 'foreigner's law' of 1986. It tried to regularize as many undocumented migrants as possible but also appeared to have the effect of attracting new migrants into Spain.[9]

Statistical data from the Spanish Ministry of Labour and Social Security indicate that at the end of 1991 and the beginning of 1992 just over 100,000 non-EC workers obtained their first one-year work and residence permits through the regularization process. Permits were restricted to a specific occupation and geographical area. Moroccans received the vast majority of these permits (48,240), followed by three Latin American nationalities: Argentinians (7,405), Peruvians (5,664), and Dominicans (5,517). Men clearly outnumbered women among the Moroccans, but they were roughly equal to women among the Argentinians and Peruvians, and a clear minority among the Dominicans. Work activities were mostly located in the service sector. Agriculture and construction were in second and third position, but accounted for far fewer jobs for migrants. Geographically similar numbers of permits were granted in Madrid (35,267) and Catalonia (32,648), with Andalusia (11,033) and Valencia (7,471) appearing in third and fourth place respectively.

The regularization process was brought to an end in 1993, with many second permit renewals and fewer permits given for family reunions. Most difficulties were experienced by agricultural and construction workers, because of the obvious constraints in obtaining a contract when the work is seasonal and temporary, and because of a rapid decrease in construction sites after the boom preceding the events of 1992 – the Olympic games in Barcelona and the World Exposition in Seville. The central government decided it was time to introduce a quota system that granted a maximum of 20,000 new work permits to non-EU nationals a year. Applications were supposed to be presented at the Spanish embassies in the countries of origin but the 1993 and 1994 quotas were put to use regularizing migrants already working in Spain rather than newcomers. The majority of the work permits were granted, in descending order, to the nationals of the Dominican Republic, Peru, Morocco and the Philippines. Domestic service was by now the most significant sector of migrant employment.

The 1995 quota specified those activities in which migrants would be granted permission to work. These activities were limited to domestic service (Filipinos, Dominicans and Peruvians) and agriculture (Moroccans). But after some months of pressure from migrant associations and other non-governmental agencies, the obligation to present papers at the countries of origin was abolished. A change of government in March 1996, when the Democratic Socialists headed by González lost power to the right-wing Aznar, provided an opportunity for migrants and other social actors to question the future development of the policy. Firstly, a new regularisation process was launched for the current year (see Table 9.4). It included many restrictions, such as the requirement of living with a close relative in Spain or having had

Table 9.3: Number of work permits granted by the quota system to non-EU migrants

First four nationalities (1993–1997)

Countries of origin	1993	1994	1995	1997*
Dominican Rep.	1,412	2,838	2,494	1,368
Peru	1,220	3,798	2,373	2,041
Morocco	586	9,714	8,387	7,689
Philippines	378	1,009	1,263	725

Source: DGOM (1999).
*in 1997 other important nationalities are Ecuador, China and Colombia (in descending order).

Table 9.4: Chronology of administrative regulations regarding non EC foreigners in Spain

1984	Law on asylum and refugee status
1986	´Law on rights and liberties of foreigners in Spain´
1991	Launch of extraordinary regularisation process
1993	Implementation of quota system
1995	Changes in the legislation on asylum and refugee
1996	Changes in the legislation on non-EU foreigners in Spain Launch of second regularization process

Source: Based on Varios Autores (1994b).

a work and residence permit at an earlier stage and since becoming undocumented. This second extraordinary regularisation was rather unsuccessful: only 24,000 applications were approved, more than a half of which were residence permits for family members, compared with the over 100,000 approved in 1991. Second, starting from 1997 the quota was again implemented. Having been fixed at a low number, 15,000 permits, it was increased to over 24,000 authorisations at the end of 1997. In the same way the 1998 quota increased the number of authorisations to 28,000 (9,154 in agriculture and catering, 1,069 in construction, 16,836 in services, and 941 others). Finally, for 1999 30,000 authorisations were granted.

Asylum seekers are perceived as a pressing problem in many European countries. In order to avoid the possible future abuse of asylum and refugee applications by migrants, changes in regulations were introduced in 1995 to strengthen control mechanisms in the process-ing of applications and to speed up handling times (Borrás 1995). Common ways of entering the country are to overstay on a tourist or student visa or to enter illegally via common borders. More recently legal methods such as quotas for work – managed by friends or relatives from Spain – and residence permits via family reunion processes are used. For the undocumented, crossing the border may be very risky, as in the well-known case of Moroccans,[10] although it can be made easier by passing through other European neighbouring countries that do not demand a visa from particular groups of non-EU nationals, such as Latin Americans.

The Profile of Migrants

Non-EU migrants in Spain are composed to a large extent of Moroccans and Latin Americans, and to a lesser extent of other African and Asian nationals including Filipinos, Chinese, Senegalese-Gambians, Pakistanis. These populations are generally concentrated in specific geographical and occupational areas. For instance, Moroccans are concentrated along the Mediterranean fringe of the Iberian Peninsula, whereas Latin Americans are found only in a couple of cities, mainly Madrid and Barcelona. Recent migration flows to Spain are still predominantly male (see Table 9.5), although women count for an important percent-age in the big urban areas (53 per cent of all migrant workers in Madrid). This is not very different from the situation in the European cities of central, northern and western Europe, which have longer immigration histories. The particularity of the south (Spain, as well as Italy, Portugal or Greece) is that these women often report migrating 'independently', and not through the traditional family reunion process – where the man migrated before and later brought his wife and children to the host country. On the contrary, most recent female migration to southern Europe was started by women and followed by other women of the family or neighbourhood. Indeed, the solo migra-tion of women from Latin America or East Asia has been profusely reported in international literature. This solo migration is not the same as movements headed by African women which are also important (see Tables 9.5 and 9.6). Despite the widespread image of female subjugation, many women migrate alone, mainly for work purposes.

From Tables 9.5 and 9.6 we can see differences between women of Latin American, African and Asian origin. While Dominican females dominate their community composition, Peruvian women have been steadily increasing in proportion over the last five years. Moroccans

Table 9.5: Non-EU migrant workers in Spain (1997); first six nationalities per sex

Countries of origin	Total	Men	%	Women	%
Morocco	67,744	56,330	83	11,414	17
Peru	14,656	5,017	34	9,639	66
Dominican Republic	12,139	1,794	15	10,345	85
Philippines	8,183	2,781	34	5,402	66
China	9,075	6,199	68	2,876	32
Argentina	6,582	4,166	63	2,416	37
Total (all origins)	176,022	115,084	65	60,938	35

Source: Cie (1999).

Table 9.6: Percentage of female non-EU migrant workers in Spain (1992-7); first six nationalities

Countries of origin:	Year						
	1992	1993	1994	1995	1996	1997	97–92
Morocco	14.6	14.8	15.3	15.3	16.3	16.8	2.2
Peru	55	56.6	58	64	64.1	65.8	10.8
Dominican Republic	85	85.2	85.6	86	85.1	85.2	0.2
Philippine	66	65.2	65.3	66.1	65.4	66	0
China	25	25.6	28	28.2	30.6	31.7	6.7
Argentina	33	33	33.3	34.3	35.3	36.7	3.7

Source: Cie (1994–9).

are still relatively few but are also increasing while becoming in 1997 the largest group in terms of numbers of women before Dominicans and Peruvians. Also among Filipinos we find a majority of women and Chinese migrants are increasingly female.

We can differentiate among groups according to their labour incorporation. African, south- and west-Asian women are less economically active and usually married. Latin American and east Asians are more economically active and single (Solé 1994), except for the case of long-established Filipinos. But being single does not mean having fewer family responsibilities. The vast majority often send money home (to

Table 9.7: Percentage of non-EU migrant workers over residents; first six nationalities (1997)

Countries of origin	Residents	Workers	%
Morocco	100,876	67,744	67
Peru	18,285	14,656	80
Dominican Republic	14,385	12,139	84
Philippines	9,675	8,183	85
China	15,232	9,075	60
Argentina	9,897	6,582	66
Total (all origins)	277,255	176,022	63

Source: Cie (1999).

parents, brothers and sisters, children, even the partner). Table 9.7 shows the strong labour orientation of all six most representative nationalities of foreign residents in Spain.

Labour Market Incorporation

While men are employed in a range of activities like agriculture, construction or commerce, women are employed mainly in private houses, cooking, cleaning and/or caring for children, the sick and the elderly. They are rarely self-employed. Most have settled in the largest Spanish cities. Having no statistical information about the level of education of women, we may distinguish between those within higher education – Peruvians and Filipinos (Escrivá 1997; Ribas 1996) – and those who are less educated – such as Moroccans and Dominicans (Lora-Tamayo 1997). However, we may find women with different levels of education in each group.[11] Education also determines labour market incorporation. There is a substantial number of nurses and teachers among Peruvian and Filipino women. They frequently take jobs involving some caring beyond pure cleaning. As qualitative work shows (see above), similarity between Spain and the Peruvian and Dominican languages is also an advantage for labour market insertion and promotion to other working areas within the service sector, though it is not so much the case in Barcelona where the Catalan language is generally used.

Apart from those activities that have been rejected by the native population, the jobs taken by recent labour migrants are limited to insecure jobs (temporary contracts and seasonal or irregular work) and poor working conditions (including salaries below the legal minimum wage and dangerous work without appropriate security and health measures). There is often a difference between the experiences of documented and undocumented migrant workers in the labour market, the latter being those who do not hold a valid work permit. These workers are potentially subject to greater exploitation because of the lack of a contract (as a guarantee of fixed work hours and salary), lack of social security entitlement and lack of union protection. The ever-increasing number of undocumented migrants is related to the creation and perpetuation of a dual labour market, in which the native population and even some legal migrants are relatively advantaged compared to undocumented newcomers. Domestic workers, in addition, suffer isolation in the work place. Foreign women are found mainly as live-in servants, generally having no more than one-and-a-half days off a week.

Social Integration

Many migrants to Spain have settled in the large urban areas, which were also targets for internal migration between the 1950s and 1970s, rather than in the rural areas from which Spanish emigration took place. Moroccans engaged in agricultural labour are the only exception to this. The diversity of national identities in Spain reveals current international immigration flows to be continuations of the internal migrations of earlier decades, with similar social and cultural barriers to integration, as in the case for Catalonia.[12] There are two other factors that helped to create new and sustain old Spanish discriminatory attitudes and behaviour. The first is the continuation of high unemployment rates among the Spanish population, as shown by Table 9.8, which are especially acute in the case of women. Over the last few decades unemployment has become one of the major concerns of the country. The second is the persistence of racist images generated in Spain and reinforced by racist experiences of other neighbouring European countries. These images are very much linked to an historically rooted anti-Islamic discourse.[13] But there are also other racist discourses, for example those concerning Latin Americans, defined as inferiors by the colonial tradition which opposed native-born Spanish descends to overseas-born original Spanish (Juliano 1994). The racist colonial experience and the anti-Semitic and anti-gypsy campaigns of previous centuries, resurface from time to time and set the scene for current expressions of racism.[14]

Table 9.8: Spanish unemployment (1980, 1985, 1990, 1995) (in millions)

Year	1980	1985	1990	1995
Active	13	13.5	15	15.5
Unemployed	1.5	2.9	2.5	3.5
Females unemployment	12.2	24.8	24.2	30.3
Males unemployment	10.7	20.3	12.0	18.0

Source: Based on Borrás (1995).

The legal and political regulation of immigration together with its social response will affect the demographic evolution of migrant populations and the possibilities for social integration (as opposed to segmented assimilation). However, we need to observe how this operates differently according to sex: whether women enjoy less benefits from the migration than men or not, and how this has influenced their status. We will concentrate here on the last issue: the status of migrant women.

The Status of Migrant Women: Conceptual Issues

Feminist research has widely questioned the traditional treatment of women within social structure and stratification studies. Such studies have generally used a gender bias that marginalized women within the analyses. Much work on social mobility, class identity and action continues to treat married women's class position, as derived from their husbands (Crompton and Mann 1986, questioning Goldthorpe). Certainly, the gender dimensions of class have not been questioned until quite recently. The participation of women in the industrial labour market was seen as marginal, and their social position was seen to derive from gender rather than class. Against that conception, feminist approaches of the 1970s and 1980s, as that of Crompton, recovered the Weberian term of 'status' and gave to it a broader content than it had been given by previous authors.

According to this position, status includes an important gender dimension (Moore 1991). Sexes have been historically divided in two gender categories where being the male has a positive connotation and being the female implies subordination. So, traditionally attributed feminine cultural practices (such as ways of dressing and speaking) receive a low status. They are connected with the conceptual division of nature and culture, the latter being a male domain. This is reflected in the sexual typification of occupations: first, the division between the domestic (private) and the public spheres in an industrial society produces the view that domestic activities are not regarded as 'work'; second, even in the 'public' sphere the incorporation of women within paid work reflects subordination and marginalization and the performance of 'appropriate' female jobs with lower social recognition and rewards.

For international migrant women other aspects need to be added to gender and class in the configuration of their status: nationality and ethnicity. It has been argued (Anthias 1992) that migrant women experience discrimination in host societies in terms of the articulation of gender, class and ethnic relations. The ethnic dimension includes the phenotypic, cultural (religion, language, etc.) and national characteristics of identification. Gregorio (1995) presents a dual schema in which migrant women in receiving societies are inserted as one of the opposite pair in the four mentioned spheres:

	Migrant women	*Native men*
Nationality	foreigner	national
Ethnicity	not white	white
	foreign culture	national or official culture
Class	poor	rich
Gender	woman	man

Even in those cases where women may achieve legal status through naturalization, for example, and also adopt cultural elements of the host society, there may still be 'physical' and/or 'cultural' difference which does not allow migrant women to reach a better position in the occupational and social scale.[15] This relates to the intersection of racism and sexism. It is often the case that qualified migrant women are forced to take unskilled feminized jobs and are poorly paid. For feminist Marxist discourse, such women play the role of a sub-proletariat, which facilitates native women's participation in the 'male' labour market. This is the case for much of the theory on the dual labour market and the position of migrant workers within it. Other authors, like Portes and Böröcz (1996), attribute this downgrading to a disadvantaged context of reception, in which migrants, independently of their human capital and class background fall into lower social positions.

Connected with the study of status in host societies is the parallel consideration of migrant women in sending areas and within their own ethnic group and/or family in the country of destination. We should not forget that international migration today is very much a phenomenon of transnationalism. Migrants develop a continuous and fluid relationship between origin(s) and destination(s) through their periodic travelling and communicating. The migration process may change, therefore, the status of (migrant) women in both contexts, that of both the sending and receiving countries. To characterize and measure gender inequality, the main factors may include the following (Lim 1995):

(1) Economic indicators of status, that is, possession of and control over resources, including knowledge, time, money and material goods;
(2) Political indicators of status, such as the ability or power to make decisions: this includes the decision to migrate; to participate in the labour force; to control the distribution of income from work; the ability to exercise control over other people; and being the mobilising force behind the migration of family members;
(3) Social indicators of status include prestige, respect or esteem accorded to women (these indicators reflect differences in socio-cultural norms and attitudes between the country of origin and that of destination).

The above help us to analyse the roles and status of women as determinants and consequences of international migration. As INSTRAW (1994) suggests, the status condition is basic for understanding those processes, including sex-selectivity in the migratory decision within the family context.[16] In summary, Lim (1995) identifies the following issues of study around the status question:

(1) Implications of sex selectivity, that is, the distribution of migrants by sex, or by sex and other variables such as age, marital status or country of origin, for the political, economic and socio-cultural contexts in which the status of women is embedded.
(2) Influence of gender relations on the motives and potential for the international migration of women.
(3) Similarities or differences between the determinants of international migration for men and women and their causes.
(4) Extent to which and manner in which laws and regulations controlling international migration are not gender-neutral.
(5) Selective impact by sex of labour market dynamics in both countries of origin and destination.

(6) Relative importance of international migration *per se* as a mechanism generating or restructuring gender asymmetries given the change in social environment that migration usually entails.

(7) Relative vulnerability of migrant women, that is, whether being female and foreign in an alien environment leads to the 'double discrimination' and 'threefold or fourfold oppression' of migrant women.

Some examples of these will be given with regard to the Spanish context in the following section.

Gain or Loss of Position?

Existing literature on immigration in Spain has only recently concerned itself with the position of non-EU women. Ioé (1997) has dealt with it in a recent work (see Table 9.9), that summarizes factors contributing to the specific social trajectories of migrant women. This presents shaping factors in the country of origin, in relation to the migratory project, and in Spain, in terms of their sphere of influence, either social or individual. The only problem is that the category 'women status' is specified in the table as the only factor of influence in the country of origin, whereas we consider the status of women in a broader sense affecting not only origin but also the migratory project and destination – Spain in our case – as well as personal dimension of migration. This 'feminine' status, as discussed previously, is socially constructed – mainly in terms of a subordinated position in gender relations which intersects with other elements such as class and ethnicity – but is individually adopted.

In terms of determinants of migration there is a tendency to think that women involved in solo (autonomous) migration, which is a very common form in Spain, are more independent than non-migrant women. However, the decision to migrate can be determined partially by family and friends, and is therefore not a total free choice. Women's migration may be part of a family strategy to survive or to maintain and increase their social position and improve their living conditions. In this sense, the study by Ribas (1996) on Filipinas in Catalonia refers to a high level of education among Filipino migrant women – higher than that of men – as a sign of high status. Nevertheless, poor employment conditions in the Philippines affect their status as the family is not able to reach or to maintain a certain level of consumption. So, migration is a response to a number of factors:

Table 9.9: Shaping factors in the social trajectories of foreign women in Spain

	In the country of origin	Migratory project	In Spain
Social contexts	Socio-economic situation Women's status Image of other countries/cultures (Spain)	Background of internal and external migration Models and history of those migrations	Social and migratory policy Labour market structure Dominant ideologies and stereotypes with regard to social, cultural and ethnic differences
Subject position	Sex and age Education and labour qualification Group of coexistence and family role, etc.	Main reason for leaving Individual or family strategy Temporal horizon of the project	Informal networks of support Family roles Command of local language, incorporation into the educational system Connection with labour market Connection with social movements (eg anti-racist organizations)

Source: Ioé (1997).

(1) In the short term, the survival of the family.
(2) In the medium term, education of children, brothers and sisters.
(3) In the long term, the rise of status and social position. For the Filipino working class the aspiration is to become white-collar workers and achieve an 'occidental' way of life.

This pattern of behaviour is also to be found among women from the other three most numerous nationalities in Spain. Therefore, women tend to shift or postpone their own aspirations in favour of the other members of the family, or they are just limited within the family frame. Moreover, research shows that depending on the timing and circumstances of emigration (whether married or single, with or without children) we find differences in the migration project. The information collected from my own fieldwork study in Barcelona gives examples of this. There is linkage of female migration, not so much to expectations of climbing a career ladder, but to the career and survival of others: children, parents, brothers and sisters, even husband. This is a special characteristic of those married Peruvian women and/or women with children. In these cases, they might experience a loss of professional and social status.[17] This may not be seen as a central problem, since a first objective when migrating – as already mentioned – was related to the welfare of others. Nevertheless, even married women, with longer residence, begin questioning their actual situation and seek more autonomy and power:

> As women in Peru we are in the background without so much freedom as you have here in Spain. I alone had to confront my husband. Till now he does not accept it, I am fighting against that 'macho' mentality. They are used not to do anything at home, they say 'that's women's affair' but for earning a life we have both to work outside. So, women play both roles, outside and inside the house. They, on the contrary, only have to study and work. Moreover, if you get free as a woman you become a prostitute, if you go out to work, the same as here, in Peru I was told to be a whore. Here it is different, it is better for women (Doris, Peruvian, 42 years old, 5 years in Barcelona).

Apart from family circumstances at origin and at destination, the receiving society has a big impact on the way women insert in the labour market and the society. As women may be able to regularize their work in domestic service, they may achieve a higher legal status than male migrants, who usually lack stable jobs. Since the establishment of work quotas in 1993 (see Table 9.4) most permits have been granted in the domestic sector, where women are overrepresented. Furthermore, because those women tend to be migration pioneers, men are often protected and supported financially by their female relatives.

However, in terms of autonomy, authority and power in work and over resources, and therefore also in everyday life conditions, men experience less constraints and more freedom than women. This has been especially reported in the case of solo Dominican migrants in Madrid by Gregorio (1996). However, migration may give women more space for autonomy and control over personal and economic resources than before departure. Indeed, this is especially the case with solo migration, when numbers from a particular origin are small. Moreover, the ethnic group or community contributes to the control of women.

For this reason, many women may avoid contact with male members of their ethnic group, as reported in the case of Moroccan women in Madrid (Páez 1993).

As Ioé (1997) also remarks, domestic service (the most important activity among women) may offer greater stability to migrants in so far as they are registered in the National Health System by their employers. However, there is also the stigma and lack of social recognition that they suffer in domestic work,[18] as it is a sector without the same legal rights enjoyed by other workers (for example, there is no right to unemployment provisions), the quasi-servile relationship established sometimes with employers, or the social isolation from the long working hours, especially in the case of live-in maids. The same authors have suggested that migrant women have been able to partially fulfil the migratory project (working in Spain, sending remittances to the families, escaping unbearable situations in the country of origin, and so forth) but in the medium and long term what is perceived today as an opportunity may become a constraint.

I have suggested (Escrivá 1997) in relation to Peruvian migration that for women with a medium-high level of education there is a downward process of deskilling through the performance of 'manual tasks'. Required skills are related to social services such as caring and attending. Many women have a degree in teaching or nursing. Serving in private houses is seen as a demeaning activity, as in Peru this is poorly regarded and poorly paid (work for indigenous women migrating from rural areas). But over time it has become regarded more positively and even accepted as one of the best forms of employment, especially when the return myth[19] is sustained. That explains why some women prefer to stay for longer periods as live-in maids rather than live-out: the expenses are less and there is a guarantee of protection in the house.

In this regard, there are four types of occupational trajectory singled out in the literature following Ioé (1997) which take place in the first period of migration:

(1) Experiences of downward mobility: this has been described in the case of Filipinos and Peruvians (Ribas 1996; Escrivá 1997).
(2) Reproduction of occupational level with higher income: the case of some women who worked as domestic servants in the country of origin or in an intermediate country.[20]
(3) Relative promotion: from inactivity or occasional activity (in terms of formal labour market) to wage employment.[21]

(4) From studying to housework – change between different forms of economic 'inactivity'.[22]

As in the case of Peruvians, continuing to live in as maids is common among those who have not experienced a downward mobility and have not reunified their families. Live-out and per-hour cleaning jobs are the norm among those who have been in Barcelona for more than three to five years, who have experienced a relative downward mobility with migration and/or have brought their family members to Spain and wish to live with them. Other activities may be found more rarely, but especially among those who have formed close relations with Spanish people; these could save some money. Finally, catering is extremely rare among Peruvian women, with the exception of those working for a family business in a Peruvian restaurant.

Table 9.10 gives a comparative picture of how the most numerically prominent migrant nationalities in Madrid are doing in terms of occupational status sometime after arrival to Spain. Only in the case of Argentinians[23] do we find a similar occupational schema to that of EU foreigners in Madrid. All other nationalities are strongly represented in low-status jobs, the Filipinos and Dominicans being those who experience a greater decline in occupational status. Not surprisingly, comparing these data with Tables 9.5 and 9.6, there is a correlation between greater feminization of migrant groups and the achievement of lower working status. This assumption fits with the schema presented above in reference to the manifold discrimination against migrant women because of unequal gender, class and ethnic relations.

One controversial issue remains on the correlation between occupational status and gender. One opinion is expressed by Ramírez (1997), who argues that Moroccan women in Spain gain autonomy and power within the family because their new role generates resources in contrast with their very poor labour market position in their country of origin. More autonomy and power are signs of a better female position. However, there is not an absolute break with the traditional female roles assigned by the members of the country of origin. Gregorio (1996) on the other hand, in her analysis of Dominican migration to Madrid, describes three stages for women's migration, leading to a not-so-optimistic evaluation of the migratory experience:

(1) The flow of solo-women migrants has its origin in the reproduction of gender inequalities which characterise their society of origin.
(2) Once in Madrid they reproduce their gender roles.

Table 9.10: Occupational status of migrant workers in Marid (%)

Origin	High	Medium	Low
EU	48.7	27.3	24.0
Non-EU	10.3	8.7	81.0
Morocco	4.1	4.7	91.2
Dominican Rep.	2.3	1.2	96.6
Peru	8.1	7.8	84.2
Philippines	1.7	1.7	96.6
Argentina	47.6	19.8	32.7
China	2.6	8.6	88.9

Source: Ioé (1997).
High: managers, technicians and professionals.
Medium: office workers, traders, sellers.
Low: agriculture, services and industry/construction manual workers.

(3) Finally, not every change is experienced as positive. Their labour incorporation in Spain and the frame of social relations are denigrating from the women's view. The labour *niche* for them is the domestic service, whereas social relations with native Spainish people involve discrimination and rejection.

Replying to this, Gallardo (1995) argued that if the migratory experience was so disappointing for women, they would tend to return home more frequently than is the case for Dominican migrants. From my point of view, since the supposed rise in gender status is accompanied by a decline in the class-ethnic status at destination but not in the country of origin, migrant workers prefer to stay and work for better positioning in the labour market, for themselves and their relatives and second generation. This sustains the idea of migratory paradise for those remaining in the country of origin.

In summary, migration for women may involve a gain or a loss of status depending on a number of factors explored earlier. Migration can be understood as a gain in terms of gender because it allows women (especially solo migrants) to improve their role within the family and community through the prestige gained by moving to the First World and earning money and knowledge. They also become important to enable the migration of others. Against this, the opinion that emigrating women practice prostitution abroad is still maintained

in the country of origin and also at destination, not only for Dominicans, as has generally been believed, but also for others like Peruvians,
damaging the social position of female migrant workers. The gain is
also relatively diminished when we concentrate on the real power
and control over resources achieved by women. For example Amanda,
a 28-year-old Peruvian, who was working as a domestic servant in
Barcelona for two years returned to Peru in 1994 and gave all her
savings to her son's father in order to invest in a new business.
However, he spent all the money improperly and had relations with
other women while she was still there. So, she ended with no money
and no steady partner any more, since she was not willing to share
him with the others. Finally, she decided to go back to Spain for the
second time.

The loss of status is very much connected with the country of
destination, above all for those experiencing downward occupational
mobility and with very few opportunities for leaving domestic service.
The latter becomes a labour market *niche* for female migrants in Spain.
Labour marginality leads to social marginalization as foreigners remain
outside national culture and domains of authority and power. Finally,
migration is evaluated by women as positive due to a gain in welfare
provision, social organization and educational opportunities: 'I like
the order here, the cleanliness, the people who are polite, I like that very
much' (Violeta, Peruvian, 22 years old, less than a year in Barcelona).
'The buildings, streets, highways, the two-floor buses and the many
cars, that I find interesting, the technology moving forward so quickly,
and the people, their politeness' (Irene, Peruvian, 46 years old, two
years in Barcelona). 'I like the way of life here, it is more advanced in
computer engineering and all those things my boyfriend wants to
further study' (Dina, Peruvian, 27 years old, three years in Barcelona).

Conclusion

In this chapter it has been argued, firstly, that Spanish immigration
policies and administrative measures are shaping the composition and
character of non-EU flows in terms of sex and nationality and labour
orientation. Other aspects of the society of origin and that of destination should be added to the analysis in order to improve understanding
of processes such as the feminization of those movements and the
centrality of the domestic service market for migrant workers. Concentrating on migrant women, the chapter discussed the existing literature
and research about the position of these female workers from social
and occupational perspective. We started from a theoretical frame,

which explains discrimination against migrant workers in complex societies in terms of the articulation of gender, class and ethnic relations (Anthias 1992).

Existing literature and research about migration is Spain are still limited, but this chapter demonstrated the range of perspectives necessary for analysing the question of women's status. Depending on the aspect referred to and the place and time of analysis we may find a gain or a loss of position for migrant women. Another question is how women themselves experience these processes. In some extreme cases they may not be able to cope with this new situation and become mentally and physically sick. Returning home, however, may still be very difficult, as they may not have achieved the objectives assigned (by them or for them) prior to departure. A less extreme description of how migrant women react against their status devaluation is presented by Gregorio (1995)[24] from a psychological view. More generally, after a period of adaptation to the new requirements – as migrant, as woman, as worker, as belonging to an ethnic group and/or nationality – women tend to feel more adjusted to the new society.

The length of time needed to adjust to the new situation and what is lost and gained in the process is something missing from existing work, since non-EU female migration to Spain is quite new. Future research will have to deal with these questions if a better knowledge of the situation of migrant women (who make up a significant percentage of migrant workers in Spain) is to be achieved. Until now, most attention has been paid to the situation of workers, whereas female dependants such as spouses, mothers, female children and girls were missing, probably due to their low numbers.

Finally, an additional area for research to focus on must be a study of the implications of migrant women's status decline or rise within (and for) the ethnic migrant group, in the society of destination, and in the society of origin. For feminist and development research, this issue is of great importance. It has to be placed very much aside from controversies on cultural diversity, which may justify the maintenance of gender and ethnic inequalities. Human migrations have occurred throughout history, bringing into play new/modified roles for people.

Acknowledgements

I would like to thank Floya Anthias and Gabriella Lazaridis for extensive comments and editorial work.

Notes

1. The following books and reports have appeared during these years: Durisotti, Garciá and Obrador (1996), Gallardo (1995), Ioé (1991, 1996, 1997, 1998), Jiménez (1996), Oso (1998), Roquero and Rodriguez (1996), Sipi (1997), Solé (1994).

2. Until the 1990s most sending countries from which most migrants originated (Morocco, Peru, the Philippines and the Dominican Republic) had free access to Spain following the tradition of openness to visitors (tourists) that had characterized Spain since the 1960s.

3. This law, as will be explained later, restricts the entrance and rights of foreigners in the country, but in the second half of the 1980s was still poorly implemented, resulting in easy entry and making it easier to remain.

4. This quota has attracted new migrants to Spain. This point will be elaborated later on.

5. This last point is related to push factors of sending areas, in contrast with pull factors listed above.

6. According to Hernández (1995), by 2050 the greyest country in the world will be Spain, closely followed by Italy, with respectively 3.6 and 3.4 persons aged 60 or above for each person below 15 years of age (UN World population estimates and projections, 1998 revision).

7. Type A permits cover seasonal and limited activities for no longer than nine months and are not renewable. Type B are one-year permits covering certain activities and geographical areas.

8. This is shown, for example, by the raising of physical barriers around the Spanish African cities of Ceuta and Melilla.

9. The regularization processes are advertised as much inside the country as outside through the mass media and also through the migrant networks.

10. Hundreds of would-be migrants, desperate to escape poverty in Africa, died while trying to cross the Strait to Spain. (IOM News, n° 3/98).

11. Gallardo (1995) argues that there is more heterogeneity among the groups than we think. Besides, although certain women, such as Dominicans from rural areas, have achieved lower degrees of education than most Filipinos or Peruvians in Spain, they are still well educated compared with their fellow countrywomen in countries of origin.

12. Solé (1995) refers to this phenomenon when comparing present international migration with previous internal movements. The author suggests that foreign migrants, like internal migrants, arrive in Catalonia without the knowledge or will to integrate into Catalan culture. When Spanish and Catalan cultural elements compete in order to become prevalent, the Spanish features (especially the language) prevail. This is especially true in the case of Latin Americans, who should in fact have an advantage in learning Catalan as a second language after their mother language, Spanish.

13. This was generated by tense relations between the populations on both sides of the Mediterranean Sea, which came into contact many times during

previous centuries. Spain has in this sense a history of a specially intense relation with Muslims and Jews, who were rejected after the Christian Reconquest.

14. The murder of Lucrecia Pérez, a Dominican undocumented migrant woman, in 1992 raised the awareness of everybody about the presence and racism against black workers. Before that and since then many other racist actions against sub-Saharan and African 'Moors' have been condemned.

15. Cultural differences may be constructed as much from the receiving society's view as from their own migrant group's view. More generally both perceptions interact and generate new visions of the others.

16. As Lim (1995) writes: Several aspects of the functions and structure of the family can be examined as affecting women's roles and status and, indirectly, migration. Research could usefully focus on the various mechanisms through which families influence the mobility of female members. These mechanisms are related to the family as a subsistence unit: to the extent that the family assigns tasks to its members, a woman's ability to migrate would depend on whether her tasks can be fulfilled by other family members. As a subsistence unit, the family determines the access of family members to resources and it is likely that women who have limited access to resources may have stronger motivations to migrate. As an economic maximization unit, the family may encourage the migration of its female members, particularly of young women moving to get married or migrating under the auspices of an extended kin network. Lastly, as a socialization unit, the family internalizes social norms and values that determine the roles appropriate for different family members, shape their kinship rights and obligations, and encourage the sense of affinity and dependence of women. But, perhaps, the most important function of the family as a catalyst for migration is the assistance that it provides through the social networks to which it belongs, each entailing a complex set of rights and obligations.

17. Most women interviewed had high degree studies in subjects such as nursing or teaching, had even had some work experience in their country of origin and had never worked as domestic servants before.

18. There is a conceptual opposition between what is considered a job and what is a 'female' task, not usually paid and valued.

19. I use the term 'return myth' meaning a desire to live back in the country of origin that is maintained, although circumstances make it more and more difficult to accomplish. The myth also helps in accepting the barriers of living in another country, as permanent settlement is not considered.

20. This is the case for example of Peruvians who migrated to Spain after a period of residence and work in Argentina (Escrivá 1997), or Dominicans who worked before in Venezuela or Puerto Rico (Gallardo 1995).

21. These cases have been profusely reported in case studies from all origins, as women are a substantial proportion of the informal workforce and their labour market participation is commonly seen as complementary but not essential. Therefore, women alternate domestic tasks with formal labour jobs depending on their reproductive cycle and economic balance.

22. This is a very unusual female trajectory in Spain, even for Moslem women, as secure and stable jobs for their male partners are rare (Solé 1994).

23. One reason for this would be that the sex composition of Argentinians in Spain is more equally balanced than – and more ethnically similar to – that of Spaniards. Therefore, sexism and racism are not so strongly directed at them, enabling them to keep similar or better job standards than in the country of origin. Another explanation has been offered by Herranz (1996) concentrating on the social, economic and political contexts in which the migratory movement took place. She differentiates two contexts for Latin American immigration to Spain. The first flow, composed of Argentinians and Chileans, occurred in the 1970s and early 1980s and found a more favourable labour market and social conditions. The second big flow has taken place since the late 1980s and was composed mainly of Dominicans and Peruvians. The latter did not find such a receptive context as their predecessors. Therefore, since the bulk of Argentinians arrived earlier, the context helped them to achieve better occupational status than other Latin Americans.

24. The author differentiates three possible reactions: (1) Claim of the own identity, (2) Retrial and inaction, (3) Negation and emulation of defining identities.

References

Anthias, F. (1992), *Ethnicity, class, gender and migration. Greek-Cypriots in Britain*, Aldershot: Avebury.

Bodega, I. (1995), 'Recent migrations from Morocco to Spain', *International Migration Review* Vol. 29, No. 3, pp. 800–19.

Borrás, A. (1995), *Diez años de la Ley de Extranjería: Balance y perspectivas*, Barcelona: Fundación Paulino Torras Domènech.

CIE (Comisión Interministerial de Extranjería) (1999) *Anuario estadístico de extranjería 1997*, Madrid: Ministerio de Interior.

Contreras, J. (1994), *Los retos de la inmigración*, Madrid: Talasa ediciones.

Crompton, R. and Mann, M. (eds) (1986), *Gender and Stratification*, Cambridge: Polity Press.

DGOM (Dirección General de Ordenación de las Migraciones) (1999), *Anuario de migraciones 1997*, Madrid: Ministerio de Trabajo y Asuntos Sociales.

Durisotti, C. García, M. and Obrador, G. (1996), 'Género e inmigración. Necesidades, participación asociativa y políticas de cambio en seis colectivos no comunitarios en el Barcelonés', Barcelona: Secretaría de la Mujer del USCOB, Febrero 1996.

Escrivá, A. (1997), 'Control, composition and character of new migration: Peruvian women in Barcelona' *New Community* Vol. 23, No. 1, pp. 43–57.

Gallardo, G. (1995), *Buscando la vida: dominicanas en el servicio doméstico en Madrid*, Santo Domingo: CIPAF.

Gregorio, C. (1996), *Sistemas de género y migración internacional: la emigración dominicana a la Comunidad de Madrid*, Doctoral dissertation, Madrid: Universidad Autónoma.

Gregorio, C. (1995), 'El proceso de integración social de las mujeres inmigrantes' in *Integración social de las mujeres pertenecientes a grupos étnicos o culturales en situación de desventaja*, Madrid: Universidad Complutense, Facultad de Psicología.

Hernández, H. (1995), 'España es el país con la tasa de natalidad más baja del mundo con 1,2 hijos por mujer' *El Mundo*, 12 December.

Herranz, Y. (1996), *Formas de incorporación laboral de la inmigración latinoamericana en Madrid. Importancia de los contextos de recepción*, Doctoral dissertation, Madrid: Universidad Autónoma .

INSTRAW (1994), *The migration of women. Methodological issues in the measurement and analysis of internal and international migration*, Santo Domingo: Instraw.

Ioé, C. (1991), *Trabajadoras extranjeras de servicio doméstico en Madrid, España*, Geneva: ILO.

Ioé, C. (1996), 'Procesos de inserción y exclusión social de las mujeres inmigrantes no comunitarias. Informe de investigación', Madrid: Instituto de la Mujer.

Ioé, C. (1997), 'Exploración bibliográfica sobre inserción social y profesional de las mujeres inmigrantes' CE: Proyecto Anima, July.

Ioé, C. (1998), 'Mujeres migrantes en España. Proyectos migratorios y trayectorias de género' Madrid: *Ofrim*, December.

Jiménez, L. (1996), *Estudio enfocado al colectivo de mujeres inmigrantes marroquíes en España: la mujer de Alhucemas*, inédito, Madrid: Dirección General de Migraciones.

Juliano, D. (1994) 'La construcción de la diferencia: los latinoamericanos' *Papers* No. 43, pp. 23–32.

Lim, L. (1995), 'The status of women and international migration' in *International migration policies and the status of female migrants*, Proceedings of the UN Expert group meeting, San Miniato, Italy, 28–31 March 1990, New York: United Nations.

Lora-Tamayo, G. (1997), *Población extranjera en la Comunidad de Madrid. Perfil y distribución*, Madrid: Delegación Diocesana de Migraciones.

Moore, H.L. (1991), *Antropología y feminismo*, Valencia: ed. Cátedra.

Oso, L. (1998), *La migración hacia España de Mujeres Jefas de Hogar*, Madrid: Instituto de la Mujer.

Páez, P. (1993), 'Cultura marroquí y migración' in G. Giménez (ed.), *Inmigrantes extranjeros en Madrid*, Tomo II, Madrid: Comunidad de Madrid, Consejería de integración social.

Portes, A. and Böröcz, J. (1996), 'Contemporary immigration: theoretical perspectives on its determinants and modes of incorporation' in R. Cohen, (ed.), *Theories of migration*, London: Sage.

Ramírez, A. (1997), *Migraciones, género e Islam: mujeres marroquíes en España*, Doctoral dissertation, Madrid: Universidad Autónoma .

Ribas, N. (1996), *La heterogeneidad de la integración social. Una aplicación a la inmigración extracomunitaria (filipina, gambiana y marroquí) en Cataluña (1985–1996)*, Doctoral dissertation, Barcelona: Universitat Autònoma .

Roquero, E. and Rodríguez, P. (1996), *La diversidad de las mujeres migrantes: el caso de la ciudad de Granada*, Madrid: Instituto de la Mujer.

Sipi, R. (1997), *Las mujeres africanas. Incansables creadoras de estrategias para la vida*, L´Hospitalet: ed.

Solé, C. (1994), *La mujer inmigrante*, Madrid: Instituto de la Mujer, colección estudios no. 40.

Solé, C. (1995), Discriminación racial en el mercado de trabajo, Madrid: Consejo Económico y Social, colección estudios, no.14.

Varios Autores (1994a), Extranjeros en el paraíso, Barcelona: Editorial Virus.

Varios Autores (1994b), Legislación sobre extranjeros, Madrid: Editorial Civitas.

Trading Intimacy for Liberty: British Women on the Costa Del Sol

KAREN O'REILLY

Introduction

British people have been migrating to the Costa del Sol in increasing numbers since the 1960s, with vast numbers settling there during the 1980s (Jurdao 1990; King, Warner and Williams 1998; Rodríguez, Fernandez-Mayoralas and Rojo 1998; Svensson 1989). Some settle permanently on the coast, carving out new lives for themselves in the relaxed and warm setting. Others visit for varying periods of time throughout the year; some staying as long as six to nine months and only returning to England to escape the searing heat of the Costa del Sol summer (cf. O'Reilly 1995). Those who have settled permanently, and who now consider Spain to be home, are generally very positive about their new lives. They enthuse about the slow pace of life, about being able to go for leisurely strolls on a mild winter's evening, about the friendly acceptance shown to them by the local Spanish, and the welcoming warmth offered by the local expatriate communities. The older migrants impress on any listener the benefits to their physical health, mental well-being and even financial wealth. According to Don, a 63-year-old migrant, 'many things are better in Spain; people live longer, healthier, more peaceful lives.[1] Younger migrants proudly report that Spain is safer and more accepting towards children, and that there is much more to do than in Britain. In fact, the first English person I spoke to as I began fieldwork in Spain told me he had never met a British expatriate who *wanted* to go home. However, in contrast, permanent migrants do occasionally experience feelings of loneliness, insecurity, boredom, and frustration but will usually only admit to these in private. The longer I stayed in Spain, as fieldwork progressed and as British migrants became more comfortable with my presence there, the more likely I was to hear about life's dissatisfactions, the trials and tribulations of being a member of a marginal minority separated from home and friends.[2] Women, especially, seemed to be expressing an emptiness and vulnerability, a disturbing or unsettling feeling caused by constant contact with the strange and unfamiliar. This chapter explores the sources of women's uncertainty in a setting that has been compared to paradise.

Methods of Approach

This chapter results from 15 months intensive ethnographic fieldwork in the municipalities of Fuengirola and Mijas in the Costa del Sol between June 1993 and September 1994 and numerous return visits over the subsequent years. The author's main purpose was to investigate, examine, and perhaps challenge, stereotypical representations of the British in Spain. Prior to the investigation a plethora of media reports had depicted the 'Brits in Spain' to the extent that, especially during the late 1980s, they had become a phenomenon: newspaper journalists wrote about them, television dramas and comedies were based on them, people talked about them. The tabloid newspaper, the *Sun*, wrote about their antics in the sun; the *Guardian* reported on their successes and failures. Radio programmes were devoted to the topic. Television documentaries were based on 'the British in Spain'. By 1992 there was a soap opera, 'Eldorado', based on their imagined lifestyle. The Britons appeared to be a fascinating topic depicted in a plethora of ways: not integrating, living lazy lives in the sun, having problems because they did not learn the language and drank too much alcohol, living like old colonials, wishing they could come home, having a wonderful time, being old and poor, criminals and coppers.

The methods used to investigate this phenomenon were necessarily qualitative, leading to what Clifford Geertz has called a 'thick description' (Geertz 1993). The aim was to avoid the imposition of further assumptions and preconceptions onto a subject already saturated with conjecture. I hoped to learn, through them, what life in Spain meant for the migrants themselves. I hoped to reveal some of the complexity of life for the British 'expatriates'. In order to achieve this I lived, with my family, as a British migrant in Fuengirola for the entire main fieldwork period. I did voluntary work with the British and became a member of several British clubs and groups. I frequented bars and social events and was also invited into many homes where I was able to conduct in-depth interviews to supplement material gained through participant observation. My children attended a local Spanish school and my partner worked amongst the British migrants doing odd jobs around the home for them. What I present in this chapter is my interpretation of their interpretation of what is going on in the lives of British migrants. It is not a direct report of the actors' view; such a report hardly needs an academic's interference. It represents an attempt (to borrow Geertz's terminology) to unravel some of those webs of significance within which the migrants are suspended and which they themselves spin. This chapter is not, therefore, arguing that *the truth* for migrants is that women feel lonely and isolated, and that all the rest is a myth. Rather, I am presenting more of the picture than any one of these truths alone can present. *Some* of what living in Spain means, for some British women, some of the time, is loneliness, isolation, even despair, and a longing for home; and some of what living in Spain means is delight and wonder.

General Features

Several authors have recognized the problems of obtaining 'hard' data on this relatively new trend in migration, both because little research has been done and because official statistics in the areas do not reflect the different migration types within the main trend (King *et al* 1998; O'Reilly, 1995; Rodríguez *et al* 1998; Valenzuela 1988; Warnes 1991). Existing statistics are difficult to obtain and to trust because of the fluidity and unofficial nature of the migrant population. It is widely accepted that figures of migrants to Spain from northern European countries are far higher than the official census enumerates (Galacho 1991; Ocaña and González 1991). The best anyone can offer is a range of figures from various sources and an acknowledgement that in terms of size the migration trend is significant (King *et al* 1998), important (Rodríguez *et al* 1998) and consequential (Mullan 1993), and that the effects locally are substantial.

Social scientists Jurdao and Sanchez (1990) hazarded a guess that over 25,000 Britons were living in Mijas in 1990, in a village whose population at the time numbered only 36,000. On the other hand 34,000 Britons were registered with the British consulate in Malaga as resident in the Malaga province in 1993. According to the census figures collected in 1994 by Mijas council, there were then 6,379 British residents living in the municipality. Fuengirola council had just 987 British residents officially registered as residents in 1994, but a local official estimated there were at least ten times that many actually living in the area.

Many, though by no means all, of the British migrants to the Costa del Sol are retirees, but this includes a number of early retirees as well as those who have reached retirement age and beyond. Rodríguez *et al* (1998) conclude from their study of retired Europeans in the Costa del Sol, that they are a relatively youthful older population and that the British migrants are more likely to have entrepreneurial or managerial occupational histories. British migrants to Spain are as likely to be men as women. My own research revealed a younger population than the one revealed by studies whose focus is on retirement migration, with an estimated average age in the high forties (O'Reilly 1996).

Women Migrants: Pleasure and Pain

Women of all ages, 'married'[3] and single, retired and working, have migrated to Spain, each with their own reasons for leaving Britain and each with their own set of experiences (good and bad) within Spain.

Older, 'married' women have usually made a joint decision, with their husbands, to retire to Spain. Having bought or rented an apartment or villa close to local amenities and to the expatriate community, many of these older women (and men) soon look beyond their own homes and families for company and amusement. Many join clubs or social groups such as FADS (the Fuengirola and District Society) or the Royal British Legion. There is a wide selection of clubs and societies in the Fuengirola area, for expatriates of all nationalities, offering a range of activities: an English theatre, Scottish country dancing, barbershop singing, walking, running, bowling, to cite just a few. Many married women also involve themselves in charity work or volunteering as a way to meet people and to generate a sense of belonging for themselves in a setting that is new and alien to them.

Beryl, for example, moved to Fuengirola in 1982, when her husband retired from his job as an electrical engineer. They bought an apartment close to the town centre and the beach and began their new lives in earnest. After a year or so, Beryl told me, going each day to the beach and to local bars for coffee became tedious for both of them and so they joined a local expatriate social club. Through the club they have met many different people. The club arranges day trips, dinner and dance evenings, bingo sessions once a week, Spanish classes, and arranges for guest speakers to attend their regular meetings. Beryl and her husband feel the club has enriched their lives in many ways. Beryl also plays bowls with a few local English women, and is a member of an organization that caters for the welfare of more unfortunate expatriates, providing advice, home nursing, equipment hire, crisis aid and a drop-in centre. Beryl told me she *needs* to do something like this: 'It gives me something to do each week. I'd get really bored otherwise.'

Beryl, like most older, married women I met, constantly impressed on me how agreeable life is in Spain. She believes people are friendlier and happier; that her husband is far healthier; that there is less trouble in the streets; and that life goes on at a slower pace than 'back home'. However, the advantages women do not stress overtly, those which are merely mentioned in passing, seem to be the most sentient. For example, older women feel free from many of the restrictions British society places on their actions and their dress. 'If I dressed like this in England, people would just stare at me. Well, I just wouldn't dare do it!' insisted Edith, a 70-year-old woman, who was wearing shorts and a brightly coloured T-shirt. Similarly, several older women told me they don't do home-baking in Spain like they used to at home. At the church coffee morning I assumed the home-made cakes one woman was selling were her own creation. 'Oh no' she told me 'I got them from the English baker's. I don't bake here! I had enough of all that.' Women do not feel the pressure to be productive in the home, to sew or to knit, or to even invite people for dinner, which they would feel in British society. 'We've come here to enjoy ourselves not get stuck in the kitchen – anyway, its too hot!' one woman told me.

Younger, married women have often moved to Spain with their husbands to jointly run a business such as a bar, estate agency, letting agents, launderette or other form of service for the local expatriate community. Of those who are not working in the family business, some gain jobs in local English schools, or with the timeshare companies; many work informally in service jobs, cleaning, serving in a bar, waitressing, teaching English, or hairdressing; and a few, especially those with young children, work as housewives. In the community I studied, British women tend not to be working with or for Spanish people. The main reason for moving to Spain, most generally insist, is for the way of life. Work, whatever form it takes, provides the financial means to that end.

Married women who are working with their husbands in a business are generally pleased to be able to spend more time with them than previously. 'In England' Tracy, a mother in her thirties, told me 'Pete was always at work and I was stuck at home with the kids. I never saw him. People think you've come to Spain to run away from money troubles but we had two successful businesses, but we never saw each other and we were always tired.' Peter and Tracy run a bar in Fuengirola.

Married women with children are less likely to feel bound to the home than they would in Britain. For one thing, there are more activities for children in Spain, they say, and, for another thing, children are more welcome in bars and restaurants than they would be back home. Mothers feel they have more opportunity to go out and mix with other people than they would have had; the children can go with them or can play in the street with the other children. Mary told me she can leave her children to play outside until midnight or even later in the summer – it is warm and light until then, there are more people about to keep an eye on them, and the streets are safer than in Britain, she believes.

Single women of all ages have migrated to this part of Spain. Those who retired are living on their pensions and, perhaps, some savings they have put by over the years. Younger women are often working, informally and/or casually, in local expatriate businesses or for local British migrants in the same sorts of occupations as the married women. Some have migrated to Spain with their parents, others visited the area, liked it, and returned to stay permanently. A few (Shirley Valentines?) went there on holiday and never came home!

Single women feel it is more acceptable to be single in Spain than it is in Britain. There is no obvious explanation for this, except that the migrants themselves have established this norm. Even in Fuengirola, generally considered to provide the perfect setting for holidaying couples, single migrant women are less likely to feel like social outcasts than they did 'back home'. They are able to walk into a bar or a club on their own without feeling uncomfortable or abnormal. They feel there is not the same pressure on them to meet a man and settle down, and that, in fact, it is quite normal *not* to be settled down. Life in Spain is for living, they insist, not for settling into a life of routine and commitments. Irene, a 65-year-old single woman told me: 'I came here because I can be myself. In England I'm a social outcast because I'm not married or *with* someone. Here no one cares. You are what you are.' Irene has a favourite bar, which she visits once or twice a week and where she can always be sure of receiving a welcome. She also goes horse riding a few times a week, and is a member of the Royal British Legion welfare committee.

Some women have moved to Spain on or after the death of their husbands. Joan (now in her eighties) told me that when her husband died she wanted to get away from the memories and the sadness and to start a new life. She bought a small apartment in Los Boliches where she can walk to shops, the beach and to the Church coffee mornings once a week. Another woman, Hazel, went to Spain after her husband died because she did not want to become a burden on her family and because 'there is so much to do around here! I have joined a painting course, I am learning Spanish, I come to FADS, and have met lots of really nice people.' Hazel had been in Fuengirola just two weeks when I met her. Other women, whose husbands have died since moving to Spain, often feel less isolated than they believe they would in Britain. One woman told me 'At least I can carry on here. There, I would be finished – no job, no husband, life is over. Then the grandchildren visit you out of pity. At least here I know they come because they want to.' Women are also more likely to feel safe in their homes alone in Spain than they did at home. This is because they believe here is less crime, at least in the Fuengirola area. This may or may not be true; what is important is that they *feel* it to be true.

As discussed above, British women in Spain generally enthuse positively about the quality of their new lifestyles. They seem eager to impress on the observer their delights with Spain, with the slow pace of life, the freedom from many social and physical restrictions associated with Britain, their new-found health and happiness. However, in some ways, this is the official discourse, communicating the corollary of the whinging Brit, rather than an honest portrayal of feelings and experiences. While spending time amongst British women in Spain I felt that this discourse had become more a rule about how to live your life than an honest expression. Occasionally, in certain private settings, when women felt secure, sure they were not being overheard, and confident that their words would not be repeated elsewhere, even to themselves, some women would confide in me their occasional feelings of loneliness, confusion and isolation; and some would admit that, once in a while, they wish with all their heart that they could just go home. These feelings are associated with friendships, or lack of them; with confusion about laws and regulations and about 'how things are done' in a strange country; with never quite feeling part of things around them; and with having left their family, friends and histories in another place.

Spanish/British Intercourse

In this section I explore the sources of these feelings of isolation, frustration and confusion, and attempt to understand why British women feel they can never quite be part of things in Spain. Shall we blame the migrants themselves for their isolation or are there circumstances to consider which enable a more complex interpretation of the situation? Floya Anthias (1992) has argued that migrant identity and subsequent actions can only be properly understood with reference to each historical context. This is what I attempt in this section.

There is no doubt that, in terms of the wider society, the British in Spain are isolated within their own communities. No one could call them integrated into Spanish society: they spend most of their time with their compatriots; they select friends, attend clubs, find work and socialize in their ethnic group. Indeed, if ethnic identity is as much to do with associational involvement as it is with either perception or self-perception of a group, as J. Milton Yinger (1986) has suggested, the British share a strong sense of ethnic identity. However, as I have shown elsewhere (O'Reilly 1996), the intention of British migrants is *not* to remain so discrete. The desire for British migrants is to mix with the Spanish, live like the Spanish, talk with the Spanish, and to share their lives with the Spanish.

It is important to understand the position of the British migrants in Spain *vis a vis* the Spanish who have 'invited' them. It is difficult to elicit any sympathy for the British in Spain as they are viewed as a powerful group whose sole intention is to take the best that Spain can offer and give nothing in return. But this is quite simply a naive interpretation of the situation, informed more by the labels used to describe them than by information gathered about them. The British in Spain are obviously not 'immigrants' in the now common-sense meaning of the term, which imputes powerlessness, minority status, and often colour, to immigrant groups (cf. Cashmore 1994: 188). However, neither are they colonizers (as is so often implied). According to the *Cambridge Encyclopaedia* a colony is 'an area of land or a country held and governed by another country, usually for the purpose of economic or other forms of exploitation'. Alternatively, a colony is a 'settlement or settlers in a new country forming a community fully or partly subject to the state from which they have emigrated' (*Collins Pocket Dictionary*). In ecology, on the other hand, colonization refers to: 'The spread of species into a new habitat, such as a freshly cleared field, a new motorway verge, or a recently flooded valley'. (*Hutchinson Softback Encyclopaedia*). The first two definitions are inappropriate for the British migrants to Spain as the area of land to which they have moved is governed neither by the country or state from which they emigrate nor by the migrants themselves. Neither is the situation one of more subtle economic domination or control as in the case of a situation often referred to nowadays as 'neo-colonialism'. The economic situation and market activity of the migrants is often marginal and is not exploitative of Spanish labour or goods (cf. O'Reilly 1996). With respect to the third definition, the loose understanding of which I suspect often informs casual accusations of colonization, Britons settling in new habitats can only be colonizing if they are understood to be a separate species from the Spanish or local inhabitants in the area in question. This is a dangerous assumption resting on notions of pure 'races' and a taxonomy of human beings. To accept this definition is to reify the notion of an ethnic group, hence returning to biological-determinist conceptions of discreteness.

Britons in Spain, rather than being labelled immigrants, emigrants or migrants, tend to be called 'expatriates'. Indeed, they use the term themselves. However, the term 'expatriate' is a value-laden term implying power, privilege and choice. It invokes a relationship between expatriate and indigenous person in which the expatriate is the more powerful or wealthy. It endows the recipient with status. The term expatriate invokes images of upper-middle class professionals working in oil-rich countries (cf. Findlay 1995), of migrant artists, scholars and writers (cf. Earnest 1968), or the migration of wealthy business personnel from richer to 'developing' countries (cf. Öberg 1994).

A 'thin description' of British expatriates in Spain, drawing on the terms *colonial* or *expatriate*, thus endows them with power, prestige and privilege that they do not actually possess. It also implies that any lack of integration is through choice, due to the putative desire to colonize an area and to recreate a patch of Britain in a warm and welcoming climate. In fact non-integration is in part due to Britons' disinterest in becoming fully participating members of Spanish society and partly the result of their historical position on the margins of this society, as tourists.

It should be remembered that Britons were not attracted to the coastal areas of Spain in order to either work or integrate into Spanish society. Nor did they come uninvited as imperialists or political colonisers, in the way that Britons (and of course other Westerners, including the Spanish) have been in the past. They were first invited as tourists when the coastal areas were marketed and 'sold' as holiday places (Punnett 1990; Jenkins 1991; MacCannell 1996). Later, when it became apparent that tourism only offered seasonal income and when foreign investment was sought as a boost to the Spanish economy, the Spanish encouraged foreigners to purchase properties and to settle in these coastal areas – but always as retirees, or visitors, or as entrepreneurs building and expanding their own businesses, not as labour supply, not for refuge or asylum: these are a very different type of migrant (Valenzuela 1988). It may have been hoped that the 'cultural mess' caused by post-war mass immigration to Western countries would eventually stabilize through the melting together of cultures, or the assimilation of one culture by another, but those immigrants were incorporated into the work force, education system and other institutions of the host society. Mass migration of Britons to Spain, however, is a very different trend. The British and other northern Europeans represented money, affluence and financial security. Their immigration was generally viewed positively in that they were bringing wealth and progress to underdeveloped areas; it was not expected that they would take anything *from* the economy. It was not until later, when it seemed such an influx of British migrants might be a drain on local or national resources, because so many were old and not as wealthy as had been hoped, that they were viewed more negatively – and still not expected to want to integrate (cf. Jurdao1990; Jurdao and Sanchez 1990).

Having moved to Spain, integration is a troublesome goal, especially when immigrants and local people are not working together. Britons looking for work would not sensibly choose Spain. Unemployment is very high in Spain and British migrants do not hope to compete in the Spanish job market. Most believe they would never be offered a job if there were a Spanish person capable of doing it, and most, additionally, are insufficiently fluent in Spanish to be able to compete equally with the local population. British migrants, therefore, tend not to look for work within the Spanish economy. Once attracted to Spain as somewhere to live they might, with knowledge of the local British communities, hope to get work within these, but this would usually be informal or entrepreneurial.

British women in Spain are therefore working either with or for other British people. Denise, for example, moved to Spain to escape a violent husband. She was initially offered work in an English bar but after nine months the owners of the bar could no longer afford to keep her on. Now Denise finds work where she can, usually casual work in British businesses or for British people. She cannot hope to compete with Spaniards for *real* jobs. An older woman, Anne, who is living on a pension, tries to increase *her* income through casual work but, since this is illegal, she works only with or for people she knows and believes she can trust, that is British people. A young woman in her thirties, Jane, is a hairdresser with her own salon in Fuengirola. Jane speaks Spanish fluently, but nevertheless tends to have only

British and other foreign customers. Anna, another hairdresser, worked in a hairdressing salon until it was taken over by a Spanish man, who told her he would have to hire Spanish people. Now she works inform-ally as a hair stylist, visiting customers in their homes. All her cust-omers are British and pay her with cash. These women have not chosen informal work within their own ethnic niche as a preference, or as a means of avoiding integration. It is merely a way of earning an income where formal employment is not an option. As Hernando de Soto so eloquently demonstrates, legality is sometimes a privilege; informal economic activity, rather than reflecting a desire not to integrate, often arises as an on-the-ground solution to an on-the-ground problem (de Soto 1989).

Britons living in Fuengirola cannot be considered integrated within wider Spanish society, either in terms of ethnic identity or in more concrete actions: they do not 'integrate' or 'assimilate'; but neither are they reconstructing a little England in the sun and neither do they have political or economic power. In fact they are excluded from the main Spanish institutions. Britons in Spain have no power to vote in general elections and as yet have not been granted the right, in Fuengirola at least, to vote in the local elections. European Union members were to have been given the right to vote in the last local elections in 1995 but there were many obstacles to registering them-selves on the electoral register, and eventually even those few who had managed to gain the correct papers were denied the right to vote at the last minute due to bureaucratic details and the failure of the two governments involved to agree reciprocal arrangements. Members of minority groups denied the right to vote in elections are generally deemed to be marginalized, excluded or ostracized, or 'on the sidelines' (de Foucauld 1992). They are not represented at either government or local levels in politics or decision making. Marginal people feel they have no part in the decision-making process, and are not full citizens of the society in which they live. This feeling of marginality may well contribute to the feelings of loneliness and isolation that women feel.

The Britons retain a discrete identity in many ways. Ethnic identifica-tion always involves an element of choice; but this choice is also subject to certain structural constraints (cf. Epstein 1978). The experi-ence for many more permanent migrants in Fuengirola is one of marginality and of powerlessness, of lack of control, of unequal access to knowledge, and even of discrimination. They are marginal in that they retain no real hope of ever being accepted members of mainstream

Spanish society. They are powerless to effect real change at the level of policy or law. They are controlled and excluded by bureaucracy, or at least feel that they are, in that they often do not know what is going on. They often do not understand the various rules and regulations that apply to them. 'Although we have lived in Spain for just over for 20 years . . . we still do not know our rights, or indeed, if we have any' wrote Mr and Mrs Brook in *The Sur in English* (9–15 July 1993). Residents wanting to apply for residence permits confront confusing procedures. Often being unable to obtain a single, unambiguous version of current regulations, many fear that application brings their case to the notice of the local authorities. If not granted residence permits, they risk being expelled from the country whereas those who do not apply face less of a risk. This quandary acts as a strong restraint against becoming full members of the new society, and thereby gaining the vote eventually.

These occasional feelings of insecurity and bewilderment are reflected in the stories of scares and bungles shared verbally and reported in newspapers with titles such as 'Tale of a Tax Scare' (*The Sunday Sun* 18 July 1993); 'Wrong Plates!' (*The Entertainer* 24–30 June 1993); and '75.000 peseta fine!' (*The Entertainer* 10–16 March 1994). 'What are they up to now at Sevillana?' one woman, a letting agent, asked on the letters page of *The Entertainer* (5–11 August 1993). Several of her clients had their electricity supply cut and were charged reconnection fees because she was late paying the bills for them. She had understood that she had a few weeks in which to pay and would be warned by letter before disconnection took place. However, the regulations had changed without her knowledge, and to her huge expense.

Confusion and ignorance worry the mothers of children in Spanish schools, where information is often passed by word of mouth and sometimes never reaches the ears of the British migrant. As an example, one school in Fuengirola set up Spanish classes for the local English children but sent the message home by word of mouth, via the English pupils. The children apparently passed on muddled messages and the classes were eventually cancelled due to lack of interest. Mothers I spoke to said they wished they had known about the classes but either found out too late or arrived at the wrong time.

In our search for an identity we (as individuals and as groups) reflect, to an extent, what people expect of us, as is made known through labelling and interaction. Britons (and other foreign nationals) in Fuengirola are marginalized by Spanish labelling. They are often referred to as 'residential tourists', establishing their status, for Spaniards, as marginal or temporary citizens, not as fully participating Spanish citizens (cf. Mellado 1993). They are thus conceptually parcelled off with the tourists. In Mijas, a village near Fuengirola, a Department for Foreign Residents was established within the local council to deal with the specific problems and interests of the local foreign population. This office gives advice to foreigners with regard to residence and work permits, tax liabilities, council fees, services and so on. It also arranges meetings with and social events for foreign residents. Interestingly enough, the same office houses and the same individuals run the tourist office for the area. Tourists and foreign residents are dealt with together. The Foreign Residents Department that Fuengirola council decided to provide was also housed with and shares the same staff as their local tourist office; in fact as a department it comes under the aegis of the Department of Tourism. The building is separate from the main council buildings, positioned in the path of the tourist trail to the local weekly market. Such treatment allows an insight into the way the foreign residents, and especially Britons since they are in the majority, are perceived by the Spanish in this area. They are not viewed as permanent settlers intending to integrate fully into Spanish society; they are tourists who stay on.

In the 1960s Julian Pitt-Rivers (1963) noted the extent of Andalusian hospitality and called it a very noble feature of the Spanish people: the stranger enjoys the special status he did in ancient Greece, where he was protected by Zeus and was welcomed and feasted (Pitt-Rivers 1963: 26). However, Pitt-Rivers suggests that this is more than mere hospitality, it is a protection of the community from too much outside influence. Treating a person as a guest maintains his or her distance and checks interference, for: 'A guest is a person who, while he must be entertained and cherished, is dependent on the goodwill of his hosts. He has no rights and he can make no demands' (Pitt-Rivers 1963: 27). This provides an interesting and useful analysis of the marginal status of the guest, which works both ways for the British in Spain who are both treated as, and identify as, guests in a foreign land.

'Nothing is likely so palpably to both encapsulate and therefore to isolate a group as linguistic barriers' suggests C. Fried (1983: 4). British people in Fuengirola often feel the Spanish are not making it easy for them to integrate or to learn the language. Police officers who can speak English, for example, will often refuse to do so, forcing the Briton to struggle along. While we were in Fuengirola a hand-written notice was posted in the police station warning foreigners, in English, not to expect to be attended to, unless they brought an interpreter with them. This is an area to which British tourists flock every year and in which the second language is English, yet, if burgled or mugged, one is expected to find an interpreter before going to the police for help!

Britons in Spain have the right to use the state health service in line with reciprocal arrangements under European community legislation, but even in areas where there is a large majority of British and English-speaking residents, there are surprisingly few interpreters or facilities providing for those with language difficulties. Very often, no allowance is made for the language or cultural differences. Several settled migrants, who would normally be entitled to use the Spanish state system, make private arrangements, often joining a local insurance scheme which includes doctor's surgery appointments, some minor treatments and English-speaking receptionist and emergency services. Though it costs them more, several people feel that they do not want language misunderstandings to get in the way when it comes to matters of health. As a result, integration between cultures suffers.

Other public service providers rarely make allowances for language and cultural differences of members of the international community. The foreigners' department at the police station in Fuengirola has interpreters, but these are not provided by the police force, they are voluntary and unpaid. In the nearest general hospital in Malaga, the situation is the same; interpreters are voluntary and as such are not always available when needed. A young British woman who had her third baby in Malaga hospital told me how lonely and isolated she felt during her stay there, mainly because she could not talk to anyone. 'I just wanted to come home' she told me 'I cried all the time'. This lack of provision, rather than either forcing or encouraging people to learn the language or to integrate, augments the exclusion of minority groups, be they 'expatriates' or 'immigrants'.[4]

Many British migrants to Fuengirola do *not* learn the local language, for whatever reason. I met people who had lived in the area 30 years and who spoke fewer than 20 words of Spanish. In fact it is possible to get by quite well without learning Spanish. As a tourist area many local services are provided for the holiday-maker and are oriented towards the tourist. Many locals learn to speak English so that they can compete with other businesses for the tourist custom. On the other hand, many permanent migrants do attempt to learn the language, especially women, but find it difficult to practise for the very reasons stated above. Local Spanish people in Fuengirola often seem more concerned to practise their English-language skills than to teach the foreign visitor any Spanish, and Spanish children, especially, seem to love to learn and to practise their English with the foreign children.

The Andalusian accent is also notoriously strong, making communication in basic Spanish very difficult, as Stanley Brandes noted during his anthropological field study in Andalusia in the seventies, 'Andalusians, scorned and ridiculed throughout the rest of the country for their distinctive accent, are masters of their tongue'. (Brandes 1980: 4). British people who learn the language before moving to Spain will usually have been taught Castillian Spanish, a Spanish quite different in dialect to Andalusian Spanish. Andalusian is spoken by many of the locals in Fuengirola with very strong accents and is difficult to understand until one gets used to hearing it. If a person is spending a great deal of her time in the company of other Britons then the chances of hearing enough Andalusian to get used to the accent is slim.[5]

Several Britons expressed frustration with their own language-learning attempts. It was the topic of many conversations during walks with the field club and whilst whiling away the time in a coffee bar. Some had tried to familiarize themselves with the language by watching Spanish television as much as possible but found this unhelpful since so many programmes were dubbed that the language heard bore no relation to the mouth movements observed. Many had abandoned all hope of successful integration into the local Spanish community as even acquiring the necessary communication skills was so problematic.

In summary, many Britons who would like to integrate more, who admire and respect the Spanish way of life and Spanish culture, and who want to learn the language, feel in some ways powerless and discriminated against. British migrants share no 'myth of return' and no romantic view of home acting as a constraint against participation in Spanish life. Many like and admire the Spanish people, and even believe they are similar in many ways. Many believe their children are integrated and go to great lengths to deny their distinctiveness and their ethnic identity in interaction with the Spanish. However, language differences persist in distancing them, enforcing a social exclusion that is further strengthened by bureaucracy and labelling, by the control of knowledge, by confusing laws, and by an absence of political representation. Not only are British migrants to Spain *expected* not to integrate, neither is participation in Spanish society facilitated or enabled. This is partially the outcome of the historical relationship between the two groups, where the migrant to Spain is viewed as a 'residential tourist' – someone who does not work and does not settle too permanently.

Making New Friends

New migrants, who cannot hope to become full members of Spanish society, are to some extent driven towards the British community for comfort and companionship and as a source of guidance while they familiarize themselves with their new surroundings. The British community welcomes newcomers, helping them to settle successfully, and as a result ties are formed and habits established that are difficult to break later on. The new migrant tries to learn Spanish but finds this difficult with so many British around and especially when she is neither working with nor even spending much time with Spanish people. She feels frustrated because she tries to mingle a bit and to integrate a little but rarely feels part of things Spanish, doesn't speak the language properly and is never quite sure of what is going on. Information that is passed on by word of mouth from Spanish person to Spanish person passes her by, and she is never quite sure whether the Spanish really want her around or whether they are just being polite. As a result, she makes friends with British people. However, these friendships are far from satisfactory.

British men in Spain occasionally admit, with regret, that they never make as good and true friends in Spain as they did in Britain, but they will not discuss this for long. They will occasionally confide in a listener that it is difficult to trust people (referring to other British migrants) when you know so little of their backgrounds and are aware they could disappear back to Britain at any moment leaving you with no further contact. However, such accounts will be reported briefly and with a tinge of sadness but then will be dismissed as the informant quickly regains his happy disposition and remembers all the advantages associated with his new life.

Women, on the other hand, will dwell on this just a little longer.[6] Marie, who runs an estate agency with her husband, Derek, confided in me one day that, even after ten years of living in Spain, she felt that she had no real friends. 'You make lots of acquaintances here', she told me, as did many other people, 'but it's hard to make real friends.' Marie misses having someone to call on in times of trouble; someone like her sons or family, she said. She went on to say 'you can tell many people here are lonely because they make excuses to come in here [the estate agency] when all they want is a chat. Its hard to get rid of them sometimes.' She, like all the other British migrants I interviewed, was referring to British people and British friends. None of them even considered trying to make Spanish friends – acquaintances maybe, but not friends.

Marie also told me, in strict confidence, that if she was to become ill or if her husband died she would go back home. 'You want to be with people you know at times like that' she said. Marie does not reveal these feelings to her husband. For the British migrants, Spain is supposed to be the best place on earth. You are not *supposed* to want to go home.

Several women complained, privately, that it is hard to make close and intimate friends in Spain and difficult even to *really* get to know someone. Jessie, a retired, married woman, told me how she, sometimes, gets incredibly bored and lonely. 'Friends here are not the same as in Wales', she said, 'they are more superficial.' Kelly, a young mother, once asked bitterly 'How can you make friends here? They all just want to live a fantasy life. Its not real!' Once again, she meant British migrants, not Spanish people. For many migrants, life in Spain is a leisured, fun life (cf. O'Reilly 1996).

Interestingly, few women believe it is family and friends back home that they miss, it is more a feeling that new friends are hard to make, or that it is difficult to move beyond the acquaintance stage. Women, generally, seem to express a feeling that friendships made later in life are of a different quality than those formed earlier (cf. Matthews 1986) but women of all ages in Spain are expressing a feeling that quality has been affected by migration.

One obstacle to the forming of new friendships is the small number of women from which to choose. Since it is so difficult to get involved in Spanish society, for reasons discussed above, British women turn to other British women. Kelly, for example, explained that as a young mother in Britain she would join her local mother and toddler club hoping to meet 'like-minded people', women with whom she felt some empathy or kinship. In Spain, she does visit the local mother and toddler club and the only other English woman there assumes they will be friends, though the only thing they share in common is the fact they are English. Even so, it easier to get talking to her than to try to initiate conversation with a Spanish woman. Furthermore, Kelly explained, 'why would any Spanish mother want to make friends with an English woman who can hardly speak her language when she has plenty of Spanish women to choose from?'

A further problem for many British migrants is that, for those who are working full time, there is no time for forging quality friendships. Individuals need time to get know something about each other on a personal level before they can interact completely, suggests Steve Duck (1998). These migrants may meet friends at work but the type of work migrant women do does not lend itself to closeness. Kim works in a bar during the evenings and cares for her children during the day. At work she is too busy to talk; during the day she is too tired. Julie works in a restaurant kitchen, alone. When she has time off she visits a couple of local British bars for coffee and a chat, but there is little time for intimacy. Marie serves in a sandwich bar; tourists pop in and out all day but no one stops for long.

This introduces a further feature of life which, for many British migrants, affects the quality of relationships they can forge. Social life, for the British in Spain, is generally conducted out of the house – in pubs, clubs, on the beach, by the pool. These public spaces do not lend themselves to intimate or intense conversation, which helps to explain the complaint that friendships are superficial: there is little opportunity or social space in which to move conversation beyond the mundane. Furthermore the community shares an ethos of fun, pleasure and leisure. There is little space for serious discussion in bars, where tourists are enjoying their temporary escape from reality, or in clubs, which are essentially fun places, or even while doing voluntary work, which often absorbs all of the participant's attention.

A further source of insecurity or isolation is that British people are often returning to Britain for one reason and another. While it is true to say that the British in Spain make friends (or acquaintances) with each other quickly and easily, it is also true that they do so because they are uncertain how long a person will stay. The British migrant community is a very fluid one, with people arriving and leaving all the time. The biggest threat to community, therefore, is internal rather than external; it is the threat of transience. As Peggy, a full resident in her seventies, told me one morning at the Church bazaar:

> You don't make many friends here, not friends, just acquaintances, isn't that right [turning to a woman looking at the clothes on the rail]. Well, one or two real friends, but mostly acquaintances. It's such a transient society. You never know when someone is going to go home you see, and people you thought were here forever . . . then something happens, like with you [turning to the same woman] and suddenly you have to go back. Last year at Lux Mundi they lost something like 36 of their regular people.

What is increasingly apparent as one hears more and more of such stories is that these migrants are continuously referring to other migrants and to their own society of migrants, not to Spanish people nor to Spanish society. Such is the extent to which they feel and make themselves marginal (living on the margins of a wider society) that the society they refer to is their own marginal one, even without this being confirmed by being expressed verbally.

Reluctance and inability to forge long-term friendships are exacerbated by frequent change and return migration. Change is something these migrants get used to. In the five months between completion of fieldwork and my next visit to Fuengirola one English language newspaper had been bankrupt and a new one initiated, run by new migrants; one bar had changed hands twice; three bars had new owners; two others were for sale; a new bar had opened; and three people I knew well had returned to Britain permanently.

Not only do people leave, but some leave unexpectedly, without warning or farewells. This can be upsetting for those who lose friends in this way, and unnerving for the rest. When one family bought a camper van, rumours circulated that their departure was imminent; but, since the couple were bar owners, and since the bar was not up for sale (as far as anyone knew), the rumours were soon quietened. However, locals awoke one morning to find their apartment vacated, all furniture and even curtains removed. A short walk down to their bar confirmed suspicions – it had been cleared out completely. The family were never seen in the area again. During a conversation about this event some time later, a fellow bar owner called Doreen told me sadly, 'People go back all the time. One year I lost four friends on one flight. But they never want to go home, they just have to for one reason or another.' On another occasion, Kelly told me, 'I have made two good friends here and they have both gone home.'

Conclusions

British women migrants to the Costa del Sol, are generally very happy with their new lifestyles and new-found liberty: they enjoy the freedom from routine, from the social restrictions on actions and dress that British society imposes, from the confinement that having children often means to women in Britain; they delight in the liberty to start again in Spain with new activities, new friends, new lifestyles. However, women migrants express feelings of loneliness, isolation and confusion which they seem ashamed to admit but which, nevertheless, are important to them. The feelings of confusion and isolation are in part caused by the severing of old ties and by the very act of migration itself. They are exacerbated by the marginal status of these British migrants within Spain; a status that has historical roots and that remains unaltered in a situation of mutual misunderstandings and poor communication. The isolation and loneliness women experience as members of a marginal group are then further exacerbated by the difficulties encountered when attempting to forge new relationships within their own ethnic group. There are problems of mistrust and doubt in a situation where personal histories are not shared and futures are ambiguous. Furthermore, within the British expatriate community, which shares a culture of fun and pleasure, of escape and leisure, there is little social space for intimacy or for the creation of the kind of deep friendship which is based on self-disclosure and mutual trust. While networks of exchange and reciprocation quickly establish the status of newcomers and provide social support for established migrants, feelings of emotional comfort and security apparently demand time, familiarity, and privacy.

Notes

1. Names and details have been altered to protect identities. Quotes are indirect as most were gathered through participant observation and written down later.

2. I have used the term 'marginal' throughout this paper intending it to be interpreted literally, without the many meanings and interpretations with which it has become imbued in academic literature on marginal groups.

3. I use the term 'married' for both married and cohabiting couples as this reflects the migrants' own use of the term.

4. As I completed fieldwork things were beginning to change in the area. In the council offices an English-speaking official was installed to help foreigners with problems related to local administration. However, the new Socialist Party mayor cancelled this provision soon after he was elected in 1995.

5. One theory which circulates as explanation for the persistence of such strong local dialects is that, post-Franco, colloquial Spanish, which he attempted to suppress, is experiencing a revival throughout the country as a whole.

6. This is not the place to visit the debate on men, women and friendship. Whether women have a greater need than men for intimate, trusting relationships or are better at forging such relationships, or whether it is the case that images of ideal friendship are expressed in terms of women's traits creating the idea that only women have such friendships, is uncertain (cf. Nardi, 1992, for full discussion). What I am certain of is that women spent more time analysing the possible causes of their dissatisfaction with relationships in Spain than did men. Men, perhaps, have learned to live in a world of acquaintances (cf. Seidler, 1989).

References

Anthias, F. (1992), *Ethnicity, Class, Gender and Migration*, Aldershot: Avebury.

Anwar, M. (1979), *The Myth of Return*, London: Heinemann.

Brandes, S. (1980), *Metaphors of Masculinity. Sex and Status in Andalusian Folklore*, Pennsylvania: University of Pennsylvania Press.

Cashmore, E.E. (1994), *The Dictionary of Race and Ethnic Relations*, Second edition, London: Routledge.

Duck, S. (1998), *Human Relationships* (2nd edition), London: Sage.

Earnest, E. (1968), *Expatriates and Patriots. American Artists, Scholars and Writers in Europe*, Durham, North Carolina: Duke University Press.

Epstein, A.L. (1978), *Ethos and Identity*, London: Tavistock Publications.

Findlay, A (1995), 'The future of skill exchanges within the European Union', in R. Hall, and P. White (eds), *Europe's Population. Towards the Next Century*, London: UCL Press pp. 130–41.

Foucauld, J.B. de (1992), 'The Scale of the Problem', in T. Johnson, *Combating Social Exclusion, Fostering Integration*, report of a conference hosted by the Commission of the European Communities, 2–3 April 1992. Brussels: Commission of the European Communities, pp. 8–14.

Fried, C. (ed.) (1983), *Minorities: Community and Identity*, Berlin: Springer-Verlag.

Galacho, F.B. (1991), Problemas de cuantificación del turismo residencial en la Costa del Sol malagueña. Una propuesta de método de medición, *in III Jornadas de Población Española*, (Torremolinos: AGE), pp. 59–70.

Geertz, C (1993), 'Thick Description: Toward an Interpretive Theory of Culture', in *The Interpretation of Cultures*, London: Fontana Press, pp. 3–30 (first pub 1973 New York: Basic Books Inc.).

Jenkins, C.L. (1991), 'Tourism policies in developing countries', in S. Medlik (ed.) *Managing Tourism*, Oxford: Butterworth-Heinemann pp. 269–77.

Jurdao, F. (1990), *Espana en Venta*, Madrid: Endymion.

Jurdao, F. and Sanchez, M. (1990), *Espana, Asilo de Europa*, Barcelona: Planeta.

King, R., Warnes, A. and Williams, A. (1998), 'International Retirement Migration in Europe', *International Journal of Population Geography*, Vol. 4, No. 2, pp. 91–111.

MacCannell, D. (1996), *Tourist or Traveller*, London: BBC Educational Developments.

Matthews, S.H. (1986), *Friendships Through The Life Course. Oral Biographies in Old Age*, Beverley Hills: Sage.

Mellado, V.M. (1993), 'The Chamber of commerce requests measures to reactivate residential tourism', in *Sur in English*, 26 November–2 December p. 5.

Mullan, C. (1993), *A Report on the Problems of Older People: British Expatriate Community in Spain*, London: Help the Aged.

Nardi, P.M (ed.) (1992), *Men's Friendships*, Newbury Park: Sage.

Öberg, S. (1994), 'Factors in Future South–North Migration', in W. Lutz (ed.), *The Future Population of the World*, London: Earthscan Publications Limited, pp. 361–87.

Ocaña, M.C. and González, C. (1991), 'El Catastro de la Propiedad Urbana como fuente para evaluar el turismo residencial', *III Jornadas de Población Española* (Torremolinos: AGE): pp. 135–41.

O'Reilly, K. (1995), 'A New Trend in European Migration: Contemporary British Migration to Fuengirola, Costa del Sol' *Geographical Viewpoint*, Vol. 23, pp. 25–36.

O'Reilly, K (1996), 'British on the Costa del Sol: Colonials or Immigrants, Residents or Tourists?', Unpublished Ph.D. thesis.

Pitt-Rivers, J. A. (1963), *The People of the Sierra*, Chicago: Phoenix Books (first impression 1961).

Punnett, N. (1990), *Travel and Tourism*, Oxford: Basil Blackwell.

Rodríguez, V., Fernandez-Mayoralas, G. and Rojo, F. (1998), 'European Retirees on the Costa del Sol: A Cross-National Comparison', *International Journal of Population Geography*, Vol. 4, No. 2, pp. 183–200.

Seidler, V.J. (1989), *Rediscovering Masculinity. Reason, Language and Sexuality*, London: Routledge.

Soto, H. de (1989), *The Other Path. The Invisible Revolution in the Third World*, London: I.B. Taurus & Co. Ltd.

Svensson, P. (1989), *Your Home in Spain* (2nd edition), London: Longman.

Valenzuela, M. (1988), 'Spain: the phenomenon of mass tourism', in G. Shaw, and A.M. Williams (eds), *Tourism and Economic Development. Western European Experiences*, London: Belhaven Press, pp. 39–57.

Warnes, A.M. (1991), Migration to and seasonal residence in Spain of Northern European elderly people', *European Journal of Gerontology*, Vol. 1, pp. 53–60.

Yinger, M. (1986), 'Intersecting strands in the theorisation of race and ethnic relations' in J. Rex and D. Mason (eds), *Theories of race and ethnic relations* Cambridge: Cambridge University Press, pp. 20–41.

Index